BLESSING AND CURSING

ASHBURNHAM INSIGHTS

Blessing and Cursing

A re-reading of Scripture by

TIMOTHY PAIN

KINGSWAY PUBLICATIONS
EASTBOURNE

First published 1987

ISBN 0 86065 535 0

*Cover photo shows front water
and the main bridge at Ashburnham Place
(colour photograph by Judges Postcards Ltd, Hastings).*

Printed in Great Britain for
KINGSWAY PUBLICATIONS LTD
Lottbridge Drove, Eastbourne, E. Sussex BN23 6NT by
Cox & Wyman Ltd, Reading.
Typeset by Nuprint Ltd, Harpenden, Herts AL5 4SE

Contents

Foreword to the Series

I am very pleased to commend this series of *Ashburnham Insights* which have come from the pen of Timothy Pain. Those of us who have watched developments at Ashburnham Place over the last few years have been particularly intrigued with the way things have developed. The careful thinking in these volumes comes from a background of faithful believing prayer for many years, and a deep concern for renewal and revival.

When there is an emphasis on experience, and when the subjective element in Christian living is to the fore, there is more need than ever for scriptural foundations. That is why we should be grateful to Tim for the obvious care he has taken to 'test everything', while at the same time to obey the apostolic injunction to 'despise not prophesyings'. Both should play their part in balanced Christian living.

Tim is not afraid to break new ground. I like the living way he writes, and I am sure these small books will have the wide readership they deserve.

Canon Michael Harper

This second set of four short books is dedicated to the memory of my grandmother, Mrs A. T. R. Jones (1894–1986).

This obstinate old East-Ender knew nothing but hardship and suffering throughout her long life. After twenty-two months of marriage she was widowed at twenty-two; Nan never recovered from this, yet lived on sixty-nine years to see thirteen of her fourteen great grandchildren. The twin sacrifices of her war-widows' pension and her wonderful praying supported many in Christian service.

Introduction

The developing series of *Ashburnham Insights* has been inspired by members of the Ashburnham Stable Family. This is a Christian community which is part resident at Ashburnham Place (a Christian training centre) and part scattered throughout the villages and small towns of East Sussex. It is our calling to maintain an unbroken 'Chain of Prayer' within the Palladian Stable which is adjacent to Ashburnham Place. We pray, by day and night, for the renewal and spiritual unity of all Christian churches in East Sussex. It is our firm conviction that the only hope of the world is in the renewal of the church, and as one expression of this we have taken it upon ourselves to share in a serious re-reading of Holy Scripture.

About ten thousand people visit us annually, and our observation and participation in hundreds of conferences has led to our conclusion that much contemporary teaching is based more on experience than on the Bible. Just as we have gained courage from each other to move from the shifting sands of tradition and experience, so we urge you to excavate and stand firm on the solid rock of Scripture.

The first set of books dealt with four issues which relate to the inner life of a local church—prophecy, tongues and explanations, intercession and baptism in Holy Spirit.

And in each slim volume I mentioned that these subjects have some evangelistic aspects. This second series deals with some facets of the life of a local church outside of the rows and semi-circles of saints on Sunday—blessing and cursing, healing, deliverance and counselling. And these four books are unashamedly evangelistic in their emphasis.

I fear that today we have two false preoccupations: one, the eternal massage of the souls of the saints; and two, power. I am sure that these books would sell much better if they were entitled 'Power healing for believers', 'Power deliverance for believers', 'Power blessing for believers', and so on. But they are written by a weak, fallible, ignorant and very vulnerable human being who is part of a community characterized by weakness, infirmity, foolishness and wordly insignificance, which is itself surrounded by thousands of people going to hell. Fortunately the members of the Ashburnham Stable Family have discovered that God's power is at its best when wrapped in human weakness. We are quite content with our frailty and infirmity but are sufficiently discontented with our unbelieving friends' eternal destiny to get up off our plastic chairs and follow the Poor Man of Galilee out into his weeping world.

This book is humbly offered as my personal re-reading of Scripture about blessing and cursing. It has been lived in, worked out and written down in community, and it is the product of much study and prayer, reading and listening, experimentation and embarrassment, banter and disagreement. A few within the Stable Family still lovingly disagree with one or two of my conclusions. Some of the material was originally worked on with the Rev Edmund Heddle for our leaders' training days, and other parts were worked on with Mr Ralph May for our ten week training courses. The final format is my own responsibility.

I have written the *Ashburnham Insights* with house-group leaders uppermost in my mind, and all the material has been refined through constant usage in groups of multiples of four. I have tried to write in a way that is simple enough to satisfy my wife, but is sufficiently thorough to persuade the local clergy. The Scripture references must all be looked up and examined as you proceed through the text.

Any acclamation should be shared between John and Marlis Bickersteth, Helen Brown, Sheila Day, Edmund Heddle, Gay Hyde, Roger Kemble, Sue Lindsay, Jo and Susie Marriott, Margery May, Ralph May, Alan Pain, David and Edna Parr, Catherine Rendall, Barbara Stidwill, Roger and Penny Wilcock and my wife Alison. Their prayers, patience, comments, research, advice, encouragement, work and love have brought these four Insights to publication.

Timothy Pain

The renewal lives by the re-reading of the New Testament.
Cardinal Suenens

Back to the Bible or back to the jungle.
Luis Palau

What the hammer? What the chain?
In what furnace was thy brain?
What the anvil? What dread grasp
Dare its deadly terrors clasp?

When the stars threw down their spears,
And watered heaven with their tears,
Did he smile his work to see?
Did he who made the Lamb make thee?
William Blake

Obed-edom had sons: Shemaiah the first-born, Jehozabad the second, Joah the third, Sacar the fourth, Nethanel the fifth, Ammiel the sixth, Issachar the seventh, Peullethai the eighth; God had indeed blessed him.... All these were sons of Obed-edom. These and their sons and brothers were well fitted for their task. For Obed-edom, sixty-two.
1 Chronicles 26:4–8

And there shall be no more curse.
Revelation 22:3(AV)

Come, Thou fount of every blessing,
Tune my heart to sing Thy grace:
Streams of mercy, never ceasing,
Call for songs of loudest praise.
Robert Robinson

Blessing and Cursing

During the last ten years or so many people have returned to the Scriptures to claim God's promises about 'greater things', 'anything you ask', 'signs following' and other such aspects of the Christian's inheritance in Jesus. As a result the members of the Ashburnham Stable Family, like so many people, have seen the lame walk, the deaf hear, the blind see, demons ejected, the broken-hearted bound up, prisoners to alcoholism and narcotics instantly set free and many other glorious demonstrations of the mighty authority Christian believers share in the authority of the name of Jesus and the power of the Holy Spirit. But there have been so very many who, despite a specific promise from God, have not been visibly helped. Such incidents have caused me to ask serious questions and to seek clear guidance from God about the cause of these apparent 'failures'. This book contains a few of the answers that I have found in my various searchings.

I have tried to help individuals who have been accident-prone to a ridiculous extent; churches with godly ministers and praying people, yet no sign of any fruit or growth; other churches which have experienced split after split in succeeding half-centuries for no apparent reason. I have been faced with the enigma of believing, baptized and

Spirit-filled Christians who have appeared to be unduly influenced by evil spirits; and I have been perplexed by families which have had such an extraordinary history running back through several generations that it has defied my imagination. My re-reading of Scripture about these and other related problems led to a study of blessing and cursing; this book contains some of my findings.

At the outset of my investigations I believed the only contemporary 'curse' was that which my wife endured with monthly regularity, and that 'blessing' was the world's response to a sneeze, a Christian greeting or, at best, a charismatic euphemism for something nice. I viewed the reality of cursing and blessing with the same cynical suspicion as those early-sixties evangelicals who came across contemporary accounts of tongues. Along with many I considered curses and blessings to be a form of medieval nonsense which could be safely dismissed with a knowing smirk.

Yet—as I studied the Tutankhamen incident, the Scharnhorst episode, other alleged curses, and missionary accounts of vodoo and the like—I began to wonder. Doubtless, some of the incidents could be explained by the power of suggestion coupled with tribal superstition, but there remained a hard core of inexplicable coincidences which, it seemed to me, could only be adequately explained by the reality of effective blessing and cursing.

With my disbelief suspended I turned to study the scriptural accounts of, and teaching about, cursing and blessing. The realization gradually dawned on me that these were not fringe activities occasionally indulged in by a few demented ancient prophets, but that cursing and blessing were central to the person of God himself. The God of the Old and the New Testaments is presented as one who both curses with awesome devastation and blesses with tangible, delightful consequences. The great

The Pharaoh

The most famous curse of all is that of Tutankhamen upon any who opened his tomb. This is blamed for the sudden death of many members of the expedition who opened and emptied his tomb. When the expedition leader, Lord Carnarvon, died of a mosquito bite, all the lights of Cairo went out. Engineers said the failure was 'scientifically inexplicable'.

One such incident can be dismissed as a coincidence, but there are many more stories like it. One of the least well known, but best authenticated, is as follows:

The Scharnhorst

During an industrial dispute a curse was placed on the German battle cruiser Scharnhorst. When she was half built she rolled on her side, killing 61 workmen and injuring 110. On the day she was to be launched, Hitler, Goering, Himmler, Hess and other Nazi leaders arrived in force—only to find that the Scharnhorst had vanished. She had launched herself in the night, crushing two barges.

Then at the shelling of Danzig in the Second World War, one of her guns exploded, killing nine men. At the siege of Oslo she was so badly damaged she had to make for home. As she swung into the River Elbe in darkness, her radar failed to pick up the approaching liner Bremen. There was a collision and the Bremen sank. It took much of the rest of the war to repair the Scharnhorst and then, when repairs were completed, the curse struck again. As she slipped out of her haven towards the Arctic under cover of darkness, a British patrol ship spotted her. The patrol radioed the British fleet, but the Scharnhorst was too fast for her pursuers. So the British commander fired a broadside on the off-chance of hitting her. It would have missed if the Scharnhorst's captain had not started a sharp turn at that moment.

That was the beginning of the end for Scharnhorst. Repeated attacks by destroyers, cruisers and the battleship Duke of York eventually sank her, with most of her crew. Two sailors who escaped by raft were found later—their emergency oil stove had exploded, burning them to death.

heroes of the Old Testament were effective cursers and blessers; Jesus and the members of the early church followed suit. This book presents my present understanding of the biblical teaching about this subject, and suggests that just as we are called to follow Christ's example in preaching and healing, so too we are called to curse and bless with his authority, and with similar clear results.

It is my prayer that these insights will contribute to the advance of the kingdom of God into the kingdom of darkness. Not every so-called 'failure' in ministry is due to a curse, but some are; not everybody will be put right by blessing, but some will. Very few unbelievers should be cursed, but the occasional one needs to be; not all believers merit frequent blessing, but we should all know how to bless effectively when called to do so by God.

I believe that it is crucial for today's church to develop a biblical understanding and practice of this subject. As we move closer to the difficult days before the return of Christ sensible believers will ensure that they become acquainted and skilled with every weapon in their spiritual arsenal: the curse and the blessing are two such weapons. They need to be re-discovered, dusted down, developed and demonstrated by local churches of every tradition and denomination.

Causes of Curses from God

I define a curse as words spoken (usually audibly, but occasionally inwardly) to an individual, family or nation, in the spiritual authority of the power of the name of God or of Satan. A true curse brings harm, destruction or judgement and can continue from generation to generation. Words spoken in cursing and blessing can determine history, which is why the Scriptures teach that great care should be taken by Christian believers with their speech. Words can have an effect which is undreamt of by most contemporary Christians.

A necessary cause

The Bible reveals Yahweh, the living God, as a God who delights to bless as far as the thousandth generation, but as a God who will curse to the third generation when there is a just cause. Proverbs 26:2 is a fundamental principle of cursing which cannot be overstated: 'The undeserved curse will never hit its mark.' This means that a curse which has no cause is utterly ineffective; in fact a tradition exists in witchcraft that a causeless curse upon a Christian boomerangs back upon the one who made it.

This principle of a necessary cause was such a part of

Jewish thought and understanding that they practised trial by cursing, a more equitable method of establishing guilt than the medieval English trial by ordeal, where, for example, an English woman under suspicion of guilt was bound and thrown in a river. If she floated she was deemed guilty and put to death, but if she sank she was posthumously declared innocent! Numbers 5:11–31 reveals the Jewish custom. In cases of uncertainty about adultery the suspected lady was cursed. If she was innocent the curse, having no cause, was ineffective; but if she was guilty the curse took effect—and what a curse! 'May Yahweh make of you an execration and a curse among your people making your thigh shrivel and your belly swell! May this water of cursing enter your bowels to swell your belly and shrivel your organs! The woman must answer: Amen! Amen!'

The first divine curse

God does not curse where there is no reason for this decisive act of judgement. Genesis 3:14–15, 16 and 17–19 are the first three recorded curses by God. The serpent was cursed because he had tempted Eve: 'Be accursed beyond all cattle, all wild beasts. You shall crawl on your belly and eat dust every day of your life. I will make you enemies of each other: you and the woman, your offspring and her offspring. It will crush your head and you will strike its heel.'

Eve was cursed because she had disobeyed God: 'I will multiply your pains in childbearing, you shall give birth to your children in pain. Your yearning shall be for your husband, yet he will lord it over you.'

Adam was cursed because he had listened to the voice of his wife and eaten from the forbidden tree: 'Accursed be the soil because of you. With suffering shall you get your food from it every day of your life. It shall yield you brambles and thistles, and you shall eat wild plants. With sweat on your brow shall you eat your bread, until you return to the soil, as you were taken from it. For dust you are and to dust you shall return.'

The curse on the serpent opposes the human race to the devil and his 'seed', his posterity; it hints at man's ultimate victory, and is the first glimpse of salvation, the *proto-evangelium*. The curse on Adam and Eve is appropriate to their specific functions: the woman suffers as mother and wife, the man as bread-earner. To these falls from their original perfection is added death, in verse 19; and the loss of intimacy with God, in verse 23.

These curses are hereditary: in Romans 5 Paul draws the comparison between our solidarity in Christ as Saviour, and our solidarity in Adam as sinner. Mankind is still affected by them today, and they will only cease to be operative when the great and glorious day of Revelation 22:3 dawns: 'and there shall be no more curse' (AV).

Anti-semitism

The Bible lists many reasons why God pronounces a curse. Genesis 12:1–3 introduces anti-semitism as one cause. Abram was blessed by Yahweh, and God promised that all those who bless Abram will be blessed by God, but all those who curse Abram will be cursed by God. Throughout history many of those nations and people who have opposed the descendants of Abram, whether Jews or Arabs, have been unsuccessful despite their apparent superiority in every area.

Genesis 12:3 uses two of the three basic Hebrew words for the verb 'to curse'. God will *arar* those who *qalal* Abram. *Arar* means to curse thoroughly and properly in a premeditated manner with the intention of bringing about great harm. It appears fifty-four times in the Old Testament and is normally only used to describe a curse by God. *Qalal* means to revile or vilify in a casual way, to esteem lightly, to make a contemptuous comment, to slight. The third verb, not used in these verses, is *qabab* which means to pierce or bore through with a hole, to execrate, to stab with words. The Arabic *kebab* is derived from it and has come to be the word used to describe the common demonic practice of sticking a pin into the effigy of a person to hurt them by an accident, illness, disaster, or even death. *Qabab* is weaker than *arar*, but stronger than *qalal*. It is a deliberate act, whereas *qalal* is a hasty reaction.

False religions

Deuteronomy 27:15–26 reveals the other principle causes of God's cursing activity. The first, in verse 15, is when a person turns away from worshipping Yahweh to follow false gods, to become involved in false religions or the occult. Those believers who contemplate visiting an astrologer or faith healer, or cultivating an interest in Islam, need to be made aware of the serious consequences which may arise from such actions. It is not only that they become vulnerable to the influence of evil spirits, but that they also face the possibility of being cursed by God. This is not something to be lightly contemplated.

For Old Testament believers this never meant that God unilaterally severed—even temporarily— their covenant relationship with him. Instead they ceased to enjoy some elements of his divine blessing during their temporal existence—to the extent of their earthly lives becoming miserable and difficult.

Some modern teachers suggest that, because we are in Christ, members of the New Covenant can enjoy all the benefits of the Old Covenant— and even more on top— without ever the possibility arising of incurring any of the punishments dealt out to those who broke the Old Covenant. But Christ did not come to abolish the Law and the Prophets; instead he came to complete them, to bring them to perfection. In Matthew 5:18–19 Jesus said, 'Till heaven and earth disappear, not one dot, not one little stroke, shall disappear from the Law until its purpose is achieved. Therefore, the man who infringes even one of the least of these commandments and teaches others to do the same will be considered the least in the kingdom of heaven.' In 1 Corinthians 11:28–32 Paul shows that many of those who are 'in Christ' are weak and ill, and some are even dead—as a punishment from the Lord. But this was a punishment with the express purpose of preventing their condemnation along with the world. A believer who is cursed by Almighty God still goes to heaven. He might arrive there earlier than anticipated, as did some Corinthians, he might have a very miserable time on earth, but his covenant relationship remains unbroken. He is still a child of God.

Slighting one's parents

Other actions which Deuteronomy 27 teaches may bring about a curse from God are to *qalal* one's mother or father. Exodus 21:17; Leviticus 20:9 and Proverbs 20:20 all show the seriousness of this action, and Jesus quoted these passages with approval in Mark 15:4 and Mark 7:10.

Other reasons

To mistreat one's neighbour, to have a wrong attitude to the helpless, to commit bestiality, incest or murder—all of these actions can put a person who has turned from following the living God under God's *arar*.

Disobedience

Deuteronomy 27:26 reveals what is the fundamental cause of any curse by God: it is deliberately to disobey a revealed command of God: 'A curse on him who does not maintain the words of the Law by observing them.' Blessing and cursing pivot upon our obedience; there is no half-way position. We either obey God and are blessed, or disobey him and are cursed—Deuteronomy 11:26–32 and 30: 15–20 make this clear. God is an extremist: if he does not bless us we are cursed, and if he does not curse us we are blessed. 2 Chronicles 34:22–28, Jeremiah 11:1–12, 17: 5–8 and 29:16–23 all emphasize disobedience as the essential cause of God's curse. Those who turn from total reliance on Yahweh to trust in man incur God's wrath, and this is constantly contrasted with the blessing awaiting those whose trust and hope is placed in Yahweh alone.

Half-hearted obedience

Jeremiah 48:10 points to the Revelation 3:15–16 principle: 'Cursed be he who does the work of the Lord half-heartedly!' God loathes those who are lukewarm far more than those who are ice-cold towards him. His curse is upon those who do his work half-heartedly, those reticent about engaging in spiritual warfare, those who think it better not to get too involved with things like exorcism, and those who would rather leave everything to the minister. This verse suggests to me one reason for the lack of blessing experienced by the English church during the twentieth century: I believe that God has cursed large sections of his church in this country. He still loves his bride; still receives her prayers, praise and worship; still longs for her repentance; but he has cursed her for her half-heartedness and disobedience, for her apathy to the poor and for her repeated immorality with the evil one.

Greed

Greed, the cancer of our age, is yet another important cause of a curse from God. This is seen in 2 Peter 2. In this diatribe against false teachers Peter lists all the characteristics of a false teacher which are abhorrent to God. But verse 14 suggests that foul greed is the most detestable attribute of all: 'Men with an infinite capacity for sinning, they will seduce any soul which is at all unstable. Greed is the one lesson their minds have learnt. They are under a curse.' These teachers are cursed children. They are still God's children, but they are cursed. The usual Greek noun for curse which is used here is *katara*, with the associated verb *kataraomai*. The Old Testament distinctions between different types of curses were not continued and so there is only one New Testament word: this accords with *arar*—the strongest type of curse. Perhaps *katara* would be better rendered by 'thoroughly curse'.

Joshua 6:18 is an associated verse which teaches that greed, or envy, attracts God's curse, but the main Old Testament passage on this thought is Malachi 3:6–12. Here God's curse is placed on the entire Jewish nation for their greed in keeping back all the gifts and tithes which are due to God. This suggests a correlation between the abysmal level of giving in some churches and their pitiful lack of blessing—or, as we could consider it, the awful barrenness which results from being cursed by God.

Misusing God's name

A final biblical reason for God cursing a person is misuse of his holy name. Jeremiah 29:23 states that those will be cursed who dare to presume to speak in the name of God without any direct order from him. And Zechariah 5:1–4 shows that those who swear falsely by his name will also be cursed. It is not the false swearing which attracts the curse, but the misuse of God's holy name. Malachi 2:1–9 is aimed at those priests who do not bring glory to God's name: 'And now, priests, this warning is for you. If you do not listen, if you do not find it in your heart to glorify my name, says Yahweh Sabaoth, I will send the curse on you and curse your very blessing.' Such leaders are to be cursed with a spiritual paralysis which will render them unable to take God's message to heart. This is a most serious passage and a real warning to Christian teachers who indulge in false teaching.

Anti-semitism, involvement in false religions, slighting parents, greed, disobedience or half-hearted obedience of God, and misusing God's name—a Christian believer who turns from God to indulge in any of these activities runs the risk of being cursed by God. We will examine the results of that in a later section, beginning on page 41.

Cursing by Men and Women

Enforced by God

Somehow, it does not appear seemly for a Christian to curse. I think that this is mainly because of the contemporary confusion between swearing and cursing, but the two activities are quite different. A believer's yes should be his yes and his no a no: we should not add any extra words to reinforce our statements. Christians should not be people who swear, but the Scriptures do teach that believers should be people who are effective cursers. Isaiah 65:15 states that God's chosen ones will curse and adds that one dreadful curse they are to use is, 'May the Lord Yahweh strike you dead.' Several biblical servants are recorded as having effectively used this curse.

Elisha used it. In 2 Kings 2:23–25 a large number of small boys jeered at him. '"Go up, baldhead!" they shouted, "Go up, baldhead!"' He turned round and looked at them, and he cursed them in the name of Yahweh. Forty-two of these youths were cleaved into many pieces by two she-bears in fulfilment of his curse: they had dared to cheek a prophet of God.

Peter used it. In Acts 5:7–11 he confronted the lying Sapphira: 'So you and your husband have agreed to put the Spirit of the Lord to the test! What made you do it? You hear those footsteps? They have just been to bury your husband; they will carry you out, too.' In response to this curse Sapphira instantly dropped dead at Peter's feet. Verse 11 must be the greatest understatement in the New Testament! However, it must be remembered that physical death here does not entail spiritual death.

Peter and Elisha were effective cursers, but how many contemporary Christians can lay claim to such a description? How many would even want such a description?

Peter's curse on Sapphira is a clear example of the Numbers 23:8 principle: 'How shall I curse one when God does not curse?' We cannot curse effectively those whom God does not curse. Balaam, that extraordinary Old Testament character, had been employed by King Balak of Moab to curse the Israelites. Numbers 22:6 makes it plain that Balaam was famous as a successful curser and blesser. Three times Balak attempted to get Balaam to curse the Jews and three times Balaam blessed them: he could only curse those whom God was cursing. This is an interesting use of the different Hebrew words for curse. Balaam could only *qabab*—pierce—those whom God *arar*—had thoroughly cursed. In Acts 5:1–6 Peter did not curse Ananias. God cursed Ananias with physical death because he had fulfilled two of the conditions for incurring a divine curse. Ananias had both lied in the name of God and had denied God gifts which had been promised to him. Peter saw that God's curse was upon the husband and so he knew that he had the authority to curse the wife if she met the same conditions. So he questioned her, then he cursed her, and the young men had to act as impromptu undertakers.

Cursing is not restricted only to men. In Judges 5:23 an angel of the Lord instructed the prophetess and judge Deborah to curse: '"Curse Meroz," says Yahweh's angel, "curse, curse the dwellers in it; for they never came to Yahweh's aid, to Yahweh's aid among the warriors."' It is interesting to note that Deborah is the only Old Testament character who is recorded as having uttered an *arar* curse; the men all used weaker *qabab* or *qalal* curses. Trust a woman to be the strongest curser!

The New Testament gives two examples of Paul cursing. The first is in Acts 13:4–12 when Elymas Magos, a false prophet cum Jewish magician, attempted to prevent Barnabas and Saul from speaking the word of God to Sergius Paulus who was the proconsul of Paphos in Cyprus. Saul looked Elymas Magos full in the face and cursed him. The curse was one of temporary blindness and Sergius Paulus became a believer, being astonished by what he had learnt about the Lord. This curse is a pivotal point in the life of Saul. With this curse Saul became Paul. After this curse he ceased to be the subordinate of Barnabas and became the real missionary leader: through this curse he came of age. Those Christian leaders who desire to push back the frontiers of the kingdom of darkness should learn about cursing; it is a most effective way of advancing the kingdom of God for those who are walking close enough to God to hear his clear instructions.

Paul's second curse is recorded in Acts 23:1–5. He was present before the Sanhedrin at the instruction of the Roman tribune in Jerusalem. Just as Paul began to speak, Ananias, the High Priest, ordered an attendant to strike Paul on the mouth. In response Paul cursed Ananias with the Isaiah 65:15 curse of the chosen ones. I believe that Paul's perennial eye problems meant that he did not realize he was cursing the High Priest, for he promptly apologized when this was pointed out to him. That Paul quoted from Exodus 22:27 shows that he understood he was using a curse; that he did not apologize for cursing but rather for breaking the Mosaic law convinces me that Paul believed it was both right and possible for a Christian believer to curse. However, I believe that Paul's apology was too late, for the words had been spoken and a speaker cannot revoke his curse because he has changed his mind. The physical blow was a valid cause, so the curse took effect and I suggest that from that moment Ananias was under sentence of death. Five years later he was assassinated while still in office as High Priest.

There are other interesting biblical examples which show that God's servants can curse. In Genesis 9:25–27 Noah cursed Canaan: 'Accursed be Canaan. He shall be his brothers' meanest slave.' The ten plagues on Egypt in chapters 7 to 11 of Exodus are really ten curses which were prophetically announced by Moses and Aaron; likewise the seals, trumpets and bowls of plagues in Revelation.

In Joshua 6:26 Joshua cursed any future person who attempted to rebuild Jericho: 'Cursed be any man who comes forth and builds this town up again! On his eldest son he shall lay its foundations, on his youngest set up its gates.' The result, over 500 years later, is seen in 1 Kings 16:34. Psalm 109 is a prophetic curse on Judas by David, and in 2 Samuel 3:26–32, David cursed Joab and his descendants. (What would you do if one of Joab's descendants came forward requesting prayer for healing of a discharging sore?) God's servants today need to learn how to curse and need to be ready to curse.

The New Testament portrays Jesus as an effective curser. In Mark 11:12–25 Jesus cursed a fruitless fig/mulberry tree—a tree which, because it had leaves, had all the appearance of also bearing fruit, but had none in reality. The disciples betrayed no surprise at Jesus actually cursing, only amazement at the short period of time which elapsed before the curse took effect. So Jesus taught them how to curse as he did. A right understanding of Mark

11:22 is crucial. Inaccurate translations have misled us by suggesting that Jesus said, 'Have faith in God,' but there is no preposition in the original Greek. The normal English translation leads us to expect an *en* or *eis* before 'God' with *theos* in the accusative or dative. However, there is no *eis* or *en* and *theos* is in the genitive case. We could write in our Bibles, 'Be having faith of God.' This transforms Jesus' teaching: to have God's faith in us is quite different from putting our faith in God. God's faith is absolute, for he is totally self-confident. He knows that he can achieve whatever he wants to do. Effective cursing becomes a possibility when we understand this.

Matthew 17:20 and Luke 17:5–6 both underline this. It is not that we need much faith to curse, only that we need the genuine article: it is quality not quantity that counts.

I suggest that there are five stages to cursing as Jesus cursed.

Knowing God's will

Cursing by a Christian is futile without the absolute certainty that God's will is known. We must never forget the Balaam principle that we cannot curse those whom God does not curse. Time must be spent listening to the Father to receive his identification of any obstacles which are so preventing God's glory from being seen that he wants these obstacles to be cursed. We need to ask the Father what are the factors, people, attitudes, and so on, which are preventing the work of God from developing. Each gospel suggests a particular type of obstacle for cursing. Mark implies that personal relationships, especially where unforgiveness exists, can be a 'mountain' to be cursed. Matthew hints that difficulty in ejecting demons may require this type of ministry. Luke, if taken with other passages about the fig/mulberry trees, suggests that those people who are like trees of good outward show but bearing no fruit are ripe candidates for 'uprooting'.

Authoritative order

These verses do not say, 'Whoever prays to me,' but, 'Whoever speaks to the mountain.' A curse is a command spoken audibly or silently to the person or situation; it is not a prayer prayed to the heavenly Father. Phrases should be used which are similar to the biblical 'Be taken up', 'Be cast into the sea', 'Move hence' and 'Be rooted up'. This will only be strange to some if they lack experience in the apostolic practice of uttering authoritative commands in ministry. The early church, and an increasing number today, spoke directly to eyes, limbs, demons, fevers and dead bodies 'in the name of Jesus', and commanded them to be changed. We often cry out in prayer, 'Do something,' but God whispers back, 'No, you do it.' This is the secret of the miracles at the wedding in Cana, the multiplication of the loaves, and Moses between the Egyptians and the Reed Sea. This executive authority, which Christ gave to the seventy-two in Luke 10:19, is ours to use today.

Receive God's faith

Home-produced faith is insufficient for cursing. The God-given confidence that the curse will be effective is needed: Paul knew that Elymas would be blinded; Peter knew that Sapphira would drop dead. When the Holy Spirit gives this gift of God's faith we are to accept the event as already being done. To believe is not to have a faint hope something could or might take place; for example, 'I think (but am not really sure) that Sapphira will die today.' Instead, to believe is to know for certain, for example, 'I believe (God has promised—and there is Ananias' body lying over there) that Sapphira will die today.'

Sustained speaking

The Greek tense used in Mark 11:23 means that we are to go on saying to the mountain, 'Get up and throw yourself into the sea.' It is not a one off command. We are to go on cursing a particular obstacle; the beginner needs persistence. When members of the Ashburnham Stable Family began to 'move mountains' and 'curse' it took ten months of sustained speaking before the mountains began to move. During the last year I, and others, have cursed three people with the curse, 'Be removed from this place, or be changed by his grace.' Two have gone and the third is definitely changing, but in each case it took over six months of weekly cursing.

Visible result

The grammatical construction of the phrases 'it will be done', 'it will move', emphasizes the certainty of fulfilment. Luke used a Greek tense which refers to a time prior to the command, for example, 'it would have obeyed', and this underlines the fact that there is to be a tangible consequence to cursing. There can be no doubt about the outcome of the curse when a Christian believer knows God's will, receives God's faith, and then continues to speak out an authoritative order.

Some people—and I am one of them—wonder how the God who worked such decisive and incisive New Testament miracles can belittle himself by getting involved in the feeble long drawn-out affairs seen today. If we argue that the delay is due to our personal failures we are implying that somehow we are involved in the actual mechanics of the miracles—whether cursing, blessing, healing or exorcism. But that is not so. God works the miracles, not us; it is he who enforces the spoken curse, our part is merely to announce it.

So why do we need to go on announcing miracles? I think that there are a number of different answers. Firstly, God delights in developing persistence and patience in our characters. Secondly, we are rediscovering the miraculous after centuries of neglect, and are still rusty, tentative and experimental. Thirdly, in our proud and instant era it must be a high priority to God to burst the bubble of our arrogant conceit and teach us the hard lesson of humility. Fourthly, we need God to underline to us the oft-forgotten truth that divine strength lies in human failure, foolishness and weakness. And fifthly, God delights in mysteries; and this, most certainly, is a mystery.

Enforced by Satan

A curse spoken by a human being is enforced either by Yahweh, the living God, or by Satan. Job 3:8 shows that curses can arouse Leviathan. No sooner does a curse which is uninspired by God pass human lips than Leviathan (another name for Satan) summons a foul minion to carry out the evil deed.

Curses against oneself

It is possible to curse oneself, and for this to be honoured by Satan. Rebekah did this in Genesis 27. She pressed Jacob to substitute himself for Esau so that he would receive Isaac's blessing. When Jacob remonstrated that this would leave him vulnerable to a curse, Rebekah spoke the awful words of verse 13 to bring the curse upon herself. The curse took effect the same day: Jacob had to leave home and Rebekah never set eyes upon her favourite son again. Isaac, nearly blind and on the verge of death, lived on for another forty-four years to see his sons reunited and prosperous, but that is the last we hear of Rebekah.

Many people today cursed their bodies when they were young. They lay in bed begging somebody somewhere, anybody anywhere, to do something about their face, their hair, breasts, legs and so on. And then in later life they wonder what—or rather who—has caused a certain physical problem. The curse must usually be dealt with before healing can begin.

In Matthew 27:24–26 the crowd cursed themselves and their children when they cried out, 'His blood be on us and on our children!' For twenty centuries the Jews have lived under a curse which I believe was placed on them by their ancestors; they have been hounded, hated and persecuted because Leviathan has been aroused. And with what vicious glee he fulfils this curse—even to this day. I believe that this curse will only cease to operate when the Jews repent and revoke the words of their forebears.

Curses by authority

A curse by one in a position of authority may also be honoured. In John 19:15–17 the Chief Priests placed their people under a different curse when they cried out, 'We have no king except Caesar.' Again Leviathan was eager to fulfil their terrible wish: for centuries the Jews were ruled by other 'caesars' until one more cruel and vindictive than all before him ruled over them with mass torture and holocaust death. I believe that Adolf Hitler, who some assert was greatly influenced by Spengler's cry, 'We need another Caesar', was both Barabbas and Caesar to the Jews. It seems to me that Hitler's suicide brought freedom from this curse and was one factor in enabling the Jews to become an independent, self-governing nation at last. The curse of the Chief Priests was only effective because they had been given authority over the whole nation. They cursed their people, and it was honoured by Satan. In Genesis 31:32 Jacob unwittingly cursed his favourite wife. It was eagerly enforced by Satan and within a short space of time Rachel died in childbirth.

Husbands can curse their wives, parents their children, ministers their people, teachers their pupils, employers their employees. This is a well-observed phenomenon; it is not normally called a curse, but it is a variation of what we are examining. A father cries, with some element of truth, 'You're useless'—and the child becomes more useless. A teacher shouts, 'You will never be as good as your brother'—and a floundering pupil drops further behind.

These are curses which are made effective by the authority of the speaker and, at times, are enforced by an aroused Apollyon—the destroyer. Occasionally, God does honour the curse of one in a position of authority when there is a just cause. The story of Jotham's curse related in Judges 9:1–57 is an example of this, but normally these are evil, Satan-honoured curses.

Cursing by those in authority in the church takes the form of excommunication. Excommunication is these days euphemistically called 'exercising discipline'. Paul's words in 1 Corinthians 5 are the basis for this practice. Paul developed the Old Testament practice of Deuteronomy 13 and ordered the Corinthians to expel a man from their midst: 'Then with the power of our Lord Jesus he is to be handed over to Satan so that his sensual body may be destroyed and his spirit saved on the day of the Lord.' This chapter seems to imply that the Christians were to cease normal social contact with the individual and to exclude him from the eucharist, but that they were not to neglect to pray for his repentance and were to encourage him to continue to attend meetings to hear the teaching of God's word.

Social ostracism and denial of access to the sacraments is, in itself, a curse because it cuts the person off from involvement in the life of the church—which is the place

God has ordained for protection from the power of curses. We will mention this further on pages 78–84. Clearly the additional measure of handing the person over to Satan is extremely serious and only to be used as a last resort.

In the past the church erred by taking it upon itself to enforce this curse with physical tortures instead of permitting God to enforce the curse in his own time and manner by allowing Satan freer access to the miscreant. Some sections of the church today make the very serious mistake of using the curse of excommunication in minor matters without realizing the awesome, devastating consequences which may result in the lives of those whom they curse in this way. Paul advocated excommunication in 'a case of sexual immorality among you that must be unparalleled even among pagans'. But I am very familiar with three instances in churches of very different traditions where those excommunicated either (a) lived too far from the church building; or (b) gossiped; or (c) intended to marry someone from a radically different Christian tradition. In one case two family deaths followed; in another, premature senility; and in the third a large number of difficult and disruptive problems ensued. The excommunicating churches are not necessarily even aware of these outcomes, let alone conscious of any connection between their 'discipline' and the family disasters.

The Scriptures grant few glimpses of Satan's servants cursing, yet they do hint at a backdrop of a wide activity in satanic cursing. Balaam is the archetype of the professional curser with a large clientele who exists today in ever-increasing numbers in Western Europe and North America. King Balak could not win the war on his own, so he turned to the demonic for help. It is now a common practice for some companies to call in demonic help and, at times, the police do the same: astrologers, spiritists and clairvoyants are all summoned to help with murder and

Steve and Christine Green— Park Road Methodist Church, St Leonards, East Sussex

Steve had been a member of his church for about five years when he told the elders that he was going out with a girl from a different church. The elders immediately wanted to vet her Christian beliefs, but Steve was unwilling to put the relationship on ice whilst Christine's background was examined. Against the advice of the elders Steve and Christine became engaged.

They then began attending alternate services at each other's church. Both found this awkward as the gulf between worship at a charismatic house church and a very high Anglican church was rather wide!

Some people at Steve's church were openly friendly, but many refused to acknowledge them. One leader appeared to be rather antagonistic and expressed his opinion that Christine's church was not a Christian church, which shocked and hurt Steve and Christine. The following day they received an ultimatum for Steve either to write an open letter resigning from the church, or be disowned publicly at the next meeting. Steve chose the first option.

The Greens say, 'The hardest thing to cope with was the social isolation and sense of rejection. Some old friends remained loyal, but for the most part we had to develop a new circle of friends. We started worshipping at a Methodist church where we knew a few people. It had a lively reputation but we felt that it lacked the sense of community of the house church.'

They still attend a Methodist church, but find it an uncomfortable compromise. They are very wary of becoming too dependent on any one particular church and try to express their Christian commitment through their home and family. Since their 'excommunication' they have had many real problems, and difficulties which date from before their marriage have intensified. They know that God alone can provide the answer but in their case the answer has been very slow in coming.

missing person enquiries. The church is at war, and curses are in the armoury of the enemy. In 1 Samuel 17:43 Goliath began the battle by cursing David, and the spiritual army of evil does the same thing today. David knew how to deal with the curse; do we?

It is impossible to estimate just how much satanic cursing goes on today, but we do know that it is considerable. The immigration into the UK from India, Pakistan, the Middle East, Africa and the West Indies has brought large numbers of expert cursers to our shores. Islam is a religion of cursing; voodoo is widely practised in the black community and is, perhaps, the most powerful and dangerous form of satanic cursing today. We turn a blind eye to such things at our peril.

The Evidence of a Curse

Once the possibility of curses has been conceded, there are important questions to be answered. It is one thing to believe in cursing, but quite another to establish the existence of a particular curse in any given instance. How can we tell if a client that we are attempting to help is affected by a curse? Is there any difference in consequence between a curse from God and a curse enforced by Satan?

Deuteronomy 28 is the key chapter here. It describes in great detail the evidence of God's blessing (verses 1–14), and the results of God's cursing (verses 15–68). It is best for the squeamish not to read these verses after a meal or just before bed!

A divine curse

A curse is not just a psychological suggestion, or the power of the human will, or a 'T' field as so many academic parapsychologists maintain, for God does not always give prior notification when he is about to curse. His curse usually comes unheralded, but circumstances soon change after its arrival. However, human curses are normally announced. In the realm of the demonic this is to gain the benefit of the power of suggestion and anticipatory fear, but the lasting impact of a curse down through several generations cannot be due to these factors alone.

It must be remembered that God's curse is principally placed upon those followers of Yahweh who have deliberately turned from obedience to specific disobedience: their blessing is exchanged for a curse. The following suggested evidences are not to be looked for among unbelievers, but only among God's people. They can be seen in individual lives, in families and in the corporate life of a local church. I believe that the long list of ghastly consequences found in Deuteronomy 28:15–68 can be broken down into six basic areas which give evidence of a curse from God.

Mental and physical sickness

Here, as elsewhere in the Scriptures, it is revealed that sickness can sometimes be the result of a curse. In these verses God promises to send mental and physical sickness upon his people when they deliberately disobey him:

> Yahweh will infect you with the plague until it has consumed you (verse 21).
>
> Yahweh will strike you down with consumption, fever, inflammation, burning fever (verse 22).
>
> Yahweh will strike you down with Egyptian boils, with swellings in the groin, with scurvy and the itch for which you will find no cure. Yahweh will strike you down with madness, blindness, distraction of mind (verses 27 and 28).
>
> You will be driven mad by the sights your eyes will see. Yahweh will strike you down with foul boils on knee and leg, for which you will find no cure, from the sole of your foot to the top of your head (verses 34 and 35).

Undiagnosed diseases; sicknesses that cannot be cured; illnesses where for some reason the cure has not worked;

the church with a quite ridiculous percentage of people continuously ill; the family with a history of severe illness for the last three generations; the individual who catches Aids or genital herpes; all of these things are suggestive, but never conclusive. If there is no response to either the healing ministry of the church or mainstream medicine then the possibility of God's curse must be considered. Questions should be asked relating to a cause in this or any of the preceding generations (Exodus 20:4–6). In cases of adoption or honest ignorance the Holy Spirit is quite able to place any necessary factual information into either the client's or the minister's mind.

Failure and defeat

Another evidence can be seen when an individual, family or church fails in every scheme or endeavour; when every enterprise appears doomed to disaster before it has begun. Perhaps it is. The essence of blessing, as will be seen on pages 59–61 is fruitfulness and multiplication, and the absence of these blessings can indicate the presence of a curse.

> Yahweh will have you defeated in front of your enemies; you will come at them by one way and flee before them by seven (verse 25).
>
> You will never be anything but exploited and plundered continually, and no one will come to your help (verse 30).
>
> You will submit to the enemies that Yahweh will send against you (verse 48).

There are many churches which import evangelists, run missions, preach the gospel fervently, and yet fail to grow. Why? I do not know whether church growth analysts include questions about cursing and blessing in their formulations, but any attempts to implement church growth principles in a cursed church will only lead to further defeat and failure, to yet more disenchantment and despair. They will not lead to blessing. 'Try harder' or 'pray more' are not the best replies to give to a chronic failure, or to a constantly defeated individual. It is much more helpful to ask gentle questions about possible areas of disobedience and incidents in recent family history.

Poverty

I am repulsed by the idea that material prosperity is an automatic consequence of Christian conversion, but it cannot be denied that God does choose to give material prosperity to some as a blessing (not as a right), and to send poverty to others as a curse.

> Accursed will be your pannier and your bread bin...the produce of your soil, the increase of your cattle (verses 17 and 18).
>
> Plant a vineyard, you will not gather its first-fruits. Your ox will be killed before your eyes and you will eat none of it (verses 30 and 31).
>
> You will cast seed in plenty on the fields but harvest little, for the locust will devour it (verse 38).
>
> Hunger, thirst, nakedness, utter destitution. He will put an iron yoke on your neck (verse 48).

God's curse of poverty normally comes through some great, unavoidable disaster which causes instant financial embarrassment and from which there is no hope of release. God's poverty always looks permanent: it is when income is below necessary expenditure and no human effort can solve the problem—short of a miracle! Such a disaster is not always a piece of misfortune; it might be a God-sent curse.

Family break-up

If multiplication is one sign of blessing, so division is a common consequence arising from a curse by God.

> Betroth a wife, another man will have her (verse 30).
>
> Your sons and daughters will be handed over to another people, and every day you will wear your eyes out watching eagerly for them, while your hands are powerless (verse 32).
>
> The tenderest and most fastidious among you will glower at his brother, even at the wife he cherishes and at the children that are left to him (verse 54).

This evidence can be seen in the Christian family where the husband and wife are at loggerheads and their children reject the faith and scatter themselves around the country; or it is visible in the church which two hundred years ago denied the doctrine of the Trinity and since then, despite returning to the truth, has suffered split after split after split. Are such situations due to curse, coincidence or honest mistakes? Only intelligent questions and the help of the Holy Spirit will provide the answer.

Oppression

Another Deuteronomy 28 evidence is seen in the Christian to whom depression, sleep problems and binding fears are a frequent problem.

> Yahweh will give you a quaking heart, weary eyes, halting breath. Your life from the outset will be a burden to you; night and day you will go in fear, uncertain of your life. In the morning you will say, "How I wish it were evening!", and in the evening, "How I wish it were morning!", such terror will grip your heart (verses 65–67).

We need to watch out for those believers who have received 'deliverance ministry' from every itinerant expert and yet have remained completely unchanged. Maybe they have even been treated by Christian psychiatrists and not been helped. We need to consider the possibility that they have been cursed by God.

Bad reputation

Three times the gospel writers used the word *kakologeo* to describe Christ's word for a curse. This means to speak evil of someone. The final evidence of God's curse, given in Deuteronomy 28, is this sense of humiliation in the eyes of men, and of perpetual disfavour from God. The person receives the impression, which may or may not be based on reality, that everybody is against him, that lots of people are speaking evil, gossiping, slandering and spreading calumny about him.

> You will become a thing of horror for all the kingdoms of the earth (verse 25).
>
> You will become a thing of horror, a proverb, and a byword to all the peoples among whom Yahweh takes you (verse 37).
>
> You will want to sell yourselves to your enemies as serving men and women, but no one will buy you (verse 68).

These are the six biblical evidences, the grounds for reasonable suspicion, that a curse from God may exist. When such results are found prayer for guidance must be made, and sensitive questioning undertaken, to establish a possible cause for the curse by God. We should not ask questions and pray merely to prove or disprove a particular theory, but rather to establish God's truth—whatever that may be.

A curse enforced by Satan

The Bible does not give any specific evidences of a curse uttered by a man, then enforced by Satan. However, we know that Satan is not a creator; he can only distort things that God has made. It is a good principle in any study to do with the demonic to realize that everything is either a corruption, distortion or counterfeit of God's glorious original. This suggests that the evidence of curses enforced by Satan could look somewhat similar to God's. My experience, and discussion with others who have worked in this area, endorses this idea. I propose the following as seven evidences of such a satanically-enforced curse; they are only empirical, and therefore are ready to be altered as experience and knowledge in these matters develops.

Suicide

Satan is 'the destroyer' and it is only to be expected that he will enforce curses in this terrible fashion. One evidence of his curse-enforcing activity is seen in the family which has an extraordinary history of repeated suicide attempts —both successful and failed—in several generations.

Gynaecological problems

Another sign is a history of repeated miscarriages, difficulties at menstruation or the menopause, and related gynaecological problems. God's original curse on Satan specified that the offspring of the woman would crush his head: he has been out for revenge ever since. His attempt at total corruption of the womb in Genesis 6:1–4 was sovereignly thwarted by God, and his revenge is seen in this satanic corruption of God's curse. When God curses he removes all hope, for barrenness is the epitome of his curse. But Satan distorts this and enforces curses with miscarriages so that hope is constantly fanned and then quickly dashed. This same demonic principle of the dangled carrot which is then rapidly withdrawn is one of the chief distinguishing features between a divine and a satanically-enforced curse. God does not play such games.

Chronic sickness

Repeated chronic sickness, both physical and mental, especially when there is no clear medical diagnosis, is a common symptom of a satanically-enforced curse. Again the evidence should be looked for in several members of a family and not only in an isolated individual. A satanic sickness normally looks as if it is just about to be healed, but the sad history is always one of repeated disappointments, of many promised cures which do not work.

Emotional breakdown

Another evidence is seen in the family which has frequent residential stays in a mental hospital; the church where successive ministers have suffered nervous breakdowns; or the family with a history of premature senility in many generations. We might think it is 'just them' or 'bad blood'. But mental and emotional breakdowns, getting better, then getting worse again, hopes raised, then dashed, suggest that Satan may be enforcing a curse.

Accident prone

A fifth result of a curse enforced by Satan can be observed when somebody has an abnormal, incredible, highly improbable rate of accidents. Everything always goes wrong. It is seen in the individual, family or church to whom disaster after disaster happens. God might curse a family with a terrible calamity but if so he does it in such a way that there can be no possible human, rational explanation, whereas Satan's accidents are comparatively

Pat Nolan—Battle Baptist Church, East Sussex

Pat was our next-door neighbour for three years from July 1982 until November 1985. During this time Pat, her husband Dennis, myself, and many of the people involved with us came to believe that Pat and her family were under the influence of a satanically-enforced curse. The following is some of the evidence that led us to this conclusion:

Pat's mother and her aunt both regularly threaten to commit suicide. Their own mother had gassed herself in 1961, and there had been another suicide associated with the family.

Pat had serious gynaecological problems that necessitated frequent hospital treatment; her mother's first child died at five hours and two years after Pat was born she suffered a serious miscarriage.

The grandmother endured an exceptionally unhappy marriage and her brother was divorced twice—quite unusual at the turn of the century. Pat's mother lived apart from her husband for over thirty years, but they never divorced each other; instead they remained in close contact yet were always at loggerheads. When the husband died, Pat's mother was left nothing in the will.

There have been six court cases between members of the family in the last half-century. The whole family history is characterized by bitterness, unforgiveness, skullduggery and strife. Each member of the family appears to be at war with a different member.

In 1920 the family owned thirty houses. On paper they were an affluent family, but they all lived like paupers. In the last sixty-six years nearly all the property has been frittered away. Their money has not been spent in wild, enjoyable living, in fact, nobody knows quite what has happened to it. Pat's father's houses were in a terrible condition. His pleasure came from trying to make money, but he got no enjoyment from using it. It simply vanished in the wake of human unhappiness.

After a terrible pregnancy, when only a miracle saved Pat's first baby's life, further gynaecological disorders drove us to prayer—and the action described on page 82.

minor. Each one has a human, rational explanation, but over a period of time the coincidences mount up. Someone can be noticed lurking behind the mayhem.

Family strife

A family history of marriage breakdowns, alienation, intense wranglings, unforgiveness and strife is yet another evidence of Leviathan roused into action by the curse of a man or woman. When God curses a family he brings separation and division, but Satan keeps the family together, with everyone hating and fighting each other. Superficially it appears that things may be fine, but underneath is bitter invective.

Material adversity

This is my final suggested symptom of a satanically-enforced curse. It is not the same as poverty. Poverty is when there is not enough income to make ends meet. Adversity is ample income in theory, but never enough money to get by in reality. For one reason or another, despite economy drives and locks on phones, the family, individual or church lives in the red. On paper they should have enough, yet in spite of the accountant's skill and friendly advice, they never prosper. It may be that they have been cursed by another—and Satan is eagerly enforcing it.

I look for several of these evidences before considering the possibility of the existence of a satanically-enforced curse. Sometimes it is obvious—but careful questions usually need to be asked, the answers verified, advice sought from a colleague, and then the wisdom and knowledge of the Holy Spirit must be given before you can proceed with any ministry.

From Curse to Blessing

The atonement of Jesus Christ is God's basic provision for the release of men and women from the earthly and eternal consequences of all curses. The cross of Calvary is the only legal basis of escape from any curse, whether divine or satanic, for only Christ's atoning, substitutionary death has dealt with the sin of the whole world. Nehemiah 13:2 looks back to Balaam and also peers prophetically forward to Calvary: 'But our God turned the curse into a blessing.' How did he do this? Galatians 3:1–14 provides the answer: 'Christ redeemed us from the curse of the law by becoming a curse for us, for it is written: "Cursed is everyone who is hung on a true." He redeemed us in order that the blessing given to Abraham might come to the Gentiles through Christ Jesus, so that by faith we might receive the promise of the Spirit' (Galatians 3:13–14, NIV). It is not just that Jesus was cursed by God when he was on the cross, but rather that he became a curse.

2 Corinthians 5:21 teaches a parallel principle: 'For our sake God made the sinless one into sin, so that in him we might become the goodness of God.' Christ was made not into a sinner, but into sin. It was by this legal fiction that Christ became answerable for the curse God laid on the world for defying the Law. Romans 8:3 and Colossians

2:14 underline this fact. Caiaphas, who was High Priest for the year, was determined to kill Jesus and could have done so easily on several occasions, but that would not have sufficed. Caiaphas wanted Christ to be crucified so that the curse of Deuteronomy 21:22–23 could be attached to him; this would be the final convincing evidence that Jesus was a blasphemous impostor. So to Christ went the curse, and to us comes the blessing. The message of Galatians 3 is not only that the cross is our means of escape from the effect of the curse, but also that by the work of Christ on the cross we can exchange our cursed state for the blessing of Abraham.

By the cross the way has been made open for us to receive the quintessence of blessing—the promised Holy Spirit; and this blessing is only available because Christ became a curse for us. On the cross Christ exhausted all the evil which is due to the descendants of Adam; he did this so that those who repent and believe may be baptized and receive Holy Spirit, and so share in the blessing due to him because of his perfect obedience. Surely this should cause us to gaze at the One on the cross with renewed gratitude, praise and love.

Some preachers manipulate the emotions by dwelling on the physical agonies endured by Christ. The early church did not do this. Tens of thousands died as he died. Many suffered crueller and more lingering deaths: Christ's crucifixion was quick and easy compared to the average Roman execution. We can only begin to guess at the depths of Calvary by taking Isaiah 53:1–12 and placing it next to Deuteronomy 28:15–68: 'Ours were the sufferings he bore, ours the sorrow he carried, but we thought of him as someone punished, struck by God, and brought low. Yet he was pierced through for our faults, crushed for our sins. On him lies a punishment that brings us peace, and through his wounds we are healed' (verses 4 and 5).

Hindsight causes us to think of the plunging spear when we read 'pierced through', but, as was mentioned on page 22, to pierce through is the supreme symbol of a curse. All the terrible curses of Deuteronomy 28 came upon Christ whilst he was nailed to the cross: there is even a prophetic hint in this chapter of Christ's quick death (verse 20), of the total eclipse from noon to three (verse 29), and of the Roman executioners (verse 49). When the crowds cried, 'Crucify' they were prescribing our release and our redemption. The curse hanging on the Jerusalem tree is the amazing basis of our salvation: the blessed One took our curse on himself, so that we cursed men could receive his blessing. Hallelujah!

Abraham was the pioneer of the pathway from curse to blessing. He believed God and took him at his word despite the obstacles of human reasoning and glaring facts: his faith was imputed to him as righteouness. Our own justification is by grace through faith, not by trying harder! We are not saved by the good works that we do, but we are saved to do God's good works; we are not saved by our obedience, but we are saved to create the possibility of obedience. Blessing is reserved for the obedient, and faith is the entrance to the highway of obedience. Faith in Christ moves us from the place of the certainty of a curse, to the position of the possibility of blessing.

The atonement is the legal basis of this exchange. However, it is one thing to have a right, but quite another to enjoy it. We may have been left a fantastic fortune of blessing, but there is a very crooked lawyer on the other side. God gave Israel the promised land, but they had to fight every inch of the way to possess it. So too we are called to spiritual warfare both to enable us to enjoy God's blessing, and to help others move from their curse to his blessing.

Blessing from God

Great damage is done by teaching that God is a schizophrenic Jekyll and Hyde. Some people consider that the Old Testament God was a terrible tyrant, a sadistic smasher who forced men to beg on bended knee. They assume that somewhere between Malachi and Matthew he transformed himself into a gentle heavenly Father who delights to give good gifts to girls and boys. But the God of Abraham has not changed. He blesses and he curses. His wrath is the only true reaction love can have to spoiling sin; his righteous indignation is the reassurance of his love. Exodus 20:4–6 reveals a jealous God who punishes to the third and fourth generations, but who also shows kindness to those who love him, right to the thousandth generation. Deuteronomy 7:7–15 amplifies this: God's cursing is limited, but his blessing is unlimited; he is faithful and true; his blessing is constant, not spasmodic. Deuteronomy 5:8–10, Nehemiah 9:17–37, Psalm 86:15 and James 1:17–18 all portray the character of this God who blesses.

The Hebrew verb for bless is *barak*, with its companion noun of *berakah*. Its root meaning is of someone kneeling down, bowing down, in fact of God bending over to make us prosperous. Its New Testament equivalent is *eulogeo*, which means to speak well of a person. *Ahere* and *makarios*, the Hebrew and Greek words for happy, are translated as *blessed* in older versions of the Bible, but we are not concerned with these words in a study on blessing—they describe a result of blessing rather than the act of blessing.

The first blessing that God spoke was to the fish and the birds: 'Be fruitful, multiply, and fill the waters of the seas; and let the birds multiply upon the earth' (Genesis 1: 21–22). Put simply it meant: 'Get mating; enjoy it; and have lots of babies.' The kernel of God's blessing is fruitfulness and multiplication—physical reproduction with lots of babies and children, and spiritual reproduction to fill the earth with the children of God.

God blessed mankind in the same way in Genesis 1:28: 'Be fruitful, multiply, and fill the earth and conquer it.' He repeated the blessing in 5:2, and in 9:1 extended it to Noah after the flood. This central thrust of God's blessing runs through Scripture and it is vital that Christians appreciate this today. Am I blessed? Am I reproductive? It is the same question. Is my local church blessed? Is it fruitful, multiplying and filling the locality? Again, it is an identical question. We are either blessed in our multiplication or cursed in our barrenness. There is no half-way state.

But some of my closest friends are physically unable to have children. What can I say to them? How do I consider them? Are they cursed friends? Well, yes, in a way they are—and so, still, am I. The Genesis 3:16–19 curses on Adam as breadwinner and on Eve as wife and mother are still in operation. The rain still falls on the just and the unjust. Christian women do not have easier labours than their unconverted neighbours. The Christian gardener does not have fewer thorns and thistles in his vegetable plot than his pagan counterpart. Though in Christ our personal cursed state has been exchanged for the blessing of God, this does not mean that aspects of God's curse on mankind—disease, the ageing process, death itself—cease to affect us. As I write this one of my sons has mumps. He has not been personally cursed with this illness, but rather he is personally affected by the generic curse on mankind of decay and disease. So it is with my childless friends. They have not necessarily been personally cursed with barrenness, but they are personally affected by the generic curse on the womb of mankind.

In Christ the door has been opened for us to experience an infinite degree of blessing. But God chooses which particular physical blessings to give to any one person or family. For some reason which he will not disclose he has not chosen to bless me with musical ability, a sociable nature or material prosperity. Instead he has blessed me with four children, considerable creativity and a warped sense of humour. It is always important not to focus on the types of blessing which God has sovereignly given to others, but rather to concentrate on whether we have rejected or buried, or are embarrassed or annoyed by his choice of blessing for us.

The level of our blessing may be determined by our obedience but the type of blessing is determined by the will of God. So what is blessing?

I define a blessing as words spoken, always audibly, in the authority of the name of God, which bring a tangible, physical, material or spiritual benefit to an individual, family, nation or church and may continue from generation to generation. Deuteronomy 8:13–15 and 28:1–14 include as evidence of divine blessing, fertility, health, victory, prosperity, good reputation, family harmony and success. When God blesses he gives any or all of these things.

The story of Abram teaches much about God's blessing.

The blessing could have been Terah's, but he disobeyed God by settling down in Haran, so the option of blessing passed to his seventy-five-year-old son, Abram. If Abram would be obedient, leave his home and country, go to a land he did not know, then he would be blessed with the seven-fold blessing of Genesis 12:1–3. A quarter of a century later the blessing spread to Sarai (17:15–22) and Abraham asked for it to extend also to Ishmael. God granted Ishmael the physical and material blessings of fertility, fruitfulness and multiplication, but he would not bless Ishmael spiritually. In the Old Testament God's physical and material blessings were freely given, but the spiritual blessing of the divine presence was restricted to those whom God chose to be within the covenant relationship. These spiritual blessings are now more widely available in Christ.

Ephesians 1:4–14 is Paul's exposition of spiritual blessing. Each clause reveals a different aspect of blessing: election, holiness, living in God's presence, adoption, the gift of grace, freedom through forgiveness, revelation and salvation. The paean climaxes in verses 13 and 14 when the Holy Spirit is revealed as the present pledge of our glorious eternal heritage of divine blessing.

God always tests those whom he chooses to bless; this is so that he can increase their blessing. Genesis 22 demonstrates the faith of both the elderly Abraham and his son Isaac, who by then must have been in his early thirties. They rose early so that Sarah could not prevent their journey to Mount Moriah. Verses 5 and 8 are the great twin statements of Abramic faith: 'We will worship and come back to you' and 'God himself will provide the lamb'. Abraham and Isaac had to walk all the way to the place of sacrifice. One was willing to forfeit his son; the other was ready to lay down his life. And so God blessed their faith-filled obedience: in verses 16–18 he showered blessings on Abraham, promising great multiplication and renown; and in Genesis 25:11, after Abraham's death, God blessed the faith-filled obedience of Isaac. God's choice of whom to bless is always unconditional, but the reception is absolutely conditional on faith-filled obedience. The details of both Abraham's and Isaac's lives demonstrate that it is not empty words when God says he blesses: his blessing brings a dramatic change in circumstances. God's blessing has measurable, tangible, physical results, and should not be reduced to the level of a cheap charismatic greeting. How we have destroyed this word by relegating it to an unthinking rejoinder to another's sneeze! Jacob wanted God's blessing, but because he went about it the wrong way God did not voluntarily bless Jacob. Only when Jacob had been humbled and lamed, and had begged for a divine blessing did there come the response of Genesis 32:29, which is quoted in 48:4 and seen fulfilled in Exodus 1:7. The blessing then passed to Joseph (Genesis 39:2–6 and 41:52) and from him on to the nation of Israel. God chose them for special blessing from among all the other nations. Why did he do this? Only because he loved them: Deuteronomy 7:7–16 shows this. And then the divine blessing passed on from the children of Israel to the people of God today. God wants to bless us too—in the same measurable, tangible, physical ways that he blessed Abraham and his descendants.

The Scriptures give three prerequisites for God's blessing on a church, family or individual—three conditions which have to be fulfilled before fertility, fruitfulness, multiplication, health, victory, prosperity, good reputation, harmony, success and God's Holy Spirit come pouring down in excessive abundance, way beyond our present experience and expectation.

Firstly, we must be in the position which God has chosen to bless. The story of Obed-edom, in 2 Samuel

6:9–11, illustrates this. He was blessed by God simply because he lived where the ark of Yahweh was dumped. 1 Chronicles 26:4–8 reveals the glorious extent of his blessing! God's Old Testament blessing was restricted to those living in the covenant relationship. His New Testament blessing—and this continues today—is restricted to those living in the New Covenant, in Christ. God's blessing is not available to those who are not living in the right place—in Christ Jesus.

The second condition of receiving divine blessing is faith-inspired obedience: obedience which is rooted in love, not in robotic legalism. In the Old Testament Deuteronomy 7:7–11, 28:1–14 and 30:15–20 all make this quite clear, as does John 14–16 in the New Testament. John 14–16 interweaves love, obedience and blessing, all culminating in the spiritual blessing of the promise of the gift of the Holy Spirit. These passages should lead individuals and churches to re-examine their level of blessing. Are we fruitful and multiplying? If not, why is there an absence of blessing? Is there any departure from faith-filled loving obedience to Christ.

The third stipulation is a right treatment of the poor. Deuteronomy 15:4–18 establishes the link between God's material blessing and the specific caring provision of the poor.

> Do not harden your heart or close your hand against that poor brother of yours, but be open-handed with him (verse 7).
>
> When you give to him, you must give with an open heart; for this Yahweh your God will bless you in all you do and in all your giving. Of course there will never cease to be poor in the land; I command you therefore: Always be open-handed with your brother, and with anyone in your country who is in need and poor (verses 10 and 11).

Deuteronomy 23:19–20 and 24:14–22 expand on this principle. It is not only wrong to be apathetic towards the poor, the despised, the penniless, the widows, orphans and strangers: it is also counter-productive! This principle is hinted at in Psalm 41:1–2, Proverbs 11:24–26, Isaiah 58:6–12, Luke 12:33 and 1 Timothy 6:18–19. It is explicitly stated in Proverbs 22:9: 'A blessing awaits the man who is kindly, since he shares his bread with the poor,' and also in 2 Corinthians 9:6–15. The most serious treatment of this requirement is given by Jesus in Matthew 25:31–46. Christ makes it quite clear that we either care for the poor and are blessed, or we are indifferent to their plight and are cursed by God. This principle is seen in action in both Acts 2:45–47 and Acts 6:1–7. Today we are faced with the obscenity of western Christians trying to slim while their third world brothers and sisters try not to starve. How will we look them in the eye in heaven? When will we be so hungry for God's blessing that we sacrifice for them, instead of sending from our left-overs? No wonder that the western church is impotent and barren. It is cursed by God for its apathy towards the poverty of its own brothers and sisters. The only conclusion I can reach is that we in the western church have no appetite for God's blessing.

This lack of a western Christian appetite for blessing is certainly true in the area of fertility. The Bible makes it plain that one aspect, perhaps the fundamental aspect, of divine blessing is babies. And what do so many of us say to him? 'No thanks!' But God is the King. The Genesis 1:28 blessing to mankind was meant literally, as is seen by the subsequent curse in Genesis 3:16–19. The effect of these curses is apparent to this day: women do give birth in pain; men do have a seemingly unconquerable difficulty in exercising gentle headship. ('Your yearning shall be for your husband, yet he will lord it over you' is, in a nutshell, the sorrow of the average woman.) Likewise the curse on

Roger and Penny Wilcock—Park Road Methodist Church, St Leonards, East Sussex

'Children always seemed to us to be an integral part of marriage. We wanted three: a nice sized family, but easy enough to feed, clothe and house. And we felt that an accidental fourth would not be too much of a disaster. Babies came as and when we planned; in March 1980, October 1981 and August 1983. However, the 1983 batch was twins! To call rearing twins 'hard work' is an understatement worth only a hollow laugh. Four children in nappies was a nightmare. Our only conclusion was that we had finished with babies.

'Then a friend had a vision of Penny pushing a Moses basket down-river, and said that she had the impression there was some way Penny was not letting go. We laughed and said Moses baskets only meant babies, and promptly forgot about it. But God began to speak to us about blessing. As we looked at the Bible we realized that blessing and fertility seemed almost inseparable: when God blessed, he gave a child. And God cared how those children were treated, loathing the child-sacrifice of the pagans. We were impressed by Jesus' words when he took a little child to himself, "Anyone who welcomes this little child in my name welcomes me; and anyone who welcomes me welcomes the one who sent me."

'We knew that we were not welcoming God through his gift of children. We resented the disturbance of childish noise and need for attention, the tie, expense and exhaustion of little people. We did not believe that God's blessing was a blessing. Then it was as if God asked whether we would be prepared to have another child. We agreed, knowing that the only sensible answer to give God is "yes", but it was with heavy hearts.

'It was only gradually that we came to accept that our fifth daughter is a love gift from our Father. We have noticed, though, that he has been able to change us and it has happened because we believed him rather than our own judgement, and because we took his word instead of our own common sense. We are, indeed, blessed.'

the man, 'With suffering shall you get your food from it [the soil].' Have you ever tried picking gooseberries? Yet we try to prevent God from blessing us by using contraceptives.

The silence of the Bible on this matter is presumably for the same reason that there is no teaching on how to stifle prophecy. From the Bible point of view why should anyone want teaching on how voluntarily to exhibit symptoms of God's curse? I think that this is another area of God's heritage that the Roman Catholic church is preserving in the face of Protestant (and charismatic) disobedience. How dare we choose how many children we have? How dare we say to God, 'You may count children a blessing, but I do not, and by my action I will now demonstrate who is in charge of my family'? How dare we say, 'We will accept the blessing of tongues, healing, prosperity, victory and success, but reject the blessing of fertility!'

Western Christians, for sane, wise and well thought out reasons, refuse the blessing of many children. Yet surely the point of Christian obedience is that it chooses the foolishness of God in preference to the wisdom of men? Evangelicals seem to be able to expound every verse of the Bible, but there is not a whisper about how to enjoy the blessing in Genesis 1:28. Whenever I publicly mention the blessing of Obed-edom I am met by gales of laughter: a laughter that sneers, 'Call that a blessing? Rather him than me!' How does God feel when we both mock and decline his blessing?

It seems to me that western Christians have rejected the notion of special individual creation and have returned to the materialistic view of the universe. They appear by their behaviour to believe in the blind, random movement of sperm and ova and to have stopped believing in 'from the womb I knew you'. God has not designed women for a life of endless child-bearing: he has programmed the birth of babies at decent intervals if proper breast-feeding takes place. And there is something called the menopause: God knows when enough is enough. But we try to master God and pretend that we know better.

Of course I am not advocating continued child-bearing when there are real medical reasons to the contrary. But I am arguing for a radical re-think of the whole issue of contraception. As far as I can see there is a correlation between the decline in Christianity in this country, and the reduction in the size of families because of contraception. When we refuse God's blessing of physical fruitfulness and multiplication does he withdraw his blessing of spiritual fruitfulness and multiplication? I certainly find it most interesting to note that most countries of the world where the Christian church is experiencing very rapid growth are the ones which enjoy high birth rates.

Blessing by Men and Women

In the Scriptures men are called both to bless the name of God and to bless other men in the name of God. The Psalms are full of exhortations to bless God and they give much practical advice on how to go about this: Psalms 16, 66, 68, 103, 135 and 145 make a good starting point for such a study. However, in this book I am only concerned with the blessing that men can receive from God and not with the blessing that men can give to God.

In Genesis 27 we read that though Isaac had blessed Jacob in error, as the result of a subterfuge, he was unable to revoke the blessing. This illustrates the principle that words spoken in blessing are so important and effective that they cannot be taken back if the blesser later changes his mind. In Matthew 12:36–37 Jesus taught that we will answer for all our *argos* words: these are our unfruitful, barren words. *Argos* is the word used, in some manuscripts, to describe the workless faith of James 2:20. Our words matter: we can minister limitation, unbelief and barrenness by what we say, and so too we can minister growth, faith and fruit by our words of blessing.

The Bible is full of men blessing men—from Noah blessing Shem and Japheth in Genesis 9:26–27, through Melchizedek blessing Abram (Genesis 14:19–20);

Rebekah being blessed by her mother and brother (Genesis 24:60); Jacob blessing Pharaoh (Genesis 47:10); Moses and Aaron repeatedly blessing the Israelites; Joshua blessing Caleb (Joshua 14:13); Eli blessing Elkanah and Hannah (1 Samuel 2:20); David blessing Barzillai (2 Samuel 19:39); the people blessing the volunteers (Nehemiah 11:2); right up to Simeon blessing Mary and Joseph (Luke 2:34); Jesus blessing the small children and then his disciples (Mark 10:16; Luke 24:50); and Paul wanting to bless the Romans (Romans 15:29). These are just a few from the host of biblical blessers. It appears that each one of them expected a tangible result from his blessing: they would have been both astonished and mystified at any suggestion that they were mouthing empty words or exchanging symbolic greetings.

In 2 Samuel 19 the rich and elderly Barzillai the Gileadite would not go to Jerusalem to allow a grateful David to provide for him in his old age. So, instead, David first kissed Barzillai, then blessed him—an act assumed to be equal to material provision. Psalm 115:14–15 mentions the blessing of fertility, and this was used annually with great effect by Eli: 'Then Eli would bless Elkanah and his wife and say, "May Yahweh grant you an heir by this woman in place of the one [Samuel] she has made over to Yahweh." And then they would go home. Yahweh visited Hannah; she conceived and gave birth to three sons and two daughters' (1 Samuel 2:20–21). The blessing of fertility was also used by Rebekah's mother and brother: 'They blessed Rebekah in these words: "Sister of ours, increase to thousands and tens of thousands! May your descendants gain possession of the gates of their enemies!"' (Genesis 24:60). So Rebekah had twins! And both Jacob and Esau went on to found great nations. When we bless we should expect similar, direct, practical results.

In Luke 10 Jesus instructed the seventy-two to bless the members of every house that they entered on their mission. 'Whatever house you go into, let your first words be, "Peace to this house!"' This is not a wish; it is a gift which is either received or rejected. In John 14:27 Jesus blessed the disciples with this same blessing: 'Peace I bequeath to you. My own peace I give you, a peace that the world cannot give, this is my gift to you.' How many contemporary Christians even occasionally bless the household of those they visit? We should. 'Peace' is no empty formality but is the coming of the salvation of God with all its associated benefits of wholeness, prosperity, blessing and harmony. If fruitfulness is the essence of God's blessing to men, peace has to be the primary blessing men give to other men.

Numbers 6:22–27 is the normative passage for men blessing men. It was the form of blessing given to the Aaronic priests, and they used it every day in the Temple of Jerusalem when they discharged their priestly responsibility of blessing the sons of Israel. Christ came, died, rose again, ascended, and baptized the church in his Holy Spirit to usher in a new nation of royal priests. This blessing, once restricted to the lips of those in the line of Aaron, can now be used for ever by all in the line of the high priest of the order of Melchizedek. Jesus Christ was the High Priest, as Hebrews 9:11 states, of all the blessings.

The Numbers 6 blessing is one of the Old Testament passages which contributes most to our trinitarian understanding. The tetragrammaton YHWH is repeated three times and the blessing is divided into three distinctive sub-blessings:

May Yahweh bless you and keep you.

May Yahweh let his face shine on you and be gracious to you.

May Yahweh uncover his face to you and bring you peace.

Each phrase can be identified with a different member of the Trinity. It is only the Father God who can make human blessing effective: and so first we announce his blessing. Just as we can only curse those whom God curses, so too we can only bless those whom he blesses. This means that human words of blessing will only be divinely implemented if they have been divinely initiated. It is the Father who keeps his people safe, the Father who cares about and looks after his children, and this first phrase of the Aaronic blessing brings the Father's protection down upon the person being blessed.

Verse 27 explains the speaking of a blessing as a calling down of the name of God upon the person being blessed. A study of the phrase 'name of God' is revealing: a biblical name is no mere label, but denotes the real personality and characteristics of the person. In the Bible, to put a name on a person is to place the individual concerned under the influence and protection of the owner of that name. It is a constant theme of Scripture that a primary function of the name of God is to protect, that the one who has God's name placed upon him will be kept safe. 1 Kings 8:29, Psalm 20, Psalm 44:5, Psalm 124 and Proverbs 18:10 all emphasize this. In John 17:11–12 Jesus prayed for the eleven disciples: 'Holy Father, protect them by the power of your name—the name you gave me—so that they may be one as we are one. While I was with them, I protected them and kept them safe by that name you gave me' (NIV). Jesus then went on to demonstrate this in John 18:1–11 by speaking the *ego eimi*, the divine name which had been revealed to Moses in Exodus 3:14. The soldiers all fell over and Jesus commanded, 'Let these others go': the disciples had been given a dramatic example of how they would be kept safe by the utterance of the name of God. This can be our privilege in blessing, for we should place the Father's name upon those that we bless.

The second phrase of the Numbers 6 blessing can be identified with the Son: 'May Yahweh let his face shine on you and be gracious to you.' It is Jesus who has caused the Father God to turn and smile at us; it is Jesus who has brought us grace and favour from God. A smiling face is a sign of pleasure and approval, and this part of the blessing brings a momentary glance from God which indicates his pardon.

The third phrase, 'May Yahweh uncover his face to you and bring you peace' can be identified with the Holy Spirit, for it is he who brings peace and the permanent indwelling presence of God, and it is in the Spirit that God permanently uncovers his face to us. In blessing we announce God's *shalom*—his peace of health, rest, security, success and prosperity— the same peace that Jesus commanded the seventy-two to bless with.

Today the practice and thinking about blessing appears to me to be muddled. In some traditions the minister/priest ends the service by announcing a blessing—normally a doxology—over the congregation. This tends to be interpreted as, 'The service has finished: now you can talk.' But surely this should be an important part of the service, for blessing can be a climax in any meeting. It should never be down-graded to the religious equivalent of the landlord calling 'Time'!

In other traditions people bless each other with the exchange of the peace: 'The peace of the Lord be with you.' But commonly this is no more than an embarrassed, mumbled wish. I believe that it should be said seriously and slowly and be filled with faith, love and expectancy; the people must be taught that they are announcing a blessing which can achieve a tangible result. In this way the 'peace' can become a highlight in any service. Yet in some charismatic gatherings the peace is only the excuse for a cosy hug, social chit-chat and an update on gossip and news. It should be the moment for ministry: the giving of God's 'peace' is the natural moment in a service for God's wholeness, victory, prosperity and blessing to be given to those people who are in need of such things.

Many churches have introduced the ministry of blessing without realizing it. They invite people forward to receive 'ministry', and by this they mean that they lay hands on the head of the person and pray over them a prayer relevant to their need. But that is exactly what blessing is, except that in a blessing the words are at times better couched in terms of a prophetic announcement rather than a prayer of petition (see page 72).

There appears to be a clear biblical link between placing, or laying, hands upon the head of a person and blessing them. In Genesis 48 Jacob blessed his grandchildren Manasseh and Ephraim by laying his hands on their heads (one hand on each head!) and in Matthew 19:13 Jesus blessed the children by laying his hands on them. When it was impossible to lay hands on each individual the biblical practice appears to be to raise both hands towards the people. Aaron did this in Leviticus 9:22, and in Luke 24:50–51 Christ did the same at the ascension.

Jesus' blessing of the disciples at his ascension is amplified in Acts 1:8–9. It appears that his corporate blessing, with hands raised, was partly a commission for particular service. This echoes Moses' blessing and commissioning of Joshua (Numbers 27:22–23), and the people of Israel's blessing and commissioning of the Levites (Numbers 8:10–17). The seven deacons were blessed and commissioned by the same means (Acts 6:6), as were Saul and Barnabas (Acts 13:3). All of these blessings and commissionings were in conjunction with the laying on of hands and were for service rather than office. This association between commissioning and blessing is only to be expected. Any person who has been given a difficult task to perform by God surely needs the aid of the blessings of peace, of safety, of spiritual fertility, of wholeness, of prosperity and so on.

Timothy's blessing/commissioning for service (but not for an office) by laying on of hands is recorded in both 1 Timothy 4:14 and 2 Timothy 1:6, and both verses refer to a gift of the Holy Spirit being given at the same time. All blessing is only a foreshadowing of the blessing of the Holy Spirit and so it is to be expected that there will be an association between blessing, laying on of hands and the gift and gifts of God's Holy Spirit. This is seen in the Old Testament in Deuteronomy 34:9, and in the New Testament in Acts 8:17, 9:17–18 and 19:6.

I suggest that there are three elements involved in men blessing men: there is a man to God dedication, a God to man blessing, and a man to man transference. Laying hands on an individual or raising hands over a crowd represents a dedication of the person or people to God: it is a giving of the person to the God who alone can guide, protect, equip, strengthen and bless. This dedication by the laying on of hands is seen clearly in Numbers 8:16 when the Levites were dedicated to their service by the people of Israel. It is also seen in Exodus 29:10, Leviticus 1:4, 4:15, 16:21 and Numbers 8:12. In these passages hands were laid on the animal to dedicate it to its useful, brief service as a sacrifice. When men lay hands on men in blessing they are dedicating the person or people to God in the same way: for a specific task as a living sacrifice.

The second element is either a plea for, or an announcement of, God's blessing upon the person. Old Testament blessing consisted mainly of pleas for God to bless; whereas New Testament blessing was usually a prophetic announcement of the imminent arrival of God's blessing. We can only bless those whom God blesses; if we are certain that the person meets God's requirements (see page 59) and we are sure that God, by his Holy Spirit, is suggesting to us that he is about to bless the person, then a prophetic announcement is in order—for example, 'The peace of the Lord be with you.' If we are not sure whether the person does meet the divine prerequisites for blessing, or we are uncertain as to God's will, it is better to petition for blessing with words like, 'May the peace of the Lord be with you.'

The third aspect of men blessing men is an element of transfer. When hands were laid on the animals to dedicate them for sacrificial service, the sins of the people were transferred to the animals. Something parallel appears to happen in blessing. It seems to me that we can normally only bless with a blessing that we have ourselves received. The Old Testament blessers usually blessed so that the person on whom they laid hands received something that they themselves had already experienced, if only in part. In the New Testament those who had received God's peace were those who dispensed it; those who had received the blessing of the Holy Spirit were those who helped others to receive it, and so on. This is why it is normally the leaders who lay on hands for blessing—on the assumption that they have most to offer! Some may argue that this is not transfer but merely greater faith: that might be so, but the experience related by Jesus in Luke 8:46 is most suggestive. Many today testify to a similar draining after ministry and blessing people—as though added to the essential elements of dedication and divine blessing is this lesser element of human transfer.

I recommend that the ministry of blessing should take place at every service. The opportunity should be given for those with a special need for peace, wholeness, prosperity, fertility and so on, to be blessed. Either the

My own experience

I began writing the Ashburnham Insights series in January 1985. I set aside one complete week per month for the first six months of the year, and repeated the pattern in 1986. During these 'writing weeks' I was able to ensure that I was freed from outside interferences. But, alas, there have been plenty of inside disruptions....

My wife gave birth to undiagnosed identical twin boys in January 1984, and in the following two years we changed over 10,000 nappies. We plumbed the depths of human exhaustion, for the blighters would not sleep. One or two hours at a stretch was all they managed, rarely coinciding! Large numbers of people prayed for us, with no obvious success. Tongues built us up, but had no soporific effect on Aaron and Barnaby.

Early in 1986 I reworked an earlier draft of this book and realized that I ought to stop praying that they should sleep, and start blessing them with God's gift to his beloved of sleep. And so a new nightly routine began which continues to this day. I adapted the Numbers 6 Aaronic blessing as follows: 'The Lord bless you and keep you. The Lord make his face to shine on you and be gracious to you. The Lord lift up his countenance upon you and give you his peace, and a peaceful night's sleep. In Jesus' name. Amen.' It worked.

Their sleep pattern considerably improved: they stopped waking an average of eight times each per night and reduced this to an average of twice each. Though still not our idea of what is ideal it is much better than before the time of blessing.

I had hoped to finish this second series before our fourth child arrived, but young Isaac beat me to the post. All the chaos of a new arrival caused inspiration to evaporate. I could not get the testimonies done. I prayed, others prayed, and nothing happened. Then a small group from the Stable Family blessed me with God's gift of creativity and three days later all clicked into place. They were finished in a few weeks.

leaders, or those who have experienced the particular aspect of divine blessing which is being sought, should lay hands on the person and give him into God's hands. They should call on the revealed name of God which is appropriate to the need—for example, the God of all peace, the God who guides, the God who protects and so on, and bless him either with a petition or an announcement, depending on which of these two is relevant.

Those members of the congregation who will be engaging in particular work for God during the week can be commissioned and blessed for their task. Students returning to college, the housewife going to advise a neighbour, the couple with non-Christian friends coming for a meal, the man going to pray for a sick friend, all of these can have hands laid on them to dedicate them for their sacrificial service and to receive the help from the Holy Spirit which they need for their particular task. At the very least this means that their service is more clearly seen as the local church at work rather than isolated individuals operating independently. At the best they will be better equipped for more effective service.

We often use the 2 Corinthians 13:13 blessing at the end of our meetings and have educated people out of blessing the floor and into blessing each other with their eyes wide open. I found this most difficult as my cultural background revolted against it. Yet slowly we are coming into the liberation of giving and receiving blessings which are real and change circumstances. The barren have received the blessing of fertility, insomniacs now sleep, the fretful are at peace, the failures have become confident as we have slowly learnt to bless in the name of God with his authority, faith and power.

Blessing is not restricted to Christian meetings. Nearly all of the biblical material deals with blessing in private conversation and personal ministry and this is where the emphasis should lie. I believe that every believer is called to become an effective blesser—and curser, so please take blessing more seriously. Do not casually say, 'Bless you'—this is lazy and meaningless. Instead, pray for God's wisdom and direction before you bless, be specific, vest it with faith, lay hands, call down the name of God, and most important of all, speak only his words. We need to gain experience in this lovely ministry by listening clearly to God's voice and by only doing what he suggests.

Helping a Cursed Person

The first stage in helping a cursed person is to know for certain that the client is cursed. Chapters 2, 3 and 4 are my attempt to help with this task. Some people find it difficult to distinguish between a satanically-enforced curse and a divine curse because of their superficial similarities, but if we listen attentively to the Holy Spirit we find that he gives clear guidance as to the type of curse. However, I offer three practical suggestions to help with diagnosis.

Firstly, God's curse is a total unchanging curse with no hope of relief, but curses enforced by Satan usually contain a glimmer of the hope of better things to come—which never materialize. Secondly, God's curse will have a cause within the last two or three generations of a Christian believer who has backslidden into gross sin. This may be immoral behaviour, blasphemous doctrine or demonic involvement. Thirdly, the result of God's curse will remain constant regardless of the spiritual state of the person being helped or the experiences they go through. However, the effect of a curse enforced by Satan will dramatically worsen at times of spiritual climax, like regeneration, baptism, receiving Holy Spirit, confirmation, church membership and so on. God's curse brings difficulties and hardship, but Satan's brings intolerable problems. This may seem vague on paper, but in practice with the help of the Holy Spirit the difference is quite obvious. I suggest that the following action should take place once the type of curse has been recognized.

Release from God's curse

Daniel 9:1–19 is the most important passage to study. Daniel recognized that the people of Israel were under God's curse and with prayer and fasting he repented personally for his own and his ancestors' sins. He did not only confess and repent of those sins he himself had committed, but also those sins committed by the national and family group of which he was part. This is the same principle which underlay Christ's baptism and Ezra's repentance in Ezra 9. As representatives before God of their people, they repented of sins they had not committed. If possible, it is helpful to identify the gross sin which caused God to curse: it can normally be ascertained by a combination of intelligent questions, historical research, and the help of the Holy Spirit. Once recognized it should be repented of, even if the person repenting did not commit the sin. You repent as if you had committed the sin, sincerely and penitently as the representative of your family. Those churches which are under God's curse for falling into unitarianism or the like in past generations, or for banning God's gifts in the present one, need to repent in similar vein to make possible any lifting of God's curse of barrenness which is upon them.

Daniel wrestled in prayer with God, pleading for his mercy to be shown, pleading for the Aaronic blessing, pleading for the Lord to act without delay. His plea was not for the people's sake, but for the sake of the name of God which they bore. The only possible way of release is to come in repentance with a firm promise of future obedience and to plead for God's mercy to be shown because the curse is bringing God's own name into disrepute.

> And now, our God, listen to the prayer and pleading of your servant. For your own sake, Lord, let your face smile again on your desolate sanctuary. Listen my God, listen to us; open your eyes and look on our plight and on the city that bears your name. We are not relying on our own good works but on your great mercy, to commend our humble plea to you. Listen, Lord! Lord, forgive! Hear, Lord, and act! For your own sake, my God, do not delay, because they bear your name, this is your city, this is your people!

The person, family or church which is under a curse of God can only throw themselves on his mercy and grace: there is no automatic escape. But my experience suggests that God is quick to bless all those who come in sincere repentance. He is the God who is full of grace and mercy.

Release from a curse enforced by Satan

If we are personally cursed by an individual (and as we wage open warfare with the forces of darkness this does and will happen) the Scriptures make the correct course of action abundantly clear. It is not to shrug our shoulders and laugh it off, but rather to counter the curse with blessing. David may have countered Goliath's strong curse with a stronger curse, but that is the only exception: elsewhere the principle is plain. Judges 17:1–3, Psalm 109:28, Luke 6:28, Romans 12:14, 21 and 1 Corinthians 4:12 all stress the importance of conquering a curse with blessing. When we receive a letter containing a curse we should reply with a written blessing; when cursed to our face we should speak a blessing. This is the way to make the curse null and void, not by casually disregarding it.

I suggest the following tentative guidelines for the

release of a person, family or church which we are convinced is under a satanically-enforced curse. Some people talk about breaking a curse. This wrongly puts the focus of ministry on the curse rather than on the person, so I prefer the phrase 'release from a curse', for it is the person who is helped, not the curse which is broken. (This is quite different from exorcism—see the *Ashburnham Insight* on deliverance.) We have to move the person from the place where the curse is operative to a place where they can be protected from it and instead receive God's blessing. The only legal basis for this exchange is the atonement of Christ: unless people are 'in Christ' and have consciously claimed by faith the benefits of Calvary they cannot begin to be released from a curse. If they are not joined to the body of Christ which is the church, and are not in reality part of a living, caring, local church, they cannot be fully protected from a curse and be blessed. It is against the church that the gates of hell cannot prevail: there is no equivalent promise for an isolated believer.

Ministry can only begin once the person is 'in Christ' and in vital fellowship with a local church. First, there should be a real repentance, perhaps over a period of time, for the cause of the curse. Again this may not involve the sin of the person repenting, but may be representative repentance for the sin of another: I suggest that the Daniel 9 and Ezra 9 principle be followed. There is no need to dig around for sins. Instead, allow the Holy Spirit to reveal what is relevant for repentance. It is often best to leave the matter for a week or so to allow time for the Spirit to bring the cause to remembrance, or to highlight the salient point. A clear confession of faith in Christ should follow the repentance. This establishes that the person is trusting only in Christ's work on the cross for his transfer from the place of curse to the place of blessing.

It is wise to establish a clear scriptural basis for release.

Isaiah 14:12–19, Ezekiel 28:17–19, John 12:31, Galatians 3:13–14, Ephesians 1:7, Colossians 1:12–14, 1 John 3:8, Revelation 18 and especially Luke 10:17–19 merit claiming in this respect. Jesus came to destroy all the works of the devil and has given to us all authority to tread underfoot the whole strength of the enemy. The person should then renounce and revoke all contact with the evil one made by himself or his immediate friends and forebears. A reaffirmation of the baptismal vow to 'renounce the devil and all his works, the vain pomp and glory of the world, with all covetous desires of the same and the carnal desires of the flesh' is most helpful. The person should be led to forgive all the relevant people, especially the one who cursed him and, if appropriate, the relative or ancestor who caused the curse.

Finally, the person in immediate spiritual authority should proclaim release. This should be the father, husband, and/or minister. He should address the evil spirit which is enforcing the curse and forbid it, in the name of Jesus, from bringing any further evil or harm upon the person, church or family. This evil spirit should then be told that henceforth the person is protected by the name of God and that by the finished work of Christ upon the cross the devilish curse is to be exchanged for a divine blessing. Hands should then be laid upon the sufferer and an appropriate blessing announced. If the person has not been filled with Holy Spirit that blessing should be sought for him. This should all be followed by a time of praise. Perhaps this ministry could be summarized as recognize, repent, renounce, release, resist, receive and rejoice! It is often necessary to bless a person daily for several weeks before a significant change and improvement is noted. Laying on of hands for blessing, unlike anointing and baptism, is not an unrepeatable act of initiation. Persistence is usually required.

Pat Nolan—Battle Baptist Church, East Sussex

From puberty onwards Pat was a modern example of the Mark 5 lady—except that her problems lasted much longer than twelve years. She also suffered from associated migraines, sometimes passing out from the pain. Pat was converted in 1967, but this had no effect on her internal disorders. She visited doctor after doctor, was examined by numerous specialists, endured countless operations for dilatation and curettage, all with no lasting improvement.

Eventually she was talked and prayed into pregnancy. Pat threatened to miscarry throughout. At first the doctors suspected a blighted ovum, then they said that there was no baby, and later on she had to spend six weeks in hospital. Eventually young Catharine was born eleven days late on November 16th 1984 by caesarean section, because she was lying in the breech position.

Pat's difficulties appeared to intensify. Her gynaecological problems got worse and she had to return to hospital in both January and then April 1985. After this hospital stay we became convinced that a satanically-enforced curse lay behind her problems. The family history outlined on page 49 was established and the dark figure of Robert Turner, Pat's great-grandfather, emerged. He had been a prominent spiritualist at the turn of the century and was involved in all sorts of dark and evil practices. We were never able to discover the cause of the curse, but its impact was only too obvious.

After a time of prayerful preparation Pat and her husband Dennis, a Baptist minister, repented for the sins of the great-grandfather and then stated that their faith for release was firmly placed in Christ alone. Next Pat renounced all the spiritualist involvement and interest of her family from the past to the present. And she forgave as far as she was able those in her family towards whom she felt some bitterness.

Dennis, as husband and minister, forbade the enforcing spirit from further harming his wife and in particular from affecting Catharine. A colleague and I blessed Pat ten minutes a day for two weeks. At first things got far worse, but the corner turned after a week and she began to improve. She returned to work in September 1985 and is now fitter and stronger than ever before.

We have found these guidelines helpful in our work at Ashburnham Place and have seen God bring tangible blessing to many people and churches which had been under the influence of an evil curse. Please do not slavishly follow them, but allow the Holy Spirit to guide you clearly and directly in each case. I pray that these suggestions will be one factor in the release of many from the bondage of Satan into the blessing of Christ.

This short book on blessing and cursing is very experimental. Little has been written or taught about the subject in recent years, and therefore this is the 'greenest' material in the developing *Ashburnham Insights* series. As the material has been worked out in the life of the Ashburnham Stable Family, in personal ministry, in teaching and in writing, I have noticed considerable local interest. At first I assumed that this was normal curiosity in something new, but the truth is that for many the ministry of blessing has been a step of faith into the supernatural which they could manage—for so many believe healing and deliverance to be beyond them. Yet once they had seen the miracles stemming from their personal co-operation with God in blessing many took the courage to risk their reputations even further. God has not let them down. And he will not let you down as you start to bless and curse those he instructs you to bless and curse. He might—at times—prune your pride, ruin your reputation, and bless those that you wish he would curse, but if you walk in faith and obedience, submit your ideas and thinking to the pages of the Old and New Testaments, and sincerely seek his blessing, you will be stretched and blessed by the new horizons of ministry which open up before you.

And may the blessing of the God of all peace be with those who have read this short book. And may the blessing of Obed-edom be upon those who have looked up all the references.

Personal Notes

Blessing and Cursing

Causes of Curses from God

A necessary cause

The first divine curse

Anti-semitism

False religions

Slighting one's parents

Other reasons

Disobedience

Half-hearted obedience

Greed

Misusing God's name

Cursing by Men and Women

Enforced by God

Enforced by Satan

The Evidence of a Curse

A divine curse

A curse enforced by Satan

Blessing from God

Blessing by Men and Women

Helping a Cursed Person

Release from God's curse

Release from a curse enforced by Satan

John Mole was educated at Oxford University and the international business school, INSEAD. In 1971 he joined Mellon Bank in Pittsburgh and after two years was transferred to the London branch. In 1975 he moved to Greece to open Mellon's Middle East and Africa Representative Office in Athens. In 1980 he moved back to London to become European Business Development Manager and in 1983 he became General Manager of the London branch.

John Mole published a comic novel, *Sail or Return*, in 1985. He resigned from Mellon Bank the same year to write full time. In 1986 he published a second novel, *The Monogamist*. His third comic novel, *Thanks, Eddie*, is published by Bantam Press in 1989.

John Mole is married, with four children, and lives in Dulwich.

'A revealing picture of what it is like to be managed . . . a chuckle on almost every page, many uproarious scenes . . . something for everyone involved in an office culture' – *Management News*

For Ben,
who also wonders why people work

Contents

Hire

'What do you do?' asked Jenny.

'Clerical. General office work. Anything really,' I said.

'Yes, but what do you do?'

After a business degree and fifteen years in international banking I wasn't qualified to do anything. It came as a shock. I thought I could just pop down to the employment agency, hand over my P45 and start work. I was a decent chap, a reliable sort of fellow. I could keep a conversation going about the dollar and the oil price and the American budget deficit. I knew which knife and fork to use, how to read an airline schedule. I could chair a meeting and make a speech and write a memo. But I couldn't do anything that would get me a job. Outside the organization for which I used to work I counted as nothing. Knowing the alphabet was the most useful thing I could think of.

'How about filing?' I asked.

When I was about ten years old I sent sixpence off to the *Rover* comic for a booklet on Learning To Swim At Home. First you practised treading water in front of the wardrobe mirror. Then you did the arm movements. For the leg movements and breathing you lay on the bed. Having mastered the basic techniques you lay on your stomach on a dining room chair and put it all together. The butterfly was hardest to do without falling on the floor. Theoretical swimming had more advantages than just staying dry. Twenty lengths on the chair was very good exercise. It was enjoyable. You learned something. It improved

your self-confidence when you went to the beach. But it was no help at all when you jumped in the water.

When I was a manager I felt the same about management education. The books I read and the seminars and courses I went on were clever and interesting. It all made sense. I came away thinking I had it all sorted out. But when I got back to the office I started floundering again. Theories of organization and motivation and planning and influencing and assertiveness and leadership and the other desirable skills and qualities of the professional manager did not seem to fit the real world.

I tried to put what I had learned into practice. Before every meeting, every speech, every memo, I asked myself who the audience was, what I was trying to achieve, what the likely result would be. But I was never certain what effect I was having on the people who worked for me. I felt I was shouting into a black hole. Did they read my carefully crafted memos or stuff them in their desks or take them home for their children to draw on? What was going on behind the blank faces at the staff meeting? Did anything I did make them work harder or more efficiently or more happily? Were they laughing at me? Did they respect me? Did they even notice I was there?

I suspected that most of what I did had a very different result from the one I intended. The more I communicated the more people said they didn't know what was going on. The more we refined our objectives the less we seemed to attain them. The more we tried to improve morale the more people left. But how could I find out what was going on? I walked about and kept my eyes open and saw people beavering away at their jobs. Did they stop when my back was turned? I listened but worried I was hearing my own echo. I tried to remember what it was like when I was a trainee and a junior. But with every rung up the ladder you forget what it was like on the rung before. If I'm ever the boss I'll do things differently, you say, until you are the boss and find yourself behaving in exactly the same way. We had attitude surveys, written questionnaires and interviews, but I had no more trust in them than any opinion poll. They tell you what people want you to hear.

Two years after I stopped being a manager I still wondered what it was like to be on the receiving end. So I went back to work to find out. I took a dozen clerical and typing jobs in the sort of offices I had been a manager in. Management books are usually written from the manager's point of view. How do you recruit people? How do you organize them? How do you get the best out of them? They look down into the organization from the top. This book is written from the point of view of the people being managed. Things look very different from the bottom of the pool.

'How about filing?' I asked.

Jenny gave me a form to fill out. On the bottom was a list of about thirty occupational skills. You ticked what level of experience you had. I had no idea what some of them meant. Bought ledger? Life claims? Some of the names I recognized from the bank I used to manage. I had read job descriptions and signed evaluations and given pep talks to nostro reconciliations clerks and foreign exchange settlements clerks and payroll clerks; I can see their faces now on the other side of the desk. I made decisions about how many we should have and what they should be paid and who should supervise them. But I had only a hazy idea of what they did all day. I ticked that I had some experience in the job titles I recognized and hoped I could muddle through.

I had no machine skills either. I had signed capital investment approval forms for computers and word processors and microfilm equipment and interviewed operators and sent people on training courses but I wouldn't know where to find the on/off switch. Half a dozen yoga lessons didn't make me proficient in Lotus. Level Three on Manic Miner and a couple of novels on a word processor was the extent of my keyboard experience. I converted forty thousand words per month into words per minute but it didn't seem worth mentioning.

I went through this ordeal with nearly twenty agencies. Some were part of chains that advertised on the tube and in the papers and were smart and modern. Others were up narrow flights of stairs, a couple of tatty wooden desks and bare boards. The smartest were those that specialized in secretaries, the scruffiest those that specialized in accountants. I was impressed with all the interviewers. They were sympathetic and polished and professional. Some of them had remarkable memories for names and where their clients lived and what sort of work they did.

'What were you doing before, John?'

'Ah. Yes. This and that.'

I thought it would look fishy that a former general manager of a City bank, out of work for two years, claiming to be a writer, should be looking for a job as a temp. At the first couple of agencies I played down what I had done before, making it sound as if I had led a feckless, reckless life, bumming round the banks of the world, a cashier here, a reconciliations clerk there, troubleshooting in payroll, a hired gun in the post room. I guess that's the accounts done, I'll be moseying along folks. I made it sound quite romantic and implausible. I didn't get anything from these agencies. Then I told the unvarnished truth, that I'd given up a good job to write novels. They thought I was potty and harmless and hard up and found me work.

Educational qualifications too were a problem at first. I wasn't sure if it was as unethical to leave out academic achievements as it was to make them up. But I didn't want to be thought overqualified. And it was perfectly true that I had five 'O' levels, just as every month in the year has twenty-eight days. Again I needn't have worried. A degree in French and German makes you neither under nor overqualified for a career in commerce. It is irrelevant. And a Master's Degree in Business Studies from the European Institute of Business Administration sounds like something they send aspiring executives in Bombay from a PO box on the North Circular Road.

By the fifth interview I was getting desperate. I sat opposite Jenny in a little windowless room with furry wallpaper. (Jenny is a popular name for recruitment consultants. I was on the books of five Jennies, which made my weekly phone-round very confusing).

'You can do wrecks, can't you, John?' said Jenny.

'Absolutely, Jenny. Wrecks, no problems. A speciality

you might say. Shipwrecks, train wrecks, you name it. Temporary Lutine bell ringer is it? Ding ding.'

She laughed. Fortunately for my clerical career she thought I was joking.

NOTE:

By management I usually mean people management. The wider aspects of business management are outside the scope of this book.

I have disguised the places I worked and the people I worked with. The need to be selective has also distorted my experience. But the incidents I describe are factual and the conversations as true as my memory allowed before I could jot them down.

In many of the management books I have read there are little case histories and anecdotes and illustrations, supposedly drawn from real life. I usually found these more interesting than the theory and skipped ahead to find them when I got bored. So in this book I have reversed the proportions. Most of it is about my experiences and the serious bits for skipping are in bold type.

And Fire

My first job was not in marine insurance. 'Wrecks' (or rather, 'recks') is short for 'reconciliations', which has nothing to do with marriage guidance either. It is an accounting job consisting of matching up entries on two different accounts. For example, one regularly reconciles one's cheque stubs to one's bank account if one has been toilet trained too early.

To be more precise, I was engaged to do nostro reconciliations at a small foreign bank in the City. There were three nostro reconciliations clerks at the bank I had managed but I only had a hazy idea of what they did. I knew nostro was Italian for 'ours' for what that was worth. I had come up through the marketing side of the bank where we were kept away from day-to-day operations.

I cycled into the City in my ten-year-old worsted suit and a wide maroon tie and a respectable enough shirt with only two buttons missing and a collar only slightly worn. I forgot to polish my shoes. I wasn't posing as a middle-aged, out-of-works recks clerk down on my luck. After two years of self-employment that is what all my wardrobe is like.

There was an added spice. One of the things upwardly mobile managers boast to each other about on the squash court is how many times they have been headhunted. Headhunted means being approached out of the blue by an executive search firm, a high-class employment agency which does not wait for job hunters to walk in but goes out to find executives with well paid and challenging jobs and asks if they would like better-paid, even more challenging jobs. The number of times one has been headhunted is as important a success symbol as a Gucci briefcase and a key to the executive lift. My scalp was hunted only once. I couldn't even brag about it because it was for a job with lower status and pay than the one I was doing at the time. So much for my reputation in the marketplace. The spice was that it was the Marketing Manager's job at the very bank where I was now about to start my new career.

I arrived at five to nine and chained my bicycle to the parking meter outside the entrance to Trident Court. Trident Court is a fancy new development with an internal atrium. Glass lifts go up and down the outside of the buildings, fountains spatter and tinkle on the floor, hanging gardens cascade from balconies. Through the network of bars in the glass roof I could see blue sky and clouds. The receptionist, who also ran the switchboard, was an elderly, grandmotherly lady. She was very pleasant and chatty until I told her I was a temp. She went back to her newspaper which she read from from cover to cover with ooh-ahs and chuckles and well-I-nevers while I passed the time with the Bank of England bulletin. I waited for an hour.

'Are you the Temp? I'm Monica. Sorry to keep you waiting. Forgot you were here.'

I was rarely referred to by name. I was the Temp. Today I was the Temp in Recks to distinguish me from the Temp in Filing and the Temp in Settlements. Temps have special status. They are the untouchables of office life. They do not receive circulars, go to meetings, get invited to official or social occasions. They are cloaked in invisibility. They materialize when someone has to take the blame. The Temp did this. The Temp did that. The Temp we had last month must have lost it. Invisibility has its advantages to managers. Temps are the first line of defence when Head Office orders a staff cut-back or a hiring freeze. They can be kept off the monthly staff returns by firing them the day before month end and rehiring them two days later, or charging them to Professional Services or Miscellaneous.

Monica, who worked in Personnel, took me from the plastic mahogany and subdued lighting of the executive floor to the metal desks and neon of operations two floors below. About thirty people sat at metal desks shuffling and ticking and passing and sorting piles of paper. Some of them gazed into computer terminal screens like crystal balls. No-one seemed to be speaking but it was noisy and confusing. As we passed, people looked up, stared at us blankly, and got back to the piles of paper. The window looked out on the atrium through a curtain of hanging plants. It was like working in a jungle tree-house. The window-ledges were piled high with files and ledgers and in some places metal cupboards had been pushed against the glass as if to keep out wild animals.

'Settlements,' said Monica.

'Ah yes, settlements.' I nodded knowingly.

We went through a pair of fire doors into another large office. This one was divided up by free-standing partitions into a complicated maze, like a stocking-filler puzzle where you have to get a silver ball to the middle. The dead-ends were work areas. The partitions were covered in a fuzzy brown material, repulsive to the touch, to deaden sound. Monica stood on tiptoe to get her bearings but was not tall enough to see over the top of the partitions. I thought of lifting her up like a ballerina but on my first day that would have been too forward. We took directions from a passing Indian gentleman and ventured through the maze.

'Accounts,' said Monica. 'You'll be working for Greta.'

This was interesting. I speculated that the work-flow in Settlements was conducive to a completely open office layout while Accounts required small isolated units. Then why did disembodied hands rise above the furry walls with files and papers, why did disembodied heads peep round the sides? It was as noisy as Settlements because people shouted to each other over the barriers or talked on the phone to the person in the next cubicle. I asked Monica.

'Accounts have always had their own offices,' she said.

'Why?'

'Dunno. They like their privacy, I suppose.'

We found my new boss. She sat in a cubicle formed by three partitions and a tall filing cupboard. Three desks were pushed together in the middle. There was very little floor space and it was mostly filled with the piles of paper and brown cardboard boxes bursting with bank statements. The desks were also covered in paper and boxes. Greta was in her early twenties. She looked tired and harassed. She had purple bags under her eyes. A cigarette smouldered in her fingers and another on the edge of the ashtray already overflowing with butts. She groomed the parts of her she could see in the mirror but was neglectful of the rest. The front of her hair was carefully combed and her pink make-up ended abruptly at the white skin under her jaw.

Monica introduced me. 'This is your temp,' she said.

'At last. You can sit there,' said Greta, pointing to the chair facing her across the desks. Monica left while she could still remember the way back. I put my coat and fluorescent cycling belt on the third chair and sat down. Greta handed a sheaf of paper across the litter that separated us. They were printed blue and looked like the gas bill.

'Can you put these into date order?'

They were deal confirmations. When a bank does a deal with a customer, for example a foreign exchange transaction, it sends out a confirmation with details of the amount, currencies, rate and so on. These were copies the bank keeps for its own records. The task of putting them into date order was not very demanding because they all had the same date on the top. I felt a growing sense of complacency. This was not going to be so difficult after all.

I had never seen anyone work so hard or intensely as Greta. She scrabbled through print-outs and files and confirmations like a dog through leaves. She added up a pile of what looked like travellers' cheques and at the same time telephoned Settlements with a query about the Frankfurt account. The fingers of her right hand whizzed over the calculator while her left hand riffled through the cheques like a card sharp while she held the telephone between her shoulder and chin and gabbled about Deutschmarks. Her brain could operate simultaneously in at least two modes. She chain-smoked king-size cigarettes. She lit them with a Snoopy lighter and took long drags, holding in the smoke as if they were joints, screwing up one eye. The acrid smell of stubs smouldering in the ashtray filled our cubicle. She bit her nails too, although I don't know how she found the time. For a brief moment she would cease her frenetic activity and stare down at the mess on her desk, stupefied at what still remained to be done. There was an instant of relief and expectation, like the dishwasher between two operations in the sequence. Then she started churning away again. It was bewildering and enervating to watch. From time to time she jumped to her feet, brushed ash off her skirt, and without a word scurried away with a handful of paper or a confirmation. I relaxed from my task and took the opportunity to extinguish the fag-ends in the ashtray. She came back even more fired up than when she had left. I wondered if a thyroid condition made her work so hard.

Meanwhile I plodded on, sorting through the confirmations. Greta would look up at me and when I caught her eye avert her gaze. After half an hour she spoke to me.

'Haven't you finished yet?'

'Nearly.' Five minutes later I handed over the pile I had been working on.

'What order is this? I said put them in date order.'

'All the dates are the same. But I was checking to make

sure,' I said, pointing to the date on top of the slip of paper.

'Of course they're all the same. That's the deal date. They were all done on the same day. You want the value date.' She stabbed her finger at another date at the bottom of the slip of paper.

'Have you ever done recks before?'

'Sure. Lots of times. I'm a bit rusty, that's all.' She did not look convinced. But I knew what a value date was. It is the date on which the money actually changes hands as opposed to the date on which the transaction is agreed. Greta was right. A lot of them were different. I set to methodically, determined to get it right.

There is nothing like personal criticism for breaking the ice. When she paused to light a cigarette I seized the opportunity for conversation.

'Do you always work so hard?'

'We're behind. There should be three of us. That's why I asked for a temp. I have to clear all the backlog of filing.' She nodded to the cardboard boxes washed up against the walls like jetsam.

'How long have you been short-handed?'

'Six months. I come in at half-past seven to get a head start. I'm usually away by half-past six.'

'You've been working at this pace all that time?'

'I'm the supervisor.'

'But you've got no one to supervise. They'll never hire anyone else if you work like this. Slow down and they'll have to get someone else.' She did not seem grateful for my advice. She looked disparagingly at the little pile of confirmations to which I had dedicated my morning.

When I had sorted the confirmations into value date order I had to fold them in half. This took another fifteen minutes. Why I had to do this was not immediately obvious and I did not like to ask in case it was standard recks procedure. Then she handed me a long computer print-out. It was a bank statement from the Zurich branch. All my confirmations concerned Swiss Franc transactions.

What I had to do was 'tick back' the confirmations to the statement to make sure that the deals had gone through and the value dates were correct. I had to write down the entries I could not account for on a separate sheet. This took me until the middle of the afternoon. It was painstaking work and not so easy as it sounded. Sometimes a single entry was covered by two or three confirmations, sometimes one confirmation had several statement entries. For example, the interest on a deposit would sometimes be added to a repayment of principal, sometimes it would be separate. I did not realize this at first so that my exception sheet was half as long as the original statement. Then the penny dropped and I started again.

Greta did not slow down. Her pace was unrelenting. At noon she took out corned-beef sandwiches from her bag and ate them while she worked. Halfway through the afternoon she took out of her bag a plastic spoon and a large slice of Black Forest gateau. She was an archetypal heart-attack candidate. At one o'clock, when I said I was going out for a brisk walk and a salad, she looked at me as if I had said something outrageous. The work-load was not self-imposed. Her industry was not a symptom of glandular or psychological disorder, which was my first assumption, but was necessary. If large payments are not made or received or are misdirected to the wrong bank or the wrong account, it can cost thousands of pounds in lost interest payments. Errors can be corrected if they are discovered before the value date. In most cases you have twenty-four hours to find them. If they are not corrected the bank that made the original mistake pays for them. Greta had taken this responsibility fully on herself.

My Swiss franc reconciliation was a very small part of this responsibility. After lunch she pointed out numerous errors in the exception sheet and set me to doing it again. She said it should have taken half an hour to do what I had done.

Only when the main accounts, dollar, sterling, and Deutschmark, had been reconciled, at about four o'clock, did Greta relax slightly. She telephoned a friend. She asked me what my name was. In return she told me something about herself. She had left school at seventeen and gone to work for a much larger bank. After three years she had moved to this bank and after a year was put in charge of reconciliations when her boss was moved up to Loan Administration. That was six months ago. She was twenty-one years old. She looked closer to thirty. She came in at half-past seven in the morning and rarely left before half-past six.

At half-past four the phone rang and Greta handed it to me. It was Jenny from the agency. I thought it was nice of her to call and see how I was getting on.

'I'm afraid they don't want you any more, John. You're not quite what they're looking for. It's nothing personal. Hello? Are you there?'

Greta had her head down, scribbling on an exception sheet. The skin on her neck had turned the same pink as her make-up. An initial numb disbelief was replaced by a turmoil of emotion. With the logical part of my mind I was grateful that I would not have to come back to this furry little cubicle tomorrow and sort confirmations until the weekend. I was grateful for the anecdote of how I was fired on my first day. I was grateful for the new experience. I was interested in how I should react. But these dispassionate thoughts were overwhelmed by the surge of anger and resentment and humiliation and hurt that welled up from the primitive part of the brain.

'Not good enough for you, am I?' I said, trying to keep my voice from sounding squeaky.

'I'm sorry. I should have told you myself.'

'How was I supposed to know what you expected of me? Telepathy?'

'It's nothing personal. Honestly.'

'Why didn't you tell me at the beginning what I was supposed to do?'

'It's nothing personal. Really.'

I handed over my time-sheet for Greta to sign. She did

not have the authority. Monica would have to sign it. I found her on the fourth floor. I kept up the attitude of injured innocence.

'So why wasn't I good enough?'

'It's not that. We wanted someone with more experience.'

'I think I could have been told what was expected, what you wanted me to do.'

'Greta is under pressure. She has a tremendous backlog.'

'She'll have it for longer if she doesn't show someone what to do.'

'I'm sorry. It's nothing personal.'

I was slow and incompetent. But I don't think that was the whole story. It would have helped Greta to have me stay for the week and get rid of the filing. I worked slowly and methodically and Greta worked as if she were possessed. It is extremely iritating when a colleague or partner does not share the same sense of urgency. I did not help myself by admiring her industry and asking her several times if she always worked that hard.

I went straight to the agency and gave the time-sheet to Jenny. She was very charming and asked if I was still available. They did not have anything just at the moment but she was sure there would be something. Just keep in touch.

'I hope I haven't messed you around.'

'It's quite all right, it happens all the time, it's nothing personal.'

It is bad form in many companies to talk about redundancies or dismissals or firings or the sack. Unwanted employees are 'let go', as if they had been longing to escape, a euphemism for the unpleasant like passing on or eternal rest. I once went on a day's course on how to 'let people go'. The trick is to make them feel it is the best thing that has happened in their lives, that they are being made redundant through no fault of their own, that their pay-off is better than anyone else is getting.

Above all you should make it sound as if the job is being got rid of, not the person, that you should leave them with self-esteem and self-confidence intact. This advice certainly makes the firer feel better. When I had to tell people that their jobs were no longer needed it helped me get over the awkwardness to tell them they were wonderful people and there was nothing personal in our decision.

But it was personal. It was deeply and devastatingly personal. I was shaken by being fired. Looking back on it now it seems trivial and amusing but at the time it made me depressed. It went deeper than not getting material for this book. Since leaving school I had thought that if necessary I could always go out and get a job, any job, to earn a living. This conviction now seemed ill-founded. If I felt like this after a day, how would I have felt after a lifetime? Being thrown out of a temping job after a day is not in the same league as being thrown out of a career and a livelihood. But it was a taste.

Why was I fired?

I blamed the agency. Greta was cross with Jenny for not sending the sort of person she had asked for.

I blamed Greta. She had given me no idea what I was supposed to do, what was expected of me.

I blamed my own tactlessness. I did not make an effort to get on with her. I questioned her industry and dedication.

I blamed personal chemistry. We did not get on.

There was probably some truth in all of these. But the most important reason was that I was incompetent.

You are what you do.

Job Satisfaction

The market was quiet. It was the period before Christmas when people do not go on holiday or change jobs before the Christmas bonus. The weather was mild and there was no 'flu around. I watched avidly for news of a cold snap or an epidemic. I signed on at more agencies. I soon discovered that the jobs that are posted on the window are no indication of what they have to offer inside. It made me genuinely depressed. The image I was projecting of a fellow down on his luck, soft spoken, avoiding eye contact, sitting hunched, fitted better and better. When I told myself that this was a lot of fun, fascinating experience, that I was writing a book, that I was not condemned to this life for real, it was as if I was talking about another person.

I took a typing test in the West End. I sat down at a word processor and copied out a passage about how Andrew Carnegie was a skilled telegrapher before he made his millions in the Pennsylvania coal fields. The two spelling mistakes in what I was copying posed a dilemma. Should I correct them in my copy and be penalized for making a mistake? In the cut and thrust of business, integrity goes by the board. I reproduced them. I did forty-five words a minute which is not as fast as Carnegie but could get me a typist's job. The minimum is thirty-five. At last I had found something I could *do*.

'And there are no mistakes,' said Jenny, sounding surprised. This was another Jenny, not the one who told me I was unwanted.

'Are there supposed to be?'

'You don't have to worry about mistakes. It's the speed that counts.'

'So when do I start? You've got plenty of secretarial jobs advertised.'

'Those aren't for men. We don't mind, of course, but the clients want girls.'

'That's sex discrimination. I'll take you to the European Court.'

'Can you do shorthand?'

'No.'

'There you are, then.'

But there were no jobs.

'What about filing?' asked yet another Jenny at an agency in the City. She was very apologetic. 'I'm ever so sorry. It's the best I can do. I had a messenger job but it went. I hope you won't get too bored. Try and stick it for a week. It'll help me out.'

'Me? Filing? I'm a whizz.'

It was at a subsidiary of a South African finance company in the City. To show keenness I got there at a quarter to nine. The name of the company, which did not mention South Africa, was on a very small brass plate inside the door of the office building. It was on the third floor. The door had a security lock opened by a number code. I rang a bell to be let in by a large bald man in a beige uniform. Inside, it was smartly decorated and furnished from floor to ceiling in beige. I browsed through the annual report from Johannesburg. The Corporate Mission Statement said that the company did not discriminate on the basis of race, colour or creed. Geraldine came out for me. She was a brisk, grey-haired lady. She showed me what number to punch to get in and out of the front door by myself. It was 1987.

'We change it every year for security,' she confided.

She took me back to the main office. There were only twenty people in the company, all on one floor. The Manager had a separate office decorated with photographs of wild animals. Geraldine, his secretary, sat in the corridor outside. The rest was open plan. There were no partitions. Clumps of beige desks were positioned far apart and in such a way that no one could look at anyone else. One clump had three dealing positions with phones and screens and keyboards. I was led to the filing area in a windowless corner and introduced to Victorina, my boss. She was a very tall girl, endowed by nature with the height to reach the top shelf of a filing cupboard without a stool. She was in her early twenties and looked fit and tanned. Her height was in her trunk not her legs so she towered over me even when she sat down. This was also convenient for sorting and collating as she could reach over two desks without difficulty. We sat in a laager made by four-drawer filing cabinets. Trays and cardboard boxes piled high with papers surrounded us. She had been away for three weeks, getting married and going on honeymoon, and needed help to catch up with the backlog.

There were three types of file: Correspondence, Business and Information. My first job was to divide up the papers into these three categories. It was not as easy as it sounds. There was a grey area between each category. Even filing has its tricks and mysteries. But I had learned my lesson from Greta. I dived in and looked industrious. I asked Victorina about herself and she told me about her husband.

'He's the Systems Manager at a stockbroker. It's a very good job. He gets a Sierra. And a good bonus. And BUPA. The trouble is most of it goes to his first wife. His children are still at school.'

'How did you meet?'

'I play netball at lunchtime. When it's not raining. His office is in a basement. The window looks onto the court. He watched me for four years. One day I heard someone ask my name and I looked down and there he was, like a rabbit in a hole. Isn't it romantic?'

I thought it was a pretty story. It gave hope to the men with their hands stuffed in the pockets of their brown macs who stand around the City netball courts ogling the long-legged girls in short skirts and loose T-shirts dancing around on the other side of the wire netting.

It took a full day to sort the pending material into three. We were constantly interrupted by people wanting files. I found this irritating. Victorina enjoyed it. She discussed the contents of a file like a librarian checking out a favourite book. She had created an elaborate check-out system that involved index cards and file out cards that had to be signed by the borrower and the filing clerk. It seemed unnecessary for a clientele of twenty people all in one room. You could just go round at the end of the day and collect them all up. Victorina was offended by this suggestion. She was possessive of her system and her territory and the service she provided.

'This place would collapse without the files, do you know that? What those people do today depends on what they did yesterday. You and I are information specialists.'

As well as a check-out system she had developed a cross-referencing system for the information files. She would not let me near this in case I messed it up. She dissected bank bulletins and stockbrokers' news-sheets and *Financial Times* special reports and the other junk mail that plops through business letterboxes into topics she thought relevant to the company's business. She showed me the Index. It was a surreal catalogue of the subjects that had caught her fancy. There were files on Soap in the Southern Hemisphere, Shortages in the Sudan, Platinum and Pollution Control, The Problems of Metal Fatigue, Israel and the Kiwi Fruit. It had a delightful, random absurdity, like reading down the spines of a collection of *National Geographics*. The week I was there no one asked for an information file. I asked Victorina if she minded.

'They know it's there. That's the important thing.'

She reported directly to the Manager. I did not see them speak. He stayed in his office most of the day, speaking on the telephone and poring over reports. People who collected and returned files stopped for a chat. She had most to do with Geraldine, the Manager's secretary, since they organized the social club together. Twice a week they had a workout in the boardroom to Jane Fonda tapes. Once a fortnight there was a game of football or netball or darts or Trivial Pursuit, men against the women.

When she went off at lunchtime to play netball in front of her new husband I had a good read of the correspondence files. I looked for titbits to feed my liberal prejudices and justify my presence to the ANC sympathizers among my family and friends. I'm not sure what I expected to find but it all seemed innocuous. After Britain and Italy the bank did most business with Zimbabwe.

'How do you feel about working for a South African company?' I asked Victorina when she came back, glowing and happy after a five-nil victory.

'The apartheid you mean? I'm not for it. But what's it got to do with me? Everyone's so friendly here. This is the nicest place I've worked.'

'Why?'

'I used to be in a big bank. There were fifty of us in one room. I'd much rather be in a small organization. You learn more. There's something new every day. It's more of a team. You're appreciated more. In most places you only get recognition from your immediate boss. Here they all appreciate what you do. And they let you get on with it.'

'There must be disadvantages.'

'If you don't get on with someone it's a disadvantage in a small place. You can't avoid them. And there's not so much scope for promotion. But it's great here. I wouldn't want to do anything else.'

Victorina's reasons to be cheerful, in the order she mentioned them, were:

- **She learnt more.**
- **There was something new every day.**

- She felt she belonged to a team.
- She felt she got recognition.
- She was left to get on with the job.

When I wrote these down I wondered if she had read articles about job satisfaction or seen a training video or taken part in attitude surveys. Her answer came out pat. Many of the conversations I had with people about their work sounded like a script. Most people know what they want out of their work.

The need which surfaced most consistently in my conversations was the need to learn. It was usually the first or second thing people mentioned. It did not matter whether it was a new manual skill or expertise or a market or just general knowledge acquired while doing the job. I heard it from men and women at all levels of the hierarchy, of all ages, in all kinds of jobs.

Settling In

'Welcome to the madhouse,' said Sharon.

I sat down in front of a blotter smothered with doodles of skinny brides in flowing wedding dresses. Sharon sat behind me. She was the supervisor. Angela sat in front of me. In front of her was Li. The fourth desk was occupied by Percy. Percy was an IBM personal computer. We had a partitioned area to ourselves facing the door to the lavatories. The door was unmarked. Directions to the lavatories were usually given as 'down the corridor, second door on the left opposite recks'. Strangers would stop at Li's desk and ask her what her job was. In reply she simply pointed behind them to the door. We were guardians of the toilets as well as the nostro balances. I asked why the door was unmarked but no one knew.

Sharon had a round, pleasant face, a high skittering giggle and a complicated hairstyle that made her look as if she had just come out of the bath. She wore tight skirts and blouses pinched under the bust and wide belts that gave her a pronounced hour-glass shape. Angela was an older, grey-haired woman with protruding teeth. She wore the same trim grey suit and black high-heels every day and carried a leather executive case. She varied her outfit with a range of blue blouses. She came from Leeds and had a Yorkshire accent. Li was Chinese from Hong Kong. She was fat and jolly and had very delicate hands. I was taking the place of Wanda who had got married and was on honeymoon in Marbella.

I was back on nostro reconciliations at another North

American bank. It was hard not to be typecast by the agencies. After a day of nostros I was classified as experienced. I was also experienced in the ways of temping. As soon as I arrived at the North American bank I asked my new colleagues what their names were, where I could hang my coat, what time I was expected to start in the morning, what time we finished, when I could go for lunch and for how long, whether there was a staff dining room, where the coffee machine was, whether there were any special house rules, where the toilets were and what my job was. I knew that this information, while not deliberately concealed, was rarely volunteered. The most you were told was where to sit.

My experience was not unique and it was not just because I was a non-existent temp. Li had joined the bank as a regular employee six weeks before. On her first day the Personnel Manager's assistant gave her forms to fill out and answered some of her basic questions about hours of work and how many luncheon vouchers she was entitled to. She was taken down to meet Archie, the Assistant Operations Manager. He spent half an hour telling her about the bank, what sort of business they did, how they fitted in to the worldwide organization. Sharon showed her where to sit and went through her daily tasks. She gave her a written job description, a legal requirement, but it wasn't very helpful since they had changed the job since it was written two years before. That was the extent of her induction into the organization. There was no easy way of finding out what all the other terms and conditions of employment were either. There was no employee handbook to refer to. Employees could get an interest-free loan to buy an annual season ticket. Li heard for the first time about season ticket loans while I was there, six weeks after she started. Sharon and Angela argued about the procedure for getting one but they could not agree. Sharon said she would take her on a tour of the bank, show her where the other departments were and introduce her to the people she would come into contact with in the course of her work. But she hadn't got round to it. The week before I arrived she had gone to a staff meeting. Several of her colleagues were surprised to see her there because they thought she was a temp. She still felt a stranger.

Her husband was also from Hong Kong. They had met when they were both at accountancy school. She gave up her studies when they started living together. They now had a three-bedroom semi in South London and a three-year-old child whom she took to a child-minder on her way to work. They were building up a private practice and spent most of the weekend seeing clients. They did the accounts for a dozen Chinese restaurants. Most of the time when we were alone we discussed food.

'Don't you get homesick?' I asked after jotting down the recipe for Szezuan fish soup.

'Terrible. We went back for two years. My husband got a good job in Hong Kong and Shanghai Bank. But we missed out here. We have to start career all over again. In Hong Kong he goes back to being typical Chinese husband. I have to stay in and look after the family. Everyone has eyes on you. Your family, your neighbours, everyone. If a woman flirts with someone else then the whole street comes round and beats you. My job here gives me independence. And status, you know. At home I am a house-slave. Here I am a professional person.'

Sometimes she came in late, distraught and upset. She would work solidly all morning, with not a word to the rest of us, breaking her concentration only to fire vituperative bursts of Cantonese into the phone. When she did this Angela would turn round to Sharon and frown and shake her head. Sharon ignored her.

Sharon and Angela usually went out for lunch. On my first day they went out for a drink with a friend in Telex who was getting engaged at the weekend. They went out for a drink about three times a week, usually on the pretext of celebrating something. There were Promotion Drinks and Transfer Drinks and Payrise Drinks and

Joining Drinks and Leaving Drinks and Engagement Drinks and Wedding Drinks and Back From Honeymoon Drinks and Sunshine Drinks (going away on holiday) and Back From The Sunshine Drinks and Reunion Drinks and New Car Drinks and Moving House Drinks and Buying A Three-Piece Suite Drinks and Getting Pregnant Drinks and when all else failed Just For A Drink Drinks. There was no precedent for a New Temp Drink but later on I was sometimes invited along, although the rounds were expensive. Sharon drank large Bacardis on the rocks and Angela Canadian Club with ice and water. We went to wine bars and cocktail bars, rather than pubs crowded with beer drinkers. To avoid paying City prices for bar snacks we ate sandwiches at our desks before we went.

During the time I was there Li always made excuses and stayed behind to read *Elements of Banking*. Once when Sharon and Angela had gone I asked her if she was teetotal.

'I drink white wine. But English people are very stand-offish. It's hard to be accepted. I am a professional person. Sharon and Angela are not professional people.'

'You don't like it here, then.'

'Oh I like it. Before I was at a stockbrokers. Working conditions were very bad. And the managers, they treat you like dirt. The office was dingy and they were always down your back. Here is light and airy and air-conditioning is good. They are very relaxed. They let you get on with job. Here I am on probation for another six weeks. Then we shall see.'

'See what?'

'I am a professional person. I wanted to be in accounts here. Not in this job. This isn't my sort of work. Sharon and Angela and Wanda are happy to do this. But they're you know . . . My husband and I are professional people. He is an accountant. I only took this job to get in the bank. They told me I would be assistant manager to Sharon when my probation finishes next month. Then I want to transfer to accounts. They're OK but they aren't our sort, are they? I have to get promotion because the child-minder is so expensive. And we send him after to private school.'

I asked Sharon about Li over a third Bacardi on the rocks. We were having Sharon's Anniversary Drink. She had been at the bank for three years and six months.

'Li's a very hard worker,' I said.

'I've had trouble with her. She'd only been here a week when she told me she was going to be my deputy. First I'd heard of it. She complained because I wasn't teaching her what my job was. I asked Archie but he'd heard nothing about it either. I thought she was trying it on. Then we went to Personnel. It was true. They'd promised her she'd be my deputy. But I don't want Li as my assistant. I'd rather have Wanda. Anyway, she wants to move into accounts.'

'Why? What's wrong with Li?'

'Nothing. She just needs to settle in. Anyway Wanda's been here longer. It wouldn't be fair.'

One morning Angela was late. She looked tired and preoccupied. We were already hard at work. Angela talked while she worked. The rubber finger stall on her index finger was a red blur. Sharon was bent over a print-out, her nose close to the paper, ticking off numbers with a sharp yellow pencil. Li pondered over a confirmation, her chin in her hands.

'My little girl was sick on my bed at three o'clock this morning. Poor little mite. It must have been the sardines. She was making a funny noise in her throat. I woke up thinking it was burglars. Sort of scratching at the door downstairs. But it was Annie.'

'Ah. Shame.'

'It went all over the counterpane. I didn't find all of it until I made the bed this morning. I had to take it to the cleaners. Over my nightie too. It woke up my little boy. Roger needs his sleep. He can't get around so easy during the day so he uses a lot of energy. He couldn't get out of bed this morning.'

'Ah. Shame.'

'I'm keeping her off food for the rest of the day. I'll go out at lunchtime to buy a chicken breast for her dinner. Roger likes that too.'

'How old are they?' I asked, anxious to ingratiate myself.

'Annie's eleven. She's only got one eye.'

'She's active though, isn't she?' said Sharon.

'It's still quite old for a Siamese,' said Angela. 'I get worried when she's poorly.'

'What about Roger?' I asked.

'He's only seven. He's a Scottie.'

'Tell him about Roger, Angela. It's ever such a shame.'

'He was run over by a motorbike two years ago. He had to have both his back legs amputated. He was in intensive care. I wouldn't have him put down. You wouldn't would you, if it was a person. My boyfriend Colin fixed him up with a little trolley. He used those little rubber push-chair wheels. The vet agreed. He refuses to put down a healthy animal.'

'He's happy as anything, isn't he, Angela?'

'Except he does need a bit of help to go to the toilet. Have you got any little ones?' she asked me.

I assumed she meant pets not children. I told them about Guinness, our dog. I related how he had gone out one Saturday night two years ago and been run over by a car. He had been in intensive care too. It had left a foreleg paralysed.

'Ah, poor little thing.'

'The vet wanted to amputate it but we thought it would change his personality.'

'Ah. Shame.'

'Because it trails along the ground it gets sore and infected. He has to wear a glove.'

'Ah. Sweetheart.'

'It wasn't easy to find anything that fitted. At first we tried toddler-sized sheepskin mittens.'

'Bless him.'

'But you can't buy them in the summer. I tried all over.'

'Ah. Shame.'

'And leather covers from piano pedals.'

'Ah. Precious.'

'And little boxing gloves.'

'Ah. The darling.'

'We made them ourselves with heavy duty PVC and nylon thread. But they didn't work. Then we discovered golf-club covers. He takes a number four wood.'

'Ah. The petal.'

'Every month or so I have the same conversation with the man in the sports shop. "Is it for you, sir?" – "No, it's for the dog" – "What's his handicap?" – "Ho Ho Ho." '

For half an hour we discussed dogs we had known. It was a safe topic of conversation, the first stage of my gradual absorption into the work group. Li did not join in. She sat with her chin on her hands, absorbed in her work.

'Do you like dogs, Li?' asked Sharon.

'When I was little girl in China if we had coughs my granny give us dog soup.' She interpreted our silence as a desire for further information. 'It was hot food, you see. Chinese food is hot or cold. Dog is hot. Fish is cold. If you have fever or boils that is hot sickness. You take cold food. If you had cough or rheumatism that is cold sickness. You take hot food. See?'

'Sounds logical,' I said.

'Mongrels are preferable for cooking to pedigree. All that inbreeding is not good. Makes the meat bad to eat. Mixed breed is better. More healthy. But a plain colour is preferable to a mixed colour or spots. Spots is the worst. Never eat Dalmatian. The best is a smooth and yellowy coat. Like Labrador. Very tasty. But I have not eaten dog since I came to England,' she added, wistfully. Once again she interpreted stunned silence as an invitation to continue. 'Cat is good for cold sickness too. But you must be very careful not to eat the fur. Not even a little bit. Bad for you.'

'Thanks for the tip,' I said.

The others didn't say anything.

Most people who voluntarily leave their jobs do so within a week of joining.

For the first day or two at a new job your sensitivities are considerably heightened. Impressions of colours and sounds and smells are intensified. You feel exposed and vulnerable. You pick up the most trivial clues about the place where you have contracted yourself to work. You hang on every word that is said to you. You make immediate and lasting judgements of the people you meet. I felt this in all the jobs I took, even the last ones when I had got used to the experience. For a permanent employee, who has made a much more significant commitment than a temp, and who is not in the habit of changing jobs, the experience is even more intense. It is in these first few days that the attitude of people to their work and their employer is formed.

The minimum requirement is that new people should be given a document with the terms and conditions of employment, benefits, house rules and so on. They should be properly introduced to their colleagues and anyone else they will come into contact with during their work. They should be shown the inside of the building where they are to work and meet at least their department head.

None of the companies I worked for did this. None of them had a well-defined procedure for inducting new people at the clerical level. It was usually left to the supervisor to show them the ropes. As the supervisor had no experience of being introduced to the company when he or she joined, there was no precedent for doing so properly.

More Job Satisfaction

Sharon put me in charge of the sterling account.

'You know what to do, don't you?' said Sharon.

'Sure,' I said breezily, 'but every bank is different. Why don't you just go through it once to make sure I follow your procedures.' Sharon sighed. She saw through that one. She handed me a wodge of computer-generated forms.

'These are confirmations. Split them. Put the two copies into two different piles.'

The print-out I was sorting into piles was confirmations of foreign exchange and money market deals that had been done the previous day in the dealing room. Each sheet contained the name of the other bank or customer we had dealt with, the amount dealt and its equivalent in dollars, and the 'value date'.

Every deal was recorded in an internal account of the bank. At the same time, money passed in and out of its accounts with other banks. These accounts with other banks are called nostro accounts. For example, if the bank exchanges dollars for francs it will pay dollars out of its dollar nostro account in a New York bank and receive francs in its franc nostro account with a Paris bank. With hundreds of transactions taking place every day, each one processed by several computers and input several times by human-beings and sent over telephone lines and satellites, mistakes will happen. They can be expensive. If, say, ten million dollars is sent to the wrong account, the correct account will be overdrawn. If interest rates are 11 per cent per annum this will cost about $3,000 a day. The job of reconciliations is to match the entries in the internal accounts with the nostros in other banks every day to see what has gone astray.

Sharon assumed I was aware of this background. After fifteen years in banking I was, in a hazy sort of way. Her technique of explaining the job was to take me through it step-by-step without explaining the reasons for what I was doing so I learned it by rote. This is probably how she had been taught herself.

'Is there a job description?'

Sharon sighed. 'Yes, we've got those somewhere, if I can find them. We lost all that stuff when we moved into the new building last year.'

'Don't bother then. Is there a procedure manual?'

'Yes, we've got one of those. We have to for the auditors.'

'Can I see it?'

'Sure. Trouble is we don't do it that way any more since we had the new computer system.'

'What if you go under a bus?'

'Angela and Wanda know. And Archie could muddle through.'

After sorting the confirmations into piles I had to highlight with a yellow felt-tip the value dates, the dollar amounts in one pile and the sterling amounts in the other pile. Anything other than dollar and sterling I threw away. Each pile was divided into 'bought from' and 'sold to' and sorted into value date order. I gave the dollar piles to Angela and kept the sterling for myself.

Next I had to take out of a drawer in my desk two large piles of confirmations. I merged them with the new piles, careful to keep them in value date order. I took out all those with today's value date and put the rest back in the drawer.

Then Sharon gave me the London Statement, the bank's internal record of the deals that had been done. I had to tick off the confirmations against the entries on the account. I asked why I had to do this as the same computer generated both the London statements and the confirmations from the same information. Sharon sighed and told me to get on with it. She was right. There were indeed confirmation tickets without entries. These I just threw away. If there were entries on the statement without confirmations I highlighted them with the felt-tip. I was mystified by this procedure, but I didn't want to make a nuisance of myself by asking.

I was then given the statement for our nostro account with the British clearing bank. I ticked off the entries that matched those on the internal account. This was not as easy as it sounds. Several entries on one statement could be merged into one entry on the other. There were reverse debits and reverse credits, cancelling previous entries. There were credits and debits that were ticked off against entries on the same statement. There were always entries on both statements that did not have matches. These were highlighted in yellow.

All through the day people came in holding scraps of paper and asked us questions about deals that had gone astray. Most of them were recent but some went back a year or so. These people were from Accounts and Cash, the section which received and paid out the cheques and drafts, and Foreign Exchange Operations. Foreign Exchange Operations is the back-up to the dealing room. When a dealer makes a deal he scribbles down the basic information on a deal ticket – the amounts, the rate, the customer. The ticket goes to Foreign Exchange Operations who check it and add all the other information necessary to put the deal into the computer and complete the transaction – the bank accounts where money will be received, the correct name and address of the other bank, a reference number. It is their job to make sure that payments are correctly made. It is Reck's job to make sure this happens and that money we expect is actually received. If we saw a missing item we told them, if they had a query they came to us. The two sections had to work very closely together.

Milla from Foreign Exchange Operations was our most frequent visitor. She had an Eastern European accent and a cheery smile. She was plump and blonde and jolly and very conscientious. It was her job to track down missing items. A bank with thousands of transactions every day is an impenetrable haystack to look through. She usually started with us. But no one had explained to her that that was what we were there for, that it was our job to help her. Every time she came in to our area, sometimes a dozen times a day, she apologized profusely for disturbing our work, blaming herself for being such a nuisance, promising she would not come back again until tomorrow. 'Here come de Big Pest', she announced every time she came in.

After reconciling the two statements and the deal tickets there were still a lot of unmatched entries. Sharon gave me another print-out with the unmatched entries of previous statements going back about eighteen months. This was the Reconciliation Sheet. There were four columns, debits and credits to the internal account and debits and credits to the nostro account with the British clearing bank. I had to search through these and look for ones that matched entries on today's statements. I was left with about twenty entries that had no match. The biggest, over half a million pounds, I had to point out to Sharon who alerted the Cash Department.

It wasn't just a question of deleting some numbers and adding others to the right columns. The columns of credits and debits on the Reconciliation Sheet and the balances on the London Statement and the Nostro had to balance-off to zero. This was done on Percy, the personal computer. At the end of the day I sat in front of the screen and called up the file called Sterling Reconciliation. I put in the closing balances of the London Statement and the nostros, updated the Reconciliation Sheet and pressed a function key. This was the moment of truth. It took half a minute to make the calculation. The screen gave me the instruction to wait, which I obeyed with bated breath. It flickered and flashed and there was the balance. If it was within a pound of zero I had done my day's work without a mistake.

Usually it was not and I had to go through all my workings. Sometimes I discovered the error within minutes, a couple of times I had to re-do the whole day's work.

I was in sole charge of the sterling account. Sharon only interfered if I asked for help or was not finished by five o'clock. I saw the daily reconciliation through from splitting the confirmations to signing the Reconciliation Sheet. It was my responsibility. I owned it. People came straight to me if they had a query. I felt important and made an effort to make sure I knew the answers.

There was no doubt about whether I had done the job expected of me. I had to make it balance to zero at the end of the day. At ten to five we cleared our desks. We weren't supposed to leave papers lying around. Li put away the print-outs. Sharon turned Percy off and locked the diskettes away in the filing cupboard. Angela took her china cup and saucer and apostle spoon to wash up. On the dot of two minutes to five the four of us were standing at the lift. We went home feeling we had accomplished something. In my old job the horizon was months, if not years. There was no beginning or end. Anything of importance was decided by committee or needed endless justification and explanation to other people in meetings or on the phone or in memos and reports. At the end of the day it was hard to look back and see what you had actually achieved.

On my first day I balanced the account on Percy first time. Sharon said I had done well. The glow of immediate pleasure took me by surprise. I had to keep reminding myself that I was not an ambitious school leaver. After a week I was balancing it by the middle of the afternoon. As a reward I was given the Hong Kong and the Singapore accounts. They were not very complicated and there were fewer errors and mis-postings.

There was not just the intrinsic pleasure of doing something well. There was as much satisfaction in finding missing items for Foreign Exchange Operations. When the discrepancy was large and substantial penalty interest at stake, we all helped to go through statements and tickets and print-outs. When it was found we would share a few moments' elation. If the discovery enabled us to claim it from another bank, there was even more satisfaction. One afternoon Archie came into our area waving a piece of paper and announced we had got back $20,000 in penalty interest from a large New York bank. Everyone cheered.

The best part of the day was asking Percy to balance at the end of the day. I always felt a thrill when I pressed the function key. This was the culmination of a day's concentration and thought and attention to detail. The delicious moments while the screen flashed 'wait' while it did its calculations were like waiting for the roulette wheel to stop. I felt an immediate glow of pride when it balanced, tinged with disappointment that the treasure-hunt was over. If it did not balance I felt a flush of annoyance, tinged with pleasure at the thought of looking for the mistake.

Unless you are a bank auditor or a recks clerk looking for mistakes I have made, you have probably skipped the last few paragraphs. If it's tedious and confusing to read, think of what it was like to write. And then think of what it's like to spend every day of your working life actually doing it.

For the first few weeks I enjoyed it. I experienced the novel sensation of not minding Monday morning. It was pleasant to settle down first thing in the morning to something mindless and chat over a cup of coffee about last night's *EastEnders* or the weekend's parties. I found the mechanical work of sorting and filing very soothing, like occupational therapy. The job needed effort and concentration but it was predictable. The whole day had an unvarying structure and routine that was reassuring. It made a pleasant change from having to look for things to do, make choices about what to tackle first, invent the day as it went along.

When I learned the job and it became routine it became as tedious as anything one does every day in the same way. There was still the thrill of balancing at the end of the day but I wondered if I would feel differently about it if I knew it was for real, that I was going to be doing it for the next few years. I asked Sharon whether she enjoyed it.

'It's like doing a jig-saw,' she confided over a Bacardi on the rocks. 'I love jig-saws. I don't usually tell people that because they think it's childish. On my birthday I always buy myself a big one. Four thousand, five thousand pieces. And I can't stop until I finish it. I sometimes stay up all night. It used to drive Ray mad when I didn't come to bed but he's used to it now. You get this funny feeling when you put the last one in, like it's all over. But usually there's a piece missing and you hunt all over the house for it and you find it down the back of the sofa and it's great. Recks is like that.'

I enjoyed reconciling the sterling account more than most of the jobs I did. The reasons were:

- **I had total responsibility for the job from beginning to end.**
- **There was a recognizable and quantifiable purpose: to save penalty interest.**
- **There was a recognizable and tangible target: to make the reconciliation balance to zero.**
- **The time horizon was short: the job had to be finished by the end of the day.**
- **There was an intrinsic satisfaction of problem-solving.**
- **Sharon was a good supervisor. She explained the task clearly, let me get on with it and praised me when I got it right.**
- **I worked in a friendly group of people who shared a common goal.**
- **The job was new to me. I was learning something.**
- **I knew I was not going to be doing it for very long.**

I was surprised to find that many of the clerical jobs I did were as satisfying as recks. Computers do the routine calculations and sorting and filing that used to be done by armies of people but this need not mean that clerks are drudges who feed the machines and sweep up after them. One of the effects of computerization on traditional office work has been to convert the recording and processing of information into problem-solving and analysis. The adding up is done but there are errors to be found, inconsistencies and discrepancies to be tracked down, conclusions to be drawn, action to be taken.

Computers

We gathered round Louise's Tupperware catalogue. She was a small, foxy-faced girl with a deep voice and sharp eyes. She was about twenty. She had a voluptuous figure which she showed off with tight skirts and plunging necklines. She had just moved to Foreign Exchange Settlements from Cash. She often came to see me on the pretext of queries which I was sure she could have answered herself. She would stand by my desk, her thigh pressed against mine, her soft shoulder brushing mine, bent over the desk with her pert bottom in the air. She smelt of musky scent and the raspberry flavoured chewing gum to which she was addicted.

'Do you like the parties?' I asked Louise.

'I never go to them. I like the things they sell but not the parties. Who wants to sit round in a room with a lot of women?' Louise's question was addressed to me, her eyes boring though my indifference to Tupperware like close-set halogen lamps. Angela and Sharon ordered salad spinners. I ordered a lemon squeezer. Louise filled out a complicated form.

'It's for the computer,' she said.

'I loathe computers,' said Angela.

'Why is that, Ange?' said Louise.

'You're just a slave to them, aren't you? You feed them and wipe up after them. They do all the work. We break down and it's good riddance. Computer goes on strike and it's the end of the world.'

'Someone's got to tell them what to do, Ange.'

'Now in my day everybody worked together. You had a decent job. You could get somewhere.'

'You were on the switchboard, Ange. You never would have done this before.'

'I know and look what happened to the switchboard. They computerized that. Does it all for you. There's no skill, you're just a nice voice. There were three of us when I started and now there's only Elsie. I should have stayed.'

'Why didn't you, Ange?'

'I didn't want to do reception. Elsie has to do reception too. I said I wasn't going to do two jobs for the same money.'

'You're all right now.'

'I want to get into marketing. Deal with real people. At least they talk to you, not like him.' Angela nodded at Percy humming to himself on the next desk.

Sharon showed me how to use Percy. It used Lotus 1-2-3, a versatile off-the-shelf program that can be adapted to any process where complicated adding and subtracting and multiplication and division are required. Sharon was very proficient. She did not simply know which keys to press in what order. She knew how the program was put together and how it worked. If something went wrong she could put it right. She was not frightened of experimenting. She had a natural aptitude for the computer. She obviously enjoyed using it and showing what she could do. I asked her if she had been on a course to learn how to use it.

'Nah. This bank's too mean. You have to pick it up yourself.'

'No one showed you?'

'Not really. You just have to work it out.'

This was not strictly true. There was a teach-yourself diskette available to anyone in the office who wanted to borrow it and could get access to one of the PCs.

Sharon logged on for me, called up the file of sterling outstandings, and showed me how to delete the items I had just matched off against today's statements. Then I had to input today's outstandings. It was fiddly work and I made a lot of mistakes. I put figures in wrong columns or forgot to put a bracket round the negatives. Each time this happened Sharon left her desk and came over to put it right. She leaned over my shoulder and her fingers fluttered over the keyboard. I had to ask several times before she would show me how to put things right myself. She logged on and logged off for me and reset the date each day. She also preferred to store the files and start the printing herself. She jealously guarded her knowledge.

Angela and Li derived satisfaction from making Percy balance their reconciliations. Both of them would bang down the final function key as if they were throwing down a gauntlet. Angela watched the screen without blinking, willing it to come up with the right answer. Li looked up at the ceiling until she heard the beep that announced the result. She looked at it out of the corner of her eye. If it balanced Angela took in a deep breath, her chest swelling. Li smirked and hid her mouth behind a delicate hand. They did not enjoy working with the PC. They knew what keys to press but they did not understand how the system worked. If they came across a problem they did not experiment but asked Sharon to help. This knowledge, and a judicious holding back of important information like how to log on, made Sharon a natural leader for anything to do with Percy.

'Who's idea was it to put the Reconciliation Sheets on Percy?' I asked.

'That was my idea,' she said. 'It used to be so time-consuming to add and delete and add up the result by hand on the machine. You had to do the whole lot, two years worth, every day, because the auditors wanted to see a complete listing. There was no short cuts. You got lots of errors. They was using Percy next door until they went on the mainframe. I kidnapped him in here. Me and the Data Processing Manager worked on it together. He was useless. He hadn't worked on PCs before and hadn't been on any courses. It was all foreign to him. I couldn't believe it. Call himself the computer expert? I knew more than him. He was a snob. He didn't want anything to do with PCs. And he was hopeless with Lotus. Anyway, we muddled through and came up with something that was better than doing it by hand. Then we had Trevor. He was a student from the City University. He was here in the summer. He was temping in the computer room as a late shift operator. He wanted to see what we had on our PC so I showed him the program. He rewrote it for us in the evenings when he got bored and now it's great. But I didn't dare tell the Data Processing Manager. He might have got upset.'

'So Trevor set it up.'

'We did it together. And I find little things to improve it all the time.'

Louise was learning how to use the PC. She had got hold of the tutorial disc. She tried to finish her work by four so she could spend the last hour of the day on the machine. She also did it in her own time, during her lunch hour or coming in half an hour early in the morning. She carried the tutorial diskette round the floor and sat down at any unattended machine she could find. Sometimes she was accompanied by Alf, the youngest of the messengers. He was about the same age as Louise. He was dark and good-looking and wore a discreet Iron Maiden badge in the lapel of his dark blue uniform. They sat down together and worked through the program, she leading him on. They argued and jostled when one of them made a mistake, their bantering full of double-entendres and sous-entendres and blatantly obvious entendres. The highlight of the diskette for Louise was when the computer played the Bandinera from the Bach B minor Suite. She turned the sound up and stared us out with her bright, close-set eyes, defying us to tell her to turn the bloody thing off.

One afternoon she pulled up a chair and sat next to me. I was updating the nostro credits. I thrilled to the scent of raspberry and saccharine.

'You don't like Tupperware parties, then,' I said.

'Dead boring. Lot of women. I had an Anne Summers party though, and that was good fun.'

'What's an Anne Summers party?'

She looked at me as though she thought my ignorance was feigned.

Which it was.

'It's like a Tupperware party. Only it's naughty underwear and sex aids and stuff. Good fun. Try anything once.'

'You often have them?' I asked.

'Never again. When you've seen it all once, it's all the same, isn't it?'

'It's what you do with it that counts.' I said. Her eyes lit up.

'A bit like Percy,' she said.

'Who's making you learn it?' I asked. I was interested to see where the impetus was coming from. There were the lessons here for the introduction of new technology. I was curious to know who had planned it.

'Nobody. Hemant lets me get on with it. He's frightened I'll make life hard for him if he doesn't.'

Karim Hemant was her boss, the manager of Foreign Exchange Operations. He was a slim, bespectacled Asian originally from Kenya. He was an expert on Lotus 1-2-3. If Sharon had a problem with Percy she would sometimes go to Hemant for advice. I could not imagine him discouraging Lousie from learning how to use a PC. She needed to feel that she was learning in defiance of authority.

'Why do you do it, then?'

'It's good fun, isn't it? Bit of a lark. It's better than sitting round twiddling your thumbs, isn't it?'

To the Data Processing Manager the personal computer was a threat. It undermined his specialist expertise.

To Angela it was another way of de-skilling her job.

To Sharon it was a new challenge, a new skill to learn and show off.

To Louise it was a game.

For all of them it was a powerful and revolutionary tool because its application was in the hands of its users.

Whatever the scale of technological innovation it will only succeed if the users help to design and install it.

Just A Change Of Name

Archie called Sharon into his office at half-past nine on Friday morning. She came out overawed with the news.

'You know Louise in Foreign Exchange Operations? She's been having some trouble with her husband. Last night he stabbed her seventeen times.'

'Is she dead?' asked Li.

'No. They let her out of hospital. She's gone to her mother's. She won't be in today.'

'Men,' said Angela.

'They'll be needing a temp, then,' I said.

It was the end of the month. The dealers had been active, taking profits and squaring positions. Also the dollar had dropped and risen again the day before. We had twice the volume of trades to cope with. The brunt fell on Foreign Exchange Operations who were one person short after Louise's misfortune. Subdued by the news we worked hard too.

In the middle of the morning Sharon took a phone call.

'Ello Mum, how are you doing?. . . you what?. . . oh . . . what about Dad?. . . aren't you telling him?. . . who'll get his tea?. . . I understand . . . is it you-know-who?. . . but what about Thursday night?. . . you'll still be there . . . see you then . . . we'll have a chat then . . .'

She hung up. The rest of us were breathlessly quiet.

'That was me mum. She's just left me dad again. She's left him a note for when he comes back from work. She's gone to live with that feller she met at her seance. It's for good this time.'

'What are you going to do?' asked Angela.

'He can get his own tea. He's done it often enough.'

'Was it sudden?'

'We knew she was seeing him. We thought it was all spiritual. My dad'll go spare.'

'Was that the medium you go to, Sharon?' asked Li.

'Not on your life. She's in Elmer's End. I go to the one in Berkeley Square with Wanda.'

'What about your mum? Is she happy?'

'I bleeding well hope so to do that. I'll see her on Thursday. We're in the same darts team. Lucky we're playing away in Romford. My dad's got a home match.'

'It's always the men who leave in China,' said Li. 'It's not so long ago the woman would be stoned in the street.'

'I wouldn't get in as deep as last time, Sharon, you've got your own life to lead,' advised Angela.

Sharon telephoned her brother and sister to tell them the news and make arrangements to meet at their dad's that night 'in case he does anything silly'.

Before lunch Archie called Sharon, Angela and Li into his office. They came out after five minutes with the news that the bank in London was being reorganized.

The bank came to London in the late sixties with the wave of foreign banks wanting to participate in the growing Eurodollar market. It built up a foreign exchange dealing room, made international loans to governments and multinationals and sterling loans to British companies.

The British banks woke up and fought back the foreign banks competing on their own territory. International recession and the debt crisis shrank the market for Eurodollar commercial lending and the appetite of the banks to take part. While this was happening the international securities markets were growing. Instead of borrowing from a consortium of banks, borrowers floated Eurobonds and other securities. Most of this business was done by merchant banks – called investment banks in America. Commercial banks who wanted to stay in the game set up separate merchant banks. These were known as 'Limiteds' because they were incorporated in London.

As well as a Limited and a Branch, this bank also had a separate entity in London called International. It housed their European Regional Management. These three groups were separately run with their own managers, operating staff, secretarial staff. The news was that all three were to be merged into one. Also that they were hiring twenty more securities dealers while keeping the operational staff numbers constant.

'The people in International won't think much of that,' said Angela, 'they think they're superior because they're, you know, in International. They look down on us in the Branch. Now we've merged I bet some of them will leave.'

'Archie said it wouldn't affect anyone. It was just a name change,' said Sharon.

'But it affected him, didn't it? He's lost his job,' said Li.

'What's he going to do?' I asked.

'He's going to be joint head of Credit. I can't see that lasting. One of them will go,' said Sharon.

'Who's your new boss then?' I asked.

'They're merging us with FX Operations. Hemant's going to be in charge. He's the new Assistant Operations Manager.'

'He's just come from Bahrain,' said Angela.

'He's Indian,' said Li.

'But they say he's all right. He's very intelligent,' said Sharon.

'I bet that's not the end of it. They don't tell you the half,' said Angela. 'There'll be people leaving again. And they'll be letting people go. You mark my words.'

We were all putting on our coats to go out for a Reorganization Drink when a big girl in a dark blue, doubled-breasted suit came in. She was not just fat. Everything about her – face, features, grin, nose, eyes, hands, feet – was on a larger scale than the rest of us.

'Wanda!' squealed Angela and Sharon together. Wanda was the girl I was replacing while she was on honeymoon and whose blotter was covered in doodles of skinny brides.

'What are you doing here?' asked Sharon.

'We came back a day early,' said Wanda, 'so I just came in to get my mortgage sorted out. You know they still haven't got an approval.'

'They're not helpful at all. They try to put you off,' said Angela.

'Well, how was it?' asked Sharon. Wanda giggled and wrinkled her large nose.

'Here. I've got the photos.' She put a large blue album on Li's desk and we gathered round to admire. They were the proofs.

'Oh, Wanda, they're lovely.'

'Is that your mother?'

'Have you chosen them yet?'

'Look at the cake.'

'It's the flowers that make a cake.'

Wanda presided over the festivities in the photographs like a pagan deity making merry with the mortals who honoured her but capable of crushing them with a single hand or withering them with a glance. I noticed that the double-breasted two-piece suit was her going-away outfit. It was customary to wear the going-away outfit to the office on the first day back when you took the photos around. It was not the first time I had witnessed the showing of the photographs. I knew that the correct etiquette when presented with the album was to say:

– What a lovely dress!

– What a pretty cake!

– Have you picked them yet?

The last refers to the photos that the bride chooses to keep in the white album that plays a tune when you open it.

'Look at that confetti. It got all over my wedding dress

but it didn't stain it at all. It was all inside my bra and knickers and it didn't stain them either.'

'How was the weather?'

'Smashing. Except for the rain. It poured down all day. We had to have all the photographs done inside the church. I didn't like my hair like that. But I got all wet when I got in the car.'

'It suits you like that.'

'The lock jammed and I was standing out there in the rain.'

'Lovely dress.'

'You can't see the pearls on the photo. I spent weeks sewing them on. There were nine hundred. Darren never saw me for weeks. I used to leave him downstairs in front of the telly while I went upstairs to sew them on. Then I had to lock it all away when he came to bed.'

'It must have been lovely.'

'The best man got lost on the way though. He came out of the Dartford tunnel and followed the wrong car. He didn't know the name of the church or the hotel. But it didn't matter because the photographer was late as well. She got held up in the rain. And the video man went to the wrong church so we don't have the videos. But it all went off all right in the end. It was lovely.'

'Look at Darren.'

'He's not really miserable. He's not smiling because I kept telling him to keep his mouth shut. When he smiles his bottom lip drops down and he looks really gormless. He enjoyed it really.'

'Where did you go?'

'Barbados.'

'Smashing.'

'It was ever so hot. Lovely. We didn't realize it was in the middle of their rainy season. When we booked Darren wondered why it was so cheap. It poured all day. It stopped one night and we saw the moon. It was lovely. We were going to come home after a week. Then I thought of shopping in Tescos and we stayed. You don't come home early from Barbados do you? I didn't put any of my swimsuits on. But we had a lovely time. There were all these palm trees and a lovely long beach with nobody on it. Darren got a new camera in the Duty Free. We took lots of pictures of the palm trees and all that.'

'Where are they?'

'He forgot to put film in the camera. But we had a lovely time.'

Wanda's visit took up all our lunchtime so we did not get our Reorganization Drink. I went with Angela to the staff lounge to make tea instead. It was crowded with low chairs and tables. On one side was a sink and a counter with a tea and coffee dispenser, a water cooler, a microwave oven and an electric kettle. There was a stack of throw-away plastic cups, designed for use with holders. The holders had been thrown away too so we used two cups, one inside the other. We all used the plastic cups except Angela who had her own blue china cup and saucer with an apostle spoon which she kept in her handbag. Angela told me, whispering, in confidence, while we waited for the kettle to boil, that she had been with the bank since it opened in London eighteen years before.

'I've seen a few things, I can tell you.'

'What have you seen, Angela?'

She tutted and pursed her lips. I persevered.

'You mean the reorganization? Or Louise?'

'Everything. They say it's just a change of name. Taradiddle. This isn't the end of it. They don't tell you the half. They're hiring twenty more dealers but who's going to do the extra work, I want to know. I suppose they'll want to move me round again. They'll expect us to change. But why should we?'

'Why should you indeed?'

'And that Wanda. I don't know why she bothered getting married, I really don't. That Darren leads her a right dance. You know what he did for his stag night? He went to Amsterdam with his mates for four days.'

After lunch we worked hard to catch up on the time lost in the morning. I had trouble with a batch of payment orders from which the commission had been separately deducted. We were interrupted by Sharon's friend Bernice from Cash.

'What am I going to do?' asked Bernice. 'My sister came round last night. She wants us all to give her some money so she can set up home. She's bought this flat and she wants to do up the kitchen. She said that if she was getting married and was moving into her first home everyone would give her a good present to start her off. But as she's a lesbian and never going to get married she thinks she's missing out. She says setting up house is the same if you're married or not. You expect your family to help out. I didn't know what to say. I mean, we've gone through her coming out and supported her and all that. My dad's always showing the video of her chained to the fence at Greenham Common. But this seems different. What do you think?'

For the next hour we explored Bernice's relationship with her sister and advised on the etiquette of her situation. My view was that a donation towards the new kitchen was appropriate but paying for a week in Malaga in lieu of a trousseau, seeing that she wasn't going to get a honeymoon out of it, was not. I was outvoted. It was decided that Bernice should not give her sister anything.

A few minutes after Bernice left Sharon's mother telephoned again.

'She's decided to go with that feller to the medium where they met. They want to know what they think about it on the other side. Uncle Jim will have something to say, I bet.'

'They just want to hold hands in the dark,' said Angela.

'I think there is something evil there,' said Li. 'My grandmother, she had powers but she didn't use them very much. She said they were dangerous.'

'You're right there, Li,' I said. 'There are evil spirits as well as good.'

'They're only your relatives,' said Sharon. 'Uncle Jim's not an evil spirit. He was ever so nice.'

'He could be an evil spirit in disguise,' said Li.

'Your best protection against evil is not to desire it, not to seek it,' said Angela.

'But the innocent are attractive prey to the forces of evil,' I warned.

'Whatever it is, that medium's to blame for me mum,' said Sharon.

Sharon and Angela finished their reconciliations by four o'clock. They spent the rest of the afternoon talking to their friends on the phone in hushed, cryptic tones about the news of the day while Li and I carried on with our work.

'It's been a full day,' I said as we put on our coats to go home.

'Lots of changes.'

'It doesn't make much difference really,' said Sharon, 'it's just a change of name.'

It had been a full day.

I have no doubt that the radical reorganization of the London operation had preoccupied senior management for weeks. Some careers were seriously affected. But it went almost unnoticed by my colleagues when it was announced. There were more momentous changes to cope with.

I had spent the previous weeks trying to understand how people in the office related to each other and to their work. The events of that day were a reminder that for most people what goes on at work is only a small part of life.

Who's The Boss?

Sharon was one of the best supervisors I had. She was very good at explaining the task and telling people they had done well. She complimented specific achievement and avoided general praise. She was also very good at correcting mistakes. It did not feel personal. One day she discovered that Li was not following the standard procedure for reconciling her accounts. Li had worked out her own method that cut corners and saved time. She also assumed, as I had done on my first day, that there would not be discrepancies between confirmations and account entries produced by the same computer from the same data.

'There are loopholes, Li.'

'But Sharon, I'm an accountant. I know what I'm doing.'

Whether it was out of of timidity or wisdom Sharon did not lay down the law. She avoided confrontation. She discussed it patiently and at the end said 'I would rather you did it like this.' She had a natural flair. But properly defined procedures would have avoided such situations arising in the first place.

I never heard anyone telling Sharon she had done well. Archie rarely came into our area. When he did he always looked preoccupied. He did not say good morning to me, but then I was only a temp. But he did not greet the others either. I did not see him speak to Li once. Sharon sometimes went into his office with queries but rarely stayed for more than half a minute. They had no other contact which I could see.

One day I was ten minutes late for work. Sharon and Angela were deep in discussion. Angela sat bolt upright on my chair with her hands on her lap facing back to Sharon. Sharon leant her head on her right hand while her left hand fed a cream doughnut into her mouth.

'I want a transfer, Sharon, I really do. They should talk to you and ask you before they plonk you somewhere. I've been here a year so I've given it a good try. If you complain they just say "You get paid don't you, what are you grumbling about?" '

'I've recommended a transfer, Angela, you know that,' said Sharon, wiping a blob of cream from her top lip.

At lunchtime I was left alone with Angela. She brought in a packed lunch in a Tupperware box. When I came back with a sandwich I suggested going into the staff lounge but she preferred to eat at her desk.

'I like to keep myself to myself.'

'You don't like it here very much, then?' I said.

'I was dumped here, wasn't I? I don't like the work. It's boring and I don't like using that thing.' She nodded to Percy.

'I thought you were used to keyboards.'

'They never used to talk back, did they? Tell you you were wrong. I should have left like Maureen. Josie was lucky. She went to telex testing. There's a lot less work. She doesn't have to do half what I have to do. She doesn't have to use computers. When I came in here I'd never even used an adding machine.'

'It's something new to learn.'

'I'm not interested, frankly. They don't want you to learn, anyway.'

'You must be doing all right at your job.'

'No one would ever tell you if you were.'

'Don't you have evaluations?'

'We have reports every year. The supervisor writes it and you sign it. It's just for the pay-rises. Everyone gets a 'C'. But what am I supposed to do? You're supposed to be able to do everything in the department, all the jobs. But I can only do this one. I've only been at it a year. Sharon's been doing it for three years. And what about Wanda? She's been doing reconciliations seven years and she only gets a 'C'.'

'What does Sharon get?'

'She was all right at her job. She got a 'C' for the work same as everyone else. But she got a 'D' for the supervisory. She's only been a supervisor for six months. But she's not very good at it.'

'How does Archie know she's not very good at it?'

'We tell him. He hears it from us. Sharon tells me I have to go to her with complaints and things, but why should I? I'd rather go straight in next door to Archie. I've known him since he joined, down in Cash.'

'Doesn't he talk it over with Sharon?'

'Oh yes. I come out and he has Sharon in and she comes out moaning that I should have told her first.'

'I bet she gets upset.'

'She can't take it. She's too moody. She's not strong enough. She won't stand up to you. You have a go at her and she bursts into tears. They ought to have a man in the job. I'd rather work for a man any day.' She wiped her apostle spoon on a pink tissue and put it carefully in the front pocket of her handbag.

'See you later. I'm off down the lane.'

When she came back she made her daily call to her mother in Wakefield. She reported on the intestinal welfare of Annie and Roger and made sure her mother was all right and someone had done her shopping and the daily help had been.

One afternoon I balanced the sterling accounts and found I was out £200. I spent all afternoon looking for it. I had still not found it by five o'clock. I was determined not to leave before I found it and stayed behind until half-past five. I was the last to leave the floor. The next day Sharon came out of Archie's office looking gloomy.

'I got into trouble for letting you stay late unsupervised,' she said. I apologized profusely.

'It's not your fault. I didn't know. It's never happened before.'

'Not in the job description, eh?'

'What job description? He only just told me I could sign temps' time-sheets. I've been taking them into him for the last six months.'

'Has anyone ever told you what to do as a supervisor? Have you had any training?'

'You must be joking. No-one's ever told me what to do. There was something about going on a course in January. Archie never tells me anything, only when I go in and ask. That's when I've got a problem. And it isn't easy with the two I've got. Angela told me today she wanted to go into marketing. First I've heard of it. She's old enough to be my mother and she resents it. I had trouble with her right at the beginning. She never wanted the job. But they mollycoddled her, tried to explain things. It didn't do any good. And I'd already gone over all that with her. Li doesn't want to be in reconciliations. She wants to be an accountant. Wanda never stops talking. Since she moved in with Darren it's all she thinks about, her work's gone to pot. I think I've got a hard group, though everyone tells me everyone has their problems. I was just asked if I wanted the job and that was it. Then six months later they ask you why you haven't done this and that. It's no excuse to say no one told me to.'

'I thought you were getting a new boss in the reorganization. Hemant. He might help.'

'They say he's quite bright. He's good on the PC. But you get used to someone, don't you? Archie knows the job. You feel you have someone to go to. He didn't bother me. He left me alone unless I needed him. Hemant won't know what we do. It's quite complicated. I'll still be going to Archie when I have a question.'

'Can't Hemant read your job descriptions?'

'Yeah, but job descriptions are no good at telling you

what the job actually is. You have to pick it up as you go along.'

'But what about dealing with Angela? Who can you go to about that?'

'You have to sort that sort of thing out yourself. The spiritualist Wanda and I go to was very helpful when they offered me this job. I get the best advice from her. She said it was from the other side but between you and me I don't think it was my Uncle Jim. I just think she's a wise person. She said imagine you're in the spirit world and can see into everyone's heart. Decide what you would do then and act accordingly.'

Sharon was not as badly off as a supervisor in the bank I managed. Her boss wrote on her annual appraisal that she had performed satisfactorily as a supervisor for the past six months but that she needed to improve.

'But I'm not a supervisor,' she said.

'Yes, you are.'

'No, I'm not.'

Yes she was. I knew she was and her boss knew she was and the Personnel Department knew she was and the six people she supervised knew she was but no one had told her. She must have been a natural leader.

'I wondered why everyone came to me with their problems,' she said.

Archie and Sharon need some guidance on the basics of supervision. A very few simple tips would make their relationships with each other and their subordinates much less stressful. But she would still have a problem with Angela.

There are many reasons why Angela was unhappy:

- **She did not like change.**
- **She was not consulted about her transfer.**
- **She was older than Sharon.**
- **She had not been trained on the PC.**
- **Her job had not been properly explained.**
- **No one listened to her.**
- **She had been mollycoddled.**
- **She enjoyed complaining.**

So what could Sharon do?

When you discuss this sort of case on management courses there is often a pat answer at the end that the bright people get and the rest kick themselves for not seeing. I was usually good at them. I used to be good at English Comprehension and Poetry Appreciation too. But in real life I rarely got the right answer. There were too many conflicting factors or not enough information or the underlying problem lay outside the office and had nothing to do with work. A professional psychologist could probably get to the bottom of it if he or she spent enough time gathering data and holding in-depth interviews.

Managers are not professional psychologists and do not have time to devote to in-depth behavioural analysis. People are more productive if they enjoy their work and get on together, but a business is not a therapy clinic. I found that if I stumbled across a solution to a problem like Sharon's, it might alleviate the immediate difficulty but created several more unpredictable ones. The motivations and perceptions and emotions of individuals working in the same place are rarely similar, often contradictory and always changing. The best you can achieve is some kind of temporary trade-off until the next crisis comes along.

Expectations

I usually telephoned for work. At four on Thursday afternoon and at half-past nine, lunchtime and four on a Friday and at ten on a Monday I telephoned the temp controller at a dozen agencies. Some agencies encourage people to come in person first thing in the morning. Anything that comes in is offered to them first. They get the best and often the only jobs. It is the oldest form of labour market.

'Sitting in, dear? Downstairs.'

I went downstairs to a large, bright basement. Two temp controllers sat at desks at one end of the room. The senior of the two, Steve, had a telephone to his ear, while Amanda sorted through a pile of time-sheets. I had registered with Steve six weeks before, and spoken a few times on the phone since. Both of them waved and greeted me by name. They did this to everyone who walked in. They pointed to an open square of comfortable chairs. Next to the seats was a door leading to the loos and a kitchen where we could make ourselves coffee. I was the second to arrive. An elegant, middle-aged woman was engrossed in the autobiography of Bertrand Russell. I exchanged nods with my fellow unemployed and took out *Down and Out in Paris and London*.

In the next half hour came a procession of stunning young women, beautifully dressed and adventurously made-up. Steve greeted them all by name. I sucked in my stomach and flicked my fingers through my hair and wished I was not wearing my baggy clerical cyclist's suit.

Some read serious tomes like *A History of Byzantium*, some read romantic novels thick as doorsteps, some the *Tatlers* and *Harpers and Queens* that were scattered on the tables in front of us. One of the girls, pale skin and raven hair and startling blue eyes, draped in an ankle-length mohair blanket, sat next to me and picked up a *Tatler*. She was Irish, as I discovered when I asked her if she regularly found work this way. Regrettably it came out as 'do you come here often' and our conversation faltered.

One reason for the silent dedication to book-learning was that we all craned to hear what Steve was saying on the phone at the other end of the room. He was ringing round the clients. He was a very good salesman. He knew his contacts as well as he knew us. He would put the phone down and call out a name and ask if he or she had a minute, as if he were interrupting. The favoured person, no longer unemployed, strolled lazily over to get instructions, while the rest of us dived back into our books. If this was the free-for-all of the labour market it was very civilized.

I tried again with the blue-eyed Irish girl.

'I'm forty-five words a minute. How about you?'

She ignored me. I relived the pangs of *stenographobia*, the fear of being laughed at by your secretary. Like many managers the first experience I had in supervising was when I got a half share in a secretary. Everyone else in the office worked with theirs in a different way. The manager, Mr Potter, read his mail in the morning while Mary sat in front of his desk with a shorthand pad at the ready. They were constantly interrupted by telephone calls that came straight through to him because she was not at her desk. She sat there for up to two hours while he talked on the phone, read reports and letters, and occasionally lifted his head to dictate letters and memos, stumbling and repetitive. It seemed to me to be a work method dating from the invention of papyrus, a highly inefficient use of labour that cost as much as I did.

When he had finished or had to go to a meeting, Mary left and sat down at her desk and typed what she had noted down. She had other things to do as well, like arrange meetings and trips and keep the diary. When she had typed the letters and memos she put them in a blotter book which she laid on Mr Potter's desk. She tried to do this as early in the afternoon as she could because he corrected at least half of them, which she had to retype before the end of the day. I asked her once why she did not do them in draft first.

'Because he corrects the draft and then I do a fair copy and then he corrects that again so I end up doing it three times instead of twice.'

I decided this was a very unproductive way of using someone's expensive time. Another reason, which I did not admit, was that I was hopeless at dictating. I had never done it before. The few times I had tried I dried up in the middle or said 'scrap that, let's start again' every third sentence. It is not a skill they teach you anywhere. It is one thing to think on your feet but another to think in perfectly formed and elegant grammatical sentences. When I dictated I had to keep my eyes off the secretary. I looked out of the window or at the ceiling because I knew that if I caught so much as a glimpse of her pencil poised over the blank paper I would dry up.

David, one of my colleagues, also had this problem. He solved it by writing everything in longhand before dictating it. This did not seem a very productive use of time, either. It saved June's time, since she took down the finished, corrected copy. But why didn't he just give her his handwritten drafts? Not only did he keep them to himself, he tried to deny they existed. He would behave as though he were dictating from his head while he glanced secretively at the teleprompt hidden among his papers. I once asked him why he did this, as his writing seemed clear enough. He told me to mind my own business. I suspect his mental movie of the busy executive incorporated scenes of bosses dictating to secretaries.

David shared his secretary, June, with Elizabeth. Elizabeth was not shackled with male role models from movies and did not like to dictate. She wrote everything down in longhand and gave the drafts to June. But they were covered in corrections. At first June ran in and out of the office every sentence. This distracted Elizabeth. Then she forged ahead with the first type draft, full of errors and omissions. Elizabeth sent back the draft with the corrections that were just as confusing as the first draft. A simple letter took several drafts. Then she tried reading over the drafts with Elizabeth before she typed them. In order to remember the corrections she wrote them down in shorthand on her pad. From this it was a short step to Elizabeth dictating from her drafts. Still she had a compulsion to correct them so June resorted to the tactic of not letting her have the blotter book until just before the post went.

I was to share Wendy with Jim. Jim was very efficient and very keen on personal time management. He used a dictating machine. This enabled him to dictate outside normal office hours or whenever he had a few minutes to spare. He had a good aural memory and his first drafts rarely needed corrections. Wendy spent a lot of time with earphones on her head. He was also good at giving instructions to Wendy. At the beginning of the day he left on her desk a neatly written list of what he wanted her to do. On my first morning with her I told her I was going to work like Jim. She would be used to that method and it seemed to me the most productive of her time and mine. Would she mind ordering me a dictating machine and a supply of cassettes? I thought she was about to burst into tears.

'I couldn't stand any more. I spend hours with bloody things stuck in my ears as it is. I'm like a machine. It's like being back in the typing pool again. I never speak to him, never see him. I don't know what he's up to half the time. And he produces so much stuff I can't believe it's all any use. He just blurts on and on into that machine. He churns out five times as much as any of the others. And I'm losing all my shorthand. You have to keep it up or you lose it. And if I lose it, I'll never get another job.'

So to keep Wendy happy I learned to dictate. She had invested time and money and pride in a skill and wanted to use it, even one as biblical as taking dictation. She liked to come in and sit by my desk for half an hour or so. Apart from the social pleasure of human contact she got a better idea of what I was doing and what the purpose of her own work was. She was better able to anticipate what we needed to do. Because I was taking up the time of both of us and because I could see her trying to make sense of what I was doing, I only generated the paper that seemed strictly necessary.

But Jim was jealous. He complained to the boss that I was taking up too much of Wendy's time. She started on my work before his. She neglected his calls and appointments. She made tea for me but he had to get his own . . .

The beautiful Irish girl put down her magazine.

'What do you look for in a boss,' I asked. 'What are your expectations?' She thought for a minute.

'That he doesn't have bad breath,' she said. 'And I can't stand having to sew on buttons.'

The girl opposite looked up from her book.

'In my last job but one, I had to take his teeth to the dentist,' she said. 'All across London.'

'That's nothing,' said the girl next to her. 'I worked for a man who'd been wounded in Vietnam. I had to take off his artificial leg and dress his stump.'

At last I heard Steve ask if I had a minute. I forced myself to put George Orwell very slowly in my pocket, to stretch lazily when I stood up and to saunter across the room as if I could take or leave his job. I sat down. He gave me a time-sheet with the name and address of the company.

'How are you on recks?' he asked.

'Tremendous. But I wanted a secretarial job. I told you. Forty-five words a minute. I can operate a word processor. I can use an audio machine. I can use a phone, make coffee, cook, sew, wash up, water plants, read a timetable, make excuses – he's at a meeting, he's not at his desk now – arrange flowers, buy birthday presents for wives, dress wounds, do heart massage, the lot.'

'There are no vacancies, John.'

'But you get plenty of vacancies.'

'They're for girls.'

'That's discrimination.'

'Do you do shorthand?'

'Shorthand is antediluvian. It's biblical. Scribes and Pharisees. Who needs shorthand these days?'

'All the secretaries who work for us.'

To save face I mulled over the time-sheet he gave me and scowled at the hourly rate, as if I had my price. On my way out I smiled at the glamorous people still sitting there but they had their noses in their books. I waited until I was outside on the pavement before I let my stomach sag and put on my bicycle clips.

Many people have to find their own method of supervising others by trial and error. Learning to ask others to do things is not easy, especially when there are no guidelines. Often the best solution is to choose a role model. But which? The paternalistic boss, the tyrant, the colleague, the supplicant?

Most people have a good idea of what they expect from the people who work for them.

Few people communicate these expectations clearly.

And even fewer find out what their subordinates' expectations of them are.

It is not easy to ask. It reverses the traditional relationship. Nor is it easy to be asked. The first time it happens there will probably be an embarrassed silence.

But unless each side knows what the other's expectations are there will be misunderstanding and confusion.

Promotion

I recognized the two receptionists in their teak-panelled redoubt, guarding a model of the Head Office in a glass case. The last time I had been in the plush reception lobby had been as guest for lunch in the colonial-style dining room. Then I wore a dark blue suit and fiddled with my tie and patted my hair and tried to remember the name of the General Manager. Now I wore the same suit, complemented with an old green cardigan with dangly leather buttons, fiddled with my beard and tried to remember the name of the Assistant Operations Manager.

I was peremptorily dispatched down to the third floor. I came out of the lift into a long green corridor. Set into a door was a window marked 'Messengers' and I tapped on it. A large lady swathed in a silvery fabric drifted over like a helium balloon and opened it. I announced I was the Temp and she opened the door to let me in. I was in the middle of a large, busy office of about fifty people, all women, with desks arranged in clusters of four. I followed her to the Assistant Operations Manager's office, a glassed-in corner of the floor. He was in his mid-thirties. To meet him on the street you would have thought he was a successful bond dealer or double glazing salesman. His hair was expensively cut and cleverly tinted. His complexion was tanned and clear. He wore a new blue suit and cotton shirt and silk tie. A gold watch bracelet dangled loosely around his wrist. He was a Northern Irishman and his name was John, which was where the confusion began that was to rule my life for the rest of the morning. The confusion continued with his thinking my name was Mark. Mark was the name of the person Jenny at the agency had told him she was sending along, but who had since found something better to do. I was a last minute substitute.

'Hello. Mark,' he said. As this was a North American bank and he had an accent I thought he was American and introducing himself according to transatlantic etiquette. So I introduced myself.

'Hi. John.' I said, shaking hands. As this was his name as well as mine he was satisfied with my salutation.

The consequence was that for the rest of the morning everyone thought I was deaf.

'Mark,' someone would say, 'can you take these down to photocopying?'

'Would you like a cup of tea, Mark?'

'Have you got the New York statements, Mark?'

As Mark was not my name I ignored them. I began to wonder why people spoke to me slowly and in loud voices and with lots of explanatory gestures and put their faces directly in front of mine to be sure I could see their lips. It was very unnerving. What was it about me that made them treat me like a halfwit? Was it an elaborate joke, an initiation rite to put newcomers in their place? I put it down to experience they had had with previous temps. The crisis came after lunch. It was common practice to telephone people on the other side of the office if you wanted to speak to them instead of walking twenty or thirty yards over to their desk. Beattie, who I had not spoken to before, telephoned me. She saw me pick up the phone.

'Mark?' she said, 'have you finished?'

'He's not here.'

'What?'

'I haven't seen him.'

'Mark! Stop messing about.'

'I said he's not here.'

'Mark. Are you all right?'

'I'll see if he's in his office.'

I put the phone down and went to John's cubicle where he was in earnest discussion with Fidelma, one of the supervisors.

'Sorry to interrupt. There's someone on my line for you and it sounds urgent. I think she's a bit upset.'

John came to my desk where Beattie was already standing, looking angry. John picked up the phone.

'She's gone,' he said, putting the phone down and looking at me accusingly.

'What are you messing me around for?' asked Beattie.

'That's her!' I said.

We went on a bit longer like this until we cleared up our misunderstandings and Beattie saw the joke. But the relationships had been formed and my identity had been established and people continued to speak to me in clear, loud voices.

It was a large bank. I asked several of my new colleagues how many employees there were but none of them knew. Glancing down the internal phone directory I guessed there were several hundred. There were many layers in the hierarchy. John was the Assistant Operations Manager. His boss was on another floor. Under John was the Deputy Assistant Operations Manager. His name was Bruce. He was on holiday. I sat at Bruce's desk next to Fidelma, the Senior Reconciliations Supervisor. She was a thin, unsmiling woman in her middle thirties with a helmet of lacquered blonde hair and a wardrobe of black dresses with white dots, the only thing distinguishing them being the size of the dots. We sat with our backs to the window on the other side of the floor from John looking over four clusters of desks. The first task I was given added to my feelings of insecurity and alienation.

'Have you done reconciliations before?' asked Fidelma.

'Life's work,' I said, 'man and boy.'

'Good. That makes a change. We had to get rid of the last two they sent along. They were hopeless. Here, we found this on Friday night. For four months we've been carrying a $423 debit and we don't know where it's come from. It shouldn't take long to find.'

She handed me a sheaf of confirmations, accounts and reconciliation sheets relating to the New York account. I felt giddy with panic. Every day there were hundreds of transactions totalling millions of dollars. There were foreign exchange deals and deposits and loans and bankers payments and cheques and scores of other different types of movement across the account.

The sum of $423 is a lot of money by human standards but a drop in the ocean of the international payment system. Once an hour Fidelma asked if I was making progress. At first I thought it was a cruel practical joke, another initiation rite to go with the loud voices and the gestures. I looked round for someone sniggering. Then I broke into a sweat with the suspicion that it was a test. If I didn't find the missing credit by a certain time I would be out on my ear. It became harder and harder to concentrate. I was very suspicious of what was said to me, the way people looked. It was made worse by sitting at the supervisor's desk where not only could I keep an eye on everyone else but they could keep an eye on me. Each time John came out of his glass cubicle I expected him to ask for my time-sheet to sign and tell me it was nothing personal. I waited for the phone to ring and Jenny to say I wasn't quite what they were looking for. I waited for that phone call every afternoon for the rest of the week.

By the end of the morning I discovered that the debit originated on the day that Bruce, the Assistant Deputy Operations Manager, had sent a telex to New York authorizing entries to be made across the account to rectify a large number of previously unreconciled items too small to be worth tracking down. We found the telex and the confirmation back from New York. Neither Fidelma nor I could work out where he had got his list of unreconciled items. What I had to do was reconstruct the steps he had taken. It was detective work. I had to put myself in his shoes, follow the workings of his mind step-by-step. It would have been much easier to ask Bruce what he had done. But he was on holiday.

Although he was on holiday Bruce came in halfway through the morning.

'Hello, Mark. I'm Bruce,' he said, opening the filing drawer of his desk. He came in again in the afternoon. And again the following morning. He was taking some banking exams and had the week off to write a paper in the Institute of Bankers Library round the corner. He came in to get things from his desk and use the photocopier. 'I'm not here,' he said, riffling through the papers in his desk and on the window-ledge behind. And it was true. He wasn't there. The others completely ignored him. It was uncanny.

'I wonder what Bruce did that for,' said Fidelma about ten minutes before he arrived the second time.

'Ask him,' I suggested.

'He's on holiday. He's not here.'

So we did not ask him. I spent a day and a half trying to piece together what someone had done three months before while that someone flitted in and out of the office like the Invisible Man.

It was not a new discovery that the normal conventions of behaviour, human relationships and even reality are suspended within offices, indeed within any formal social organization, that they are substituted by a more convenient or efficient set of conventions. What I found interesting was how quickly and effortlessly an outsider such as I was absorbed by them. I knew nothing depended on keeping this job, it did not matter if I was fired again. I knew I was only there for a week. I knew this was not my career, my livelihood. I had no desire to include reconciliations in a list of accomplishments. I had never seen these people before, I would never see them again. I knew that I did not belong, that I was an outsider, an observer. Despite knowing all this I was anxious about failing, keen to do a good job, keen to find that $423. I wanted to pass the test, to be accepted. Perhaps part of it was pride. It was humbling to be an MA, MBA, Vice-President, General Manager who could not hold down a clerk's job. But this does not fully account for the need to be accepted by this group of people. It was an emotional commitment engendered by the situation in which I found myself. And it happened with every job I took. I was not only an observer but a full participant in the groups I temporarily belonged to.

I felt sorry for Fidelma. She was uneasy in her job. Beattie, who became my best friend, explained that Fidelma had been promoted to Senior Reconciliations Supervisor two months ago. Before, as an ordinary Reconciliations Supervisor, she had sat at a cluster of desks and been a *prima inter pares* of four women. Now she had moved away to the window where she could see and be seen by the whole office. Her responsibilities had changed. She had three supervisors reporting to her. She had to allocate work and make sure it was done. She had to report absences, sign self-certified sick notes, organize what time people went to lunch and many other administrative duties that changed her status.

'She's gone all funny,' said Beattie, 'she can't take a joke no more.'

My relationship with Fidelma was not a comfortable one. It was a struggle to get her to say hello in the morning. I think she blamed me for the deafness fiasco. Nor was she impressed with my work rate on the $423 debit. For the rest of the week the only verbal exchanges she initiated with me were reprimands. For example, I went out for lunch on the first day through the door I had come in, the one with the window marked messengers. She ran after me and told me sharply it was strictly forbidden. I looked round for other means of egress but could only see the window and the door to the lavatory.

'That's the way I came in.'

'That's because it was opened for you.'

'Can I go out through it if someone opens it for me?'

'You use the official door, round the corner.'

She also reprimanded me for making personal telephone calls. If I had calls to make I should make them in my lunch hour from a public call-box. The calls and their destinations of each telephone were logged. No one was allowed to make personal calls. I was also rebuked for chatting with Beattie, putting my coat on the window-ledge, eating a sandwich at my desk, whistling, doodling on Bruce's blotter, looking out of the window and sitting at an empty desk without work. When I had finished something I was expected to ask around the girls for more to do. Feeling sympathy for Fidelma's inadequacies did not stop me feeling resentful and uncooperative for the rest of the day. After a couple of days I plucked up courage to ask if she had had any training in supervision.

'What for? You learn on the job round here.'

She was not the only unhappy person and I was not her only victim. I was used to being ignored as the Temp but there was little ordinary civility among the others either. A person would arrive in the morning, take her coat off, sit down at her desk and her arrival would scarcely be registered, let alone greeted by the others. They carried on counting tickets or ticking statements. In the late afternoon, when the bulk of the work was done, there were occasional outbursts of laughter, occasional conversations, but they soon died away. Conversations were brief, about clothes, jewellery, commuting, going down the lane. Work, office conditions and the bank were never discussed. Not only was there little interaction between people sitting close to each other but there was very little visiting between areas, although they seemed to know each other. They used the telephone instead of walking over to each other. I saw no one come into the office who was not of the department. There was a rest room with a drinks machine and a few chairs where sandwiches were meant to be eaten. I ate lunch there twice. People queued up for drinks without speaking. It was like a library. We chewed in silence, staring into the middle distance, or read the newspaper. John stayed in his office most of the day. During the week I saw him speak only to Fidelma about problems with the computer. Their relationship, inside the office, was purely functional and unsmiling. From time to time he patrolled through the desks, flicking his left wrist so the gold bracelet jangled. It seemed that he ran an organized, disciplined office area with very little time-wasting, in which everyone knew what they were supposed to be doing.

There was a suggestion scheme. A printed cardboard point-of-display box proclaimed the Bankwide Suggestion Scheme – People Count – We Want Your Feedback – We Need Your Ideas. The box was stuffed with printed forms on which to write comments and suggestions. I should have liked to read the details of the scheme and study the small print on the leaflets but the box was on top of an eight-foot cupboard at the back against the wall and I did not want to attract criticism from Fidelma by climbing up to get it.

With great relief I finally sorted out the $423 debit. 'About time too,' said Fidelma. She put me onto reconciling the unimportant accounts that the others did not have time for. I was given the weekly bank statement for Hong Kong dollars, for example, that we held in Hong Kong. I had to compare it with the SWIFT statements we sent to them. SWIFT is a worldwide communication system, a cross between a telex and a computer, by which banks tell each other what they want paid out of their accounts and what they expect to receive. I ticked off items that appeared on both statements and wrote down on a reconciliation sheet what was left. The amounts were recorded and added up on an antique fruit machine called Walther. I paced my work so that I would always look busy when Fidelma was around but have enough slack to chat to Beattie when she was not.

Beattie was my friend. She was a black woman from St Lucia who took a motherly interest in my welfare. She told me where to hang my coat, what time lunch was, where to get coffee, where the toilets were. She had been there for three years and had worked her way up the currencies from the little-used Malaysian Ringits and Barbados dollars through the pesetas and lire to the French francs reconciliation of which she was now the guardian. She had four children. She and her husband sang in a gospel choir in Streatham. When Fidelma was out of the room we exchanged musical arrangements of psalms we both knew, humming under our breath and giggling. She made sure I was included in the drinks orders. Two or three times a day someone would go round with an in-tray taking orders for the drinks machine. There was a wide variety of refreshment available on the machine. They were selected by punching in a number. You were supposed to know what number you wanted and call it out to the person taking the orders. Fortunately Beattie knew the numbers off by heart. Mine was a 39 in the morning (Tea no sugar) and a 149 in the afternoon (Fizzy Ribena.) The latter, 149, was a popular choice.

Beattie also lent me her toilet pass. To get to the gents you went out of the office, past the lifts, and through a security door onto a small landing with a broom cupboard on the left and the gents on the right and a fire escape straight ahead. But to get back through the security door into the office you needed a magnetic pass to insert into the electronic lock. I did not realize this the first time. After hammering on the door for a quarter of an hour I waited until someone else came in. The alternative was to go down the fire escape but I did not know if this would set off alarms. Besides it was several floors down. Fidelma reprimanded me for being away from my desk and asked me where I'd been all that time. I explained and asked for a pass. But temps were not allowed to have passes. Beattie said I could borrow hers when I wanted to go. I could not help feeling uncomfortable with this arrangement. When she wasn't there I had to borrow one of the other girls'. Then I discovered a bell push on the side of the electronic lock. This attracted the attention of a messenger who came and let me in. I used this for two days or so until I discovered that it clanged like a fire bell all over the office. 'The Temp's been again,' I could hear them say. So I went in pubs at lunchtime.

I asked Fidelma on Friday morning if I was to come back next week. She said they had already told Jenny at the agency they did not want me. There was no one off sick and Bruce was coming back from holiday and they were on top of the work. I did not mind if this was true or not. I did not care. I was glad to be out of that sullen and oppressive atmosphere.

The first supervisory job is always the most difficult, particularly if you start on Monday with people you were equals with on Friday afternoon.

The easiest way to exercise authority is through prohibition. Don't do this. Don't do that. We learn it as children. The more insecure we are the more defensively and negatively we behave. We become yes-men to our boss and no-men to our subordinates.

In all the companies where I worked none of my bosses had guidance in how to supervise before they became supervisors. A few had been on courses after a few months in their new position. There is an argument for doing it this way. They will recognize situations from experience and make better use of the theory.

But then it is too late. Attitudes and self-confidence and relationships with subordinates are formed in the first few days. By the time they have got another few rungs up the hierarchy and are sent on management training courses it is immensely difficult to break out of old habits of dealing with people.

Those habits are self-perpetuating throughout the organization. Without any other guidance new bosses model themselves on their old bosses.

Some kind of training in positive supervision and motivation might not have stopped Fidelma being a misery-guts. But it might have helped her concern for order and efficiency to be more productive.

Communication

I had to change tubes three times and walk a mile to get to Acme Auto Parts in Dollis Hill. Where the M1 meets the North Circular Road there are many companies dedicated to the maintenance and refurbishment of motor vehicles. Panel-beating specialists, paint specialists, rebore specialists, silencer specialists, brake specialists, clutch specialists, suspension specialists – it was an automotive Harley Street. Even the shops on the Broadway all had signs in the window 'Everything Must Go'. They were discount stores and cut-price supermarkets. Woolworths was the quality store. The whole area was in transition. I had my breakfast bacon sandwich in an Irish caff between a Greek grocer and an Indian newsagent. The caff served kebabs, the grocer sold samosas and the newsagent sold Irish papers. Opposite the caff was a red brick church converted into a mosque, although it still had a cross on the steeple.

Acme Auto Parts was set back off the road in a small industrial estate approached by a potholed road. They specialized in commercial vehicles. This was the Head Office. They had several branches throughout the country. I was to report to the Accounting Manager, Mr O'Rourke. I went in the main door. Young men in blue overalls, sporting the blackheaded pallor of those who spend their lives with machinery, had not heard of him. The most junior was sent to ask upstairs while I admired the posters of naked girls turned on by gaskets and piston rings and brake linings.

The boy came back with a young woman different in

every visible respect from those on the posters. She led me under the counter, through a metal door and up some stairs to the second floor of the building. I followed her through tall racks of metal shelves loaded with spare parts. Half the upper floor was a warehouse tended by men in long brown coats. The other half was offices, the nerve centre of Acme Auto Parts' nationwide empire. It did not have the conspicuous luxury of the City offices I was used to but it was light and spacious, divided up by metal and glass partitions. The desks and cabinets and metal parts of the partitions were painted various shades of dark green. Half the office was one big room with a dozen desks housing Stock Control and Dispatch and Invoicing. The other half was Accounts, divided into half a dozen smaller offices. In one corner was the office of the Managing Director, Mr Kelly. This was made by solid simulated-teak partitions so it was impossible to see inside. He had a separate door to the staircase so he could slip in and out without being seen. Outside the door was a black plastic visitor's chair and a brass ashtray on a pole. It was two minutes to nine and all the desks were empty.

My guide led me to a smaller glass cubicle in the opposite corner. A pimply young man looked up from a ledger. One side of his spectacles had been expertly fixed with invisible Sellotape. I stood in front of him, still dripping with rain.

'Ah. Well. Mr Mole is it?' I nodded.

'It's reconciliations, isn't it? Do you mind doing some checking and adding up for me first?' He asked tentatively, as if I were likely to storm out of the office in a fury at being asked to do something outside the job description.

'I'll do anything you like,' I said.

'That's great. Here. All you have to do is add up the columns. Pencil in the totals at the bottom.' He handed me a sheaf of typed accounts. I took them, still standing in my dripping raincoat. He looked at me inquiringly as if he wondered why I was still standing there.

'Ah. Well. I suppose you'll need somewhere to sit. I'll show you.' He led me through a large cluttered office with half a dozen desks to a smaller room with three desks and a computer printer. He pointed to a desk, empty but for a calculator. On the wall beside it was a calendar featuring hydraulic hose in an Alpine setting but no human interest. No tits and bums on the first floor.

'There y'are. You have everything you need? Great.'

I put the papers on the desk and sat down in my dripping raincoat.

'Ah. Well. You can hang your coat up over there.' He pointed to a coat stand in the large cluttered office. I stood up again, took my raincoat off and followed him back. He took a stubby pencil out of his pocket and gave it to me. 'You might be needing this.' I went back to the desk and started adding up the figures on the calculator.

At nine o'clock sharp people started to come in. They all clocked in by the door at a polished wooden clock that made an old-fashioned ping. They took off their coats and went straight to their desks. There were about twenty-five women, the majority of whom were in middle years. Half a dozen were in their late teens or early twenties. There were three male clerks. A woman in her mid-fifties came into my office and took off a fur coat, the filaments sparkling prettily in the light from the ceiling neon. I looked up but she did not seem to notice me. She sat down, changed her shoes and unlocked her desk. She took out trays of pay-packets which she began to sort through. A younger woman came in, nodded to the older woman when she looked up and sat down at the third desk. She had a plump, fresh face and glossy black hair, the sort of girl you imagine feeding chickens in a farmyard scene or slicing cheese in an old-fashioned Sainsburys. She changed her shoes and combed her hair in the reflection of the terminal screen on her desk. She did not look at me. Once again I felt the familiar temp's sensation of being disembodied, insubstantial, invisible, that I did not exist. It was reassuring that they did not say anything to each other either.

The desks were arranged so that we all sat with our

backs to each other. At ten past nine a woman came in, bent down beside me, said 'excuse me' and reached into the well beside my feet for a pair of black shoes. She did not say anything to the others. Nothing more was said until ten o'clock. The older woman tutted over the tray of pay-packets. The younger woman transcribed information from a pile of yellow invoices onto the screen. I totted up the figures on the calculator. At ten o'clock an old man in a grey warehouseman's coat came in with a cardboard box. 'Anything today, Pamela?' He asked the older woman. 'No thanks, Sid,' she said, without looking up from the time-sheets she was checking. He stood by the younger woman's desk. 'Anything today, Philomena?' Philomena ordered a bacon sandwich. Sid left without looking at me. I pinched myself. Before he came back with the orders the tealady came round. She put a mug of tea in front of me without prompting. I was consumed with warm feelings of gratitude. When she asked if I took sugar tears came to my eyes.

Pamela was in charge of payroll and petty cash. At noon she opened up a hatch in the wall by her right shoulder. It opened into the warehouse. Men in blue overalls queued up and she handed out brown envelopes and answered questions about overtime and tax and stamps. People also telephoned her throughout the day with queries. She was not chatty on the phone but nor was she taciturn. Sometimes she left the office to see Mr O'Rourke or Mr Jones, the Finance Director. Mr Jones sat in an office between the Managing Director and Mr O'Rourke. He was in his mid-forties with close-cropped grey hair, gold-rimmed glasses and an extensive collection of matching tie and handkerchief sets. Philomena left the office more frequently. After she had finished inputting the invoices she began checking one computer print-out against another. Every half an hour or so she carried one print-out to the large cluttered office next door where a blonde woman of about the same age was doing similar work. They pored over the print-out, keeping their backs to O'Rourke and Jones, and whispered to each other.

Later on in the morning I was engrossed in checking a particularly long string of figures. I finished and looked up from my work. Pamela and Philomena had gone. I looked out into the rest of the office. Not a soul. It was deserted. Even O'Rourke had gone. I sniffed the air for smoke. Surely if there had been a fire alarm I would have heard it. It was the reverse of the usual temp's feeling of insubstantiality. This time it was everyone else who had become invisible. Nothing so dramatic. It was two minutes past one. They had all gone for lunch and left me there.

I whiled away the time I spent commuting to Dollis Hill reading seminal works of management theory. Inspired by a classic study of relationships among mule spinners in Philadelphia in the nineteen-thirties I decided to log the social interactions of my little office. This was easy because there were not very many. I jotted them down on the back of a tally roll. These were the results for the first day:

Type of interaction	Pamela	Philomena	Me
Telephone calls from outside	6	0	0
Telephone calls originated	2	0	0
Short absences (5 mins)	7	3	0
Other absences (5–30mins)	2	7	0
Business interchange with outsiders	14	2	2
Social interchange with outsiders	2	2	0
Business interchange with each other	4	3	1
Social interchange with each other	11	11	2
Total number of incidents of interaction within our office	39	18	5

Notes:

1) These were the interchanges in working hours. In the lunchbreak Philomena went shopping. Pamela sat for most of the time at her desk eating egg salad rolls and reading the *Daily Express*. When I came back with a ham and tomato roll for my lunch I remarked that it had started raining again but this is not logged above since a) It did not occur in working hours; b) She did not reply.

2) I have not recorded Sid's two visits to us in connection with Philomena's bacon sandwich nor the two visits of the tea-lady, as I was unsure whether to categorize them as business or social.

3) One of my two social interchanges was with Philomena when I asked where the toilets were. The other was with Pamela when she said good night.

4) Two business interchanges were with Mr O'Rourke when he brought me some figures to add up in the middle of the morning and the middle of the afternoon. These were as follows: 'He y'are.' 'Thanks.'

5) I had one business interchange with Pamela. I had finished adding up what I had been given and was flipping through the calendar that portrayed hose couplings in a variety of exotic settings.

'Don't you have anything to do?' she asked.

'I've finished,' I said.

'Oh.'

This exchange took place just before noon and was the first time we had spoken to each other.

6) Of the nine separate social interchanges between Pamela and Philomena seven I would not categorize as conversations. They were:

Good morning – Good morning. (1 interchange)
Cold in here, isn't it? – Yeah. (3 interchanges)
Gone chilly, hasn't it? – Terrible. (1 interchange)
Stopped raining then – Has it really? (1 interchange)
Good night – Good night. (1 interchange)

There were three 'conversations', which I define as more than two consecutive phrases. The first, which took place over morning tea, was a detailed exchange of information as to whose family had the most number of birthdays in the Christmas period, defined as the last two weeks of December and the first two weeks of January. The second took place before lunch. They took it in turns to relate in detail the execution of the previous day's laundry. The third, over afternoon tea, concerned the unpredictability of the weather over the Christmas period and the English climate generally.

This describes only the pattern of social intercourse within the room where I was working. Pamela had several good-natured exchanges with men who came to her window for pay-packets or information. I saw Philomena on isolated occasions chatting briefly and smiling with the people next to her during her absences when she had queries or worked at other terminals. I did witness laughter in the office on a number of occasions during the week. I was never close enough to identify its cause. But generally everyone worked continuously and industriously in silence.

I do not attach very much importance to the quality of interchange between me and the other two. I deliberately initiated nothing to see what would happen. There may be something about me that causes people to shun social contact with me. Nor did I consciously rebuff approaches and I was not aware that any were made. But I was surprised at the paucity of social contact between the two of them and with others. It wasn't that they didn't get on or my presence inhibited them. The rest of the office was like it too. It reminded me of a psychiatric ward in which everyone was under sedation. In such circumstances the slightest occurrence attained monumental importance. What might in other circumstances seem trivial, such as variations in the ambient temperature and whether program five includes fast spin and how many relatives were born on Boxing Day, became very interesting. I spilt tomato pips from my sandwich on December's cash-flow forecast, an incident which stuck out sufficiently for me to record it.

Things loosened up a bit on the second day. I decided not to be self-effacing but to be extrovert, to see what effect positive, outgoing behaviour would have. I was beaten to it by Pamela. As soon as she walked in she said 'Good morning. Er. We don't know what to call you.' We introduced ourselves. When Sid came for the breakfast orders Pamela and Philomena said they did not want anything and he shuffled out. I went out after him and asked if he would get me a bacon sandwich. His relief was palpable. He said four times, very apologetically, 'I should have asked you yesterday.' It was as if he had no mechanism, no precedent for breaking the ice. I felt that they were all uncomfortable at being so uncommunicative. There was no culture of friendliness and co-operation. I thought it strange that a group of mature, middle-aged women could be shut up for eight hours together in a room without talking to each other.

After a promising start we lapsed into the pattern of the day before. It was a strain for me constantly to initiate contacts, like saying good morning as I passed people in the corridor or when they came to take things from my desk. There was a sullen, broody atmosphere, the reason for which I could not fathom. The tone was set by the managers. Mr Kelly, the Managing Director, either slipped in and out of his private door without being seen or he sat at his desk all day. The only times I saw him were when he walked through the office after lunch each day with a cigar. Mr Jones, the Finance Director, started with surprise if you said hello. On the third day I asked him how things were and he was at a loss for words. I don't think he was shy, since he talked fluently enough on other occasions, he was simply taken aback.

In many ways it was a model office. People arrived on time. They did not take any more lunch break than they were entitled to. They did not waste time in idle chat. There was little visiting between desks. They did not make or receive private telephone calls. They got on with their work. They seemed to have cured one of the traditional complaints of office life, the mania for meetings. While I was there I saw no panics or fire-drills or emergencies or crises. Everything was under control. It was a spare, lean, industrious group. A fair day's work for a fair day's pay.

So I got on with my work too. I finished adding up the month-end accounts. I started the task for which I had been hired. It consisted of reconciling the differences between the cash book and a daily computer report of cash sales. The cash book was a daily report from each branch of what had been paid into the bank at the end of the day. It was accompanied by a paying-in slip. The cash sales report was generated from information on invoices for the goods sold. In theory the two should have matched. But it was not as simple as it sounds. Every day there were part payments, refunds, cancelled orders, credit notes issued and honoured. Mistakes were made in adding up, customers were short-changed or given too much, input errors were made. Sometimes the discrepancy would be as small as 1p, sometimes as large as £25. Each of them had to be accounted for. Reconciliation of the daily differences had not been done for three months.

First I had to discover what the underlying system was, what gave rise to the entries and what the reports meant. This was not easy. A new computer system had been installed six months before and there were still teething problems. Although he was nominally responsible for it, Mr O'Rourke was not entirely clear himself how it worked. He had been with the company six months. He had not visited any of the branches and had never met the person on the ground floor of our own building who was responsible for counting the cash at the end of the day. Even making allowances for his shyness this surprised me. He was at my desk when I asked him why certain invoices were batched together one day and left separate another. He gave what seemed to be a reasonable explanation. When he had gone Philomena whispered that that wasn't the reason at all. She did the input for our branch, and some days she could not get on the terminal until late so she batched them manually to save time. I began to suspect that there were cracks in the smooth facade of the operation.

I went back to the source documents, the original invoices and advice notes. They were stored in large cardboard boxes, too heavy for one person to lift. The system for arranging them was that an empty box was put down wherever there happened to be space – on top of a desk or on the floor by the window or on top of another box. The day's batch was tossed in until the box was full. I had to get Mr O'Rourke to come and help me shift the boxes until he detailed Sid as my assistant. Then I had to find the batch relating to the day I was interested in and tick off the amounts against the report and the paying-in slip. It was painstaking work but not as tedious as adding up columns of figures. There was the pleasure of the search for discrepancies and the triumph of discovery. The pleasure was dulled by the frequency of mistakes. It is no fun looking for needles in haystacks if you keep kneeling on pincushions. The mistakes were not only due to carelessness but to inadequate checking procedures. When a batch of figures was input, for example, it was not immediately balanced. If there was a shortfall in the cash till at the end of the day, not just pence but pounds, it was simply noted on the bottom of the paying-in slip and nothing was done. These errors and omissions were let through at each stage of the system until there were months' worth for me to reconcile.

On the third day I noticed that someone had been there before me. There were ticks and double ticks against certain figures. Most of them were figures I was looking for, too. Pencilled figures in margins turned out to be the discrepancies I was looking for. Truant numbers were underlined. I pointed this out to Mr O'Rourke. 'That must have been for something else,' he said. When he had gone, Pamela whispered that I should look in the bottom drawer of the desk. Under a pair of shoes and a box of paper hankies

I found a sheaf of papers with detailed reconciliations of the accounts I was working on.

'Who did these?' I asked.

'Linda,' said Pamela. 'She left. Last August, wasn't it, Philomena?'

'Doesn't Mr O'Rourke know?' I asked.

'It was just after he joined.'

'Why doesn't anyone tell him?'

Pamela shrugged. 'He never asked.'

I wasn't about to tell Mr O'Rourke either. Linda had got me off to a head start. I could take it easy. Although Linda's paperwork was secret it was obvious that most of the major errors that she had discovered had been rectified. After she left no one had reconciled the accounts and there were glaring deficiencies. I found a batch of invoices that had not been posted at all, amounting to nearly two thousand pounds. This might not sound much in the context of a daily turnover of several thousand, but to an accountant used to tracking down the last five pence it is enormous.

In addition to errors and omissions there was duplication of work which to my unpractised eye seemed unnecessary. It was Sharon's job to verify that the invoices listed in the batch matched the invoices in the stock control report. This was for the cost accounting system. Tracey checked that VAT from the same batch of invoices had been correctly input and the VAT report was correct. They competed for the same terminal. The same person could have done both jobs. On Friday Sharon discovered that an invoice had been incorrectly input as a credit note and given an incorrect posting number. Tracey did not discover this for herself until Monday afternoon when an exception report was produced by the computer. Yet they sat opposite each other.

At lunchtime I gave a few of Linda's reconciliations to Mr O'Rourke. He complimented me on how fast I worked. He took them into the next room to show Mr Jones. Mr Jones told Mr O'Rourke to tell me to lay them out differently, the columns in a different order. When Mr

O'Rourke gave me my new instructions I asked what the reason was. He did not know.

I made an effort to break the ice again. I suspected that Pamela was the source of everyone's moroseness. I thought she might have been shy or depressed or slightly deaf, which would explain why she ignored me. Once when she was out of the room I spoke to Philomena.

'It seems a nice place to work,' I said.

'Huh. Sometimes. About once a month.'

'Been here long?'

'Hardly anyone's been here long. I've been here seven months. Pamela's been here years, though.'

'There seem to have been changes here recently.'

'Recently! Ever since I've been here. People leave all the time. They put things on the computer all the time. They change the way of doing things. You get used to doing things one way and then they change it.'

'Why do they change things?'

'I dunno. They just do.'

Pamela came back and Philomena swivelled back to her terminal. I spent the hours in silence, working slowly through piles of batches and reports. I gave up being cheerful and chatty, it did not seem to have any effect.

It was no longer a model office. Although it gave the outward appearance of calm efficiency it was the most confused, disorganized and inefficient place I had ever worked in. You didn't have to be an industrial psychologist to know why. It was because no-one talked to each other. There was no exchange of views or information about anything, whether personal or work-related. There was no sharing of problems or experience or expertise. The relationship between people in the office was only marginally more meaningful than that between travellers in a railway carriage. So things were falling between the stools and down the cracks and under the table.

The lack of communication explained the inefficency, the lack of interest in other people's jobs, the lack of co-operation in problem-solving. But what explained the lack of communication? Change usually generates tension and gossip and information exchange and, above all, complaint. But here there was nothing, not even a grapevine. Even the kitchen where the tea was made was quiet, as if no one had been introduced.

My first hypothesis was that communication was not being fostered by senior management. Perhaps there was no informal communication because there were no formal channels. I asked Pamela where the staff noticeboard was and she said there wasn't one. There was no staff handbook. There were no staff functions, no Christmas party, no office sweep for the Grand National or the Derby, no outings or social evenings. When I asked Philomena and Pamela why there were no social events they seemed surprised that I should think such things possible.

Mr Jones and Mr O'Rourke did very little communicating between themselves and virtually none to the staff. Sitting in open, glass offices they set an example of isolated industry. Once or twice a day Mr O'Rourke stood in the doorway of Mr Jones' office and they held a brief discussion. But in my previous experience, if management creates an information vacuum people will fill it with gossip and rumour. This did not happen. There was no communication on any level and I could not understand why.

The answer, when I discovered it, was blindingly obvious. I asked Philomena outright over afternoon tea why no one talked to each other. The reason was that they were not allowed to. It was against the rules. That's why Linda left and others before her. After several warnings they had been fired for talking on the job.

'He's had me in the office four times for talking since I've been here,' said Philomena. 'Once more and I'm out.'

It was a salutary discovery. Mr Jones and Mr Kelly lived in a world without management theory. Organizational behaviour and development and motivation and all the other high falutin' notions that I had been immersed in for the past few months were as irrelevant to the way they ran their business as kinship among the bushmen or potlatch among the Kwakiutl. Clock-in, no talking, get to work. It was breathtakingly simple and very enviable. It took all the stress out of people management. It was the most extreme instance I came across of a traditional management style but it was by no means unique. The sullen, broody atmosphere of the first North American bank derived from a similar style. From a strictly utilitarian viewpoint, whether it was pleasant or humane or satisfying for the employees is neither here nor there. If people don't like it they can leave. The objection is that it does not work.

I was booked by the agency to stay longer. There were probably more interesting facets of management style to be discovered. But by the end of the fourth day I couldn't stand it any more. I told Mr O'Rourke I wasn't coming back in the morning. He looked very disappointed. But he did not say anything.

In most situations, and especially in times of change, for example when new technology and systems are being introduced, people can learn from each other, help each other, share experience and expertise.

Communicating freely and creatively about work is inextricably bound up with other forms of social communication. Stamp out idle chat and you stamp out productive discussion too. The most oppressive places I worked were also the most inefficient. People will not share their work experience if they do not share other things as well.

The tree of life of an organization is the grapevine.

The most dynamic and efficient places I found buzzed constantly with speculation and rumour and complaint. Official communication channels merged in with gossip so that they were almost indistinguishable. There was no less frustration and dissatisfaction than in other places, but it was expressed and could be dealt with and used to improve the productivity of the organization.

Feedback

The closest I came to the Lutine bell was Records in an insurance company on the fringe of the City that had been acquired by a transatlantic conglomerate. My responsibility was to check that the addresses on a computer print-out matched the addresses on a large batch of brown envelopes. Keith, Rhoda and Daff, who comprised Records, did not know why I was doing this. The Head of Administration assured me that since an explanation would have taken up a large proportion of the small amount of time I was engaged for, it could be dispensed with. I shall never know.

On my second day there was an important meeting for all staff at 10 o'clock. Keith, Rhoda and Daff left me in charge of their office. It had been called by the Head of Human Resources, an expatriate from Head Office who was on a six-month assignment to install a new staff administration system. Rhoda explained that Human Resources was what they used to call Personnel before the takeover. I asked why they changed the name.

'Makes it sound more important than it really is, yeh? They always use longer words than they have to over there.'

'I don't like it,' said Keith. 'Sounds as if we're all some sort of raw material.'

'And who are the Inhuman Resources?' added Rhoda.

I asked if they knew what the meeting was about.

'The morale here's terrible,' said Rhoda. 'Last month fifteen people resigned in one week, yeh? There were four people made redundant the week before. They joined the company at the same time as I did. That's worrying, isn't it? I mean, what's behind it all? There was a manager who'd been here twenty-five years and he was given the push. It's the senior managers who are leaving too, not just the clerical staff. They can't care very much for the staff, can they, if they let that happen? We've got 25 per cent temps, and you know what that means.' She clapped her hand to her mouth. 'No, I've got nothing against temps. I didn't mean that. But you can't be expected to know the job right off, can you?'

'Having so many temps means it's easier for them to close down, doesn't it?' said Keith. 'They just keep it going until most people have gone so they don't have to pay out so much redundancy. I've seen it all before.'

Keith was the supervisor. He was about fifty, although he looked younger. His hair was ginger, mottled with grey. His fair moustache was hardly visible. He had started in the original insurance broking company as a junior clerk thirty-three years before. Since then he had been promoted twice, to clerk and then senior clerk. When he joined it had been a family firm. It had been acquired and merged and now taken over by a transatlantic conglomerate. Change had washed over Keith. He had been coming to the same room in the same building for thirty-three years. Every evening he left the office to visit his wife who had been in hospital for several years after a car accident. They had no children. Keith's desk was like a mantelpiece at home. A pipe rack, a tobacco pot, a colour photograph of his wife in a wooden frame, a small brass ship's wheel on a wooden stand, a silver tankard commemorating twenty-five years' service and other bits of bric-a-brac were arrayed on the side where it was pushed up against the wall. Every night at ten past five he locked them away in the bottom drawer. On the wall were several pretty black-and-white etchings of churches and graveyards. He had done them himself. He sketched on Saturdays and etched on Sundays.

Rhoda was in her late thirties. She had been with the company ten years. She had a face from a Flemish painting, high forehead and pink cheeks. She had a habit of tapping her pencils and felt tips against her right front tooth so by the end of the day it was black. She was pregnant and wore thick stockings and large tartan smocks over angora sweaters. I asked her if she was going to come back when she had the baby.

'Not if I can help it. I've done my time. It depends when Steve gets his divorce. Then we'll get married.' Her desk was always cluttered and she liked to give the impression she was always behind with her work.

Daff was in her middle twenties. She had been with the company five years. She was tall and thin and had long straight blonde hair. She dressed in pretty Laura Ashley dresses with bows at the back. She smiled constantly as if she were keeping a funny secret. On my first day, feeling sensitive and paranoid, I thought she was laughing at me. Her interest was religion. She read booklets with titles like Our Mission and The Way. She sang in two church choirs and her boyfriend was a lay preacher. Her glow of inner serenity was unshaken by her incurable clumsiness. She had a talent for tripping over on a smooth surface or knocking over stacks of files without apparently touching them. She was not allowed beverages at her desk unless it was entirely covered with blotting paper.

They came back from their meeting just after eleven. I had expected to see them reassured, if not reinvigorated by the prospect held out to them by the Head Office spokesman of a bright future for the company, opportunity for all of you, our best assets are our people, meeting the challenge of the future, share in the success, immense growth possibilities, blah blah blah. But they were furious. All three were seething with anger.

'No one knew what he was talking about.'

'And when we asked questions he didn't listen.'

'He was so evasive.'

'He ignored what people were saying.'

'Did you see the way he laughed when Harry asked a question?'

'He didn't answer it properly, either.'

'They think we're fools.'

'No one believed him.'

'They couldn't give a damn.'

'I think they want us to leave.'

'But only the good people go.'

'What's the point of having a meeting unless they answer the questions, and are honest, and they listen?'

I felt a pang of sympathy for the Head of Human Resources. He probably thought he had done a great job. Put it on the line. Make them know you care. I always hated explaining company policy. You have no contribution in making it, you don't know what lies behind it, you can't alter it and you have no discretion about it. The chances are high that you don't understand it well, either. But to the people you are addressing you are the embodiment of the policy. It is difficult for a spokesman to lose face by saying he doesn't understand it or agree with it. And even harder to answer questions without being evasive or defensive. I learned never to hold mass meetings to explain policy, particularly if it affected terms and conditions of work.

'It wasn't even about the company. It was about the new pay system.'

'It sounded just like the old one to me.'

'It was all about how our pay-rises are worked out and how the jobs are graded.'

'Half of them didn't understand it.'

'What about my question about the mortgage?'

'Did you understand it, Keith?' asked Daff.

'There are points for each job, yeh?' said Rhoda.

'That's not right. There's points for the person,' said Daff.

'It can't be,' said Rhoda, 'it's got to be for the job.'

'For the person.'

'For the job. What do you think, Keith?'

'Each job is given a salary grade, a band they call it. If you're at the bottom of the band you get a bigger pay-rise and if you're at the top you get nothing at all.'

'See, Daff? There's a salary for each job, yeh? And there's a mid-range point, yeh? Now this year the rise is going to be a lousy 3 per cent, yeh? But that's 3 per cent of the mid-range, so the low earners get more and the high earners get nothing.'

'Where do you get the 3 per cent from?' I asked.

'They go round the other insurance companies. They do a survey,' said Daff.

'And what about raises for merit or performance?' I asked.

'That's on top. But you can't go higher than your salary range,' said Rhoda.

'You never know, anyway. When you get a pay-rise it's written on a little scrap of paper. They give it to the supervisor, who gives it to you. They don't call you in or anything. The manager just plonks it down on the desk. They could at least put it in an envelope. There's no point in asking what it's for, they don't know. I once complained and so now they put mine in an envelope. But you'd think they'd tell you what your rise was for, whether there was anything in it for merit.'

'You can work it out for yourself, Daff.'

'Why don't they write the salary system down so people can read it?'

'Then they'd have to stick to it, wouldn't they?'

'Anyway, this is boring,' said Rhoda. 'I fancy a baked potato.'

We left for the pub together. Usually one person stayed behind to man the telephones but today they didn't care. Although I had only been there a week and was not in their situation, I was roped in as a neutral observer. They talked about the grading system all the way to the pub. We each had a pint of lager. Keith stood the round and we bought him a baked potato and salad. We sat at a low table by one door.

'Didn't he say anything at all about the changes?' I asked.

'No. They keep that to themselves.'

'Why do they always keep it so close to their chest?' wondered Daff. 'They never tell us anything ahead of time.'

'Perhaps they don't know themselves,' I said, recalling the fog of indecision that enveloped management offices I had known. The complaint that 'they up there' knew everything and wouldn't communicate it to 'us down here' I had heard at every level of organization I had inhabited. But Keith and Rhoda would not accept the possibility that their bosses were bumbling along blindly from day to day.

'They know all right. They know. They just don't tell us.'

'Look what happened last month,' said Rhoda. 'We've got this Customer Services section, yeh? It handles the little accounts and the private customers. The company decided to get rid of its private customers. One day they were given a stack of letters to send out with the monthly statement. It was from the management saying that we were stopping private business and asking the customers to close their accounts and find other brokers. That was the first the Customer Services people had ever heard of it. What a way to find out. Well, what was going to happen to their jobs? They were up in arms. What a way to treat people, yeh? They don't care. They just don't care.'

While Rhoda was speaking, Keith started to wink and frown at her. She turned round on her stool. Passing behind, lifting her handbag over Rhoda's head to squeeze past, was a young woman in a camel coat. Rhoda's hand flew to her mouth.

'I didn't hear that,' said the young woman in the camel coat, with an embarrassed smile.

'Who's that?' I asked.

'The assistant to the Head of Human Resources.'

'It's a pity she didn't hear it. If the Personnel

Department doesn't listen to what the staff is saying, what chance have the managers got?'

'They wouldn't be interested. I don't care. It's a mess,' said Daff. 'You know what I was doing this time last year? I was doing input down in Claims. There were three of us. Then on the Friday we were told that they were closing our section and I was being moved up here. They didn't say a word about it before. Right out of the blue. I said I didn't want to go. I don't know the work. But they said that's all there was.'

This discussion went on over lunch and through the rest of the afternoon and the rest of the week. The Head of Human Resources may not have set people's minds at rest at his meeting but he had certainly ignited debate and gossip. People from outside would pass by and add more fuel to the flames. There were hushed telephone conversations and huddles in the corridors and whispers round the coffee machine. George from Investments came by with hard news. He was normally a cheerful fellow who sometimes came to see us with queries. Today he looked gloomy. A section head was retiring and was not being replaced.

'And what about Betty, she's been waiting for that job for years . . . they've done away with an eighteen or twenty thousand-a-year position . . . who's going to do all that extra work, I want to know . . . it was all sprung on us . . . I'm not going to put myself out . . . this company won't be bothered . . . they don't care . . . that's how they get all the good people to go . . . look how many have left already . . .'

I made one more attempt to suggest that the same conversations were going on in the management suite, that their bosses might be as confused and as worried as they were. But this was dismissed as naive, like my inquiry as to whether there was an internal newsletter.

'Not likely,' said Daff.

'There's one over there. Head Office puts it out. They send it to us. It's irrelevant to us here. It's mostly about barbecues and picnics and people getting awards. It's interesting to see what they get up to. But we have nothing over here,' said Keith.

'We're the plebs,' said Daff.

'How do you find out about things then?' I asked.

'It all goes along the grapevine.'

On Friday Keith held a staff meeting. One of the first innovations of the Head of Human Resources when he arrived from 'over there' was a meeting which every supervisor had to hold twice a month. They were expected to go to a separate conference room, draw up a written agenda and produce minutes. Then the supervisors went to a meeting with their own supervisors and so on up the hierarchy. Eventually this upward cascade of intelligence would get to the General Manager. Likewise information would trickle down to all levels of staff. Everyone received an instruction booklet entitled 'Improved Communication—Your Chance To Be Heard'. There were tips on how to chair a meeting and how to listen and how to be an effective participant.

They left at four o'clock. I was not invited. I felt wounded because I had been accepted and had taken part in their discussions. I was also interested to see how they behaved in a formal situation and how they expressed their anxieties in the minutes. I said good night, thinking they would still be at it by the time I left. They were back within a quarter of an hour. I asked Daff what they talked about. 'Nothing much. It's all been said, hasn't it?' she said. True. I couldn't think what they could have discussed that had not been chewed over at our desks.

The next day at four o'clock Keith went to the staff meeting with his supervisor. They did not see each other every day as we did. With all the rumours flying around I could imagine them talking far into the night. He came back at five past five and started putting his ornaments into the desk.

'Well?' said Rhoda.

'They wanted to ban smoking on the floor. It was

Betty. Ever since she gave up she's been a terror. I talked them out of it.'

'What else did you talk about?' I asked.

'That was all that was on the agenda. That was enough. You haven't seen Betty when she gets worked up. She'd have kept us there all night.'

I hoped that management would find this intelligence useful when it cascaded up to their ears. Perhaps they would include non-smoking areas in the next attitude survey under 'working conditions'. Perhaps there would be a ban on smoking in the corridors or in the lunch room to keep the non-smokers happy. The Head of Human Resources would point to the pile of minutes he collected twice a month and think what a good idea it was to have staff meetings, you really got to know what employee concerns were.

On the day I left the newsletter from Head Office arrived. I retrieved it from Rhoda's waste-paper basket. It was eight pages long, printed on glossy paper. Most of it contained news from the transatlantic subsidiaries. The centre spread had a photograph of the Chief Executive delivering a speech to a famous business school on the subject of Corporate Excellence. He was standing at a rostrum. He looked lean and fit and intelligent. 'CEO DELIVERS KEYNOTE SPEECH'. An editorial note said that they were reprinting it in full to reinvigorate the caring spirit of the company and remind us all that its past and future success depended on a concern for people, whether employee or customer or shareholder.

'Our concern for people . . . means something to our employees . . . people don't talk salary dollars in our bank, they talk performance and point levels . . . we place a tremendous emphasis on our training programs . . . people like to be understood . . . we emphasise employee counselling . . . we can't afford to have our good people ruined by somebody who may not be a good boss . . . so there's feedback, constant feedback. This is important – people like to be understood. They like to think somebody cares aside from their immediate boss . . . when we decide on a major change in our organization we do it incrementally and slowly – so that it is understood by the people in our organization. After all, if an idea is going to work, we need the support of those people . . . major change has to be accepted by people in all parts of our delivery system . . .'

It went on and on. The organization he was describing was a model of Human Resources management and as remote from Keith and Rhoda and Daff as Utopia or Erewhon.

In his speech, the CEO was describing the policy statement in the front of the annual report, a procedure manual, a set of forms, a set of minutes, the staff noticeboard, a timetable of meetings and briefing and counselling sessions. He was not describing what really happened. He was not describing what people in his company did and felt.

I do not think the CEO was deliberately misleading his audience. He probably believed what he said. His own management style, the one he used on his executive board and department heads, may well have been founded on the principles he proclaimed to the business school audience. But it did not filter through the padded doors of the executive suite. It is very hard for managers at any level, especially the more senior ones, to escape from a fantasy world of their own making. They can easily become prisoners of their own rhetoric. He was describing the organization he would like to create, that he did his best to create, that people told him he was creating. The evidence from the minutes and the feedback from his subordinates reinforced his delusion.

A more cynical explanation is that what the CEO was talking about did not apply to lowly clerks overseas. In which case, where was the cut-off point for enlightened management? Did it apply only to the professional grades or only the domestic branches? And who drew the line? If there was a line, I think it unlikely that the CEO drew it. The organization that existed in his mind and in his reports to the board and speeches to business schools was real to him. But it was not real to most of the people who worked for him.

Motivation

'How do you feel about Cancer Research?'

'I'm for it.'

'Ha Ha Ha. I mean working there.'

'Emptying the ashtrays?'

'Ha Ha Ha. Looking after the luncheon vouchers, actually.'

Jenny said the foundation had very nice offices. They were air-conditioned. Margaret would meet me at the door and take me along to the office and take me through the job and show me the subsidized restaurant. That would make a change. It sounded like a welcoming, friendly place.

The doorman wore a black suit. He called several numbers trying to find Margaret while I sat in the lobby browsing through illustrated leaflets on leukaemia and lung cancer. I felt dizzy and overcome with hot flushes. Twice I stood up to tell the doorman not to bother, I didn't feel like the job anyway, I had something less malignant lined up. I called myself a coward and sat down again. Another doorman in a black suit suggested they try Noreen in Finance. Noreen would know where Margaret was. This was correct. Margaret was on holiday. It was Margaret I was replacing, which is why she wasn't there to meet me. No one else knew anything about me.

'It's OK. I'll just slip quietly away.'

Noreen came down for me before I could escape. She was about forty, with a pretty face, wry smile, close-cropped black hair, a Liverpool accent. She wore a business-like grey skirt and blue blouse and dark tights and jogging shoes. I assumed she was affecting an American style but I found out later she had bad feet. We shook hands and I followed her to the lift. It smelt of hospital disinfectant and I felt dizzy again. We walked along a green-painted corridor lined with Jackson Pollock type abstracts and doors marked with wasp yellow and black nuclear warnings. As well as raising money for research at universities and hospitals, the foundation had its own laboratories. I felt on less threatening ground when we went through a door marked Chief Cashier. She introduced me to Ernest, the bearer of the title. He was a tall, overweight man with a round face and delinquent comb-over and rolled-up sleeves who looked as though his shirt was hanging out even when it wasn't. He smoked sweet Dutch tobacco in a curly pipe. He brooded in the middle of a waste-paper merchant's paradise. The office was by design light and airy with windows overlooking a park but was made dark and cramped by piles of print-out and files and cardboard boxes that reached the ceiling and obscured all but a couple of panes of the window. He was very genial and we shook hands warmly. He took me through a connecting door into a sparse, but lighter, office and introduced me to Willy. Willy was a short, cheery, ginger-haired man in his thirties with a week's growth of beard that he had just brought back from holiday.

'Designer stubble, eh, Willy?'

'It's because of my spots.'

He was the Deputy Chief Cashier and my immediate boss. Noreen was the Assistant Chief Cashier. I was simply the Cashier.

I was to share a small, untidy office with Noreen. It was defined by modern partitions but there were ragged holes in them that looked as though they had been chewed away by the cables that flopped out of them. Ducting and cables dangled from the ceiling. It was hot and airless. It smelt of stale tobacco and wet plaster. There was no natural light. We were illuminated by a fluorescent tube and a wooden standard lamp with a pink tasselled shade that was the personal property of Noreen's auntie. The room was divided in two by a moveable screen about the height of my chin. Noreen sat on one side, facing the screen with her back to the wall. My place was in a narrow galley made by the partition at my back and the cash window at the front. The window opened onto the corridor. Until eleven o'clock and after four, and for an hour at lunchtime, it was concealed from the public by a wooden door that it was my duty to open from the outside. The window itself was equipped with a Hygiaphone, a device of perspex and glass that cleverly admitted money but not germs. I asked Noreen if it was guaranteed to exclude carcinogenic viruses and she thought I was joking. She told me that until recently they were all in a large general office that stretched back to the window. Records had taken over all except our little section. When they were in a large general office they could cover for each other at the cash window and did not need temps. There had been rumours that they would be moved to better accommodation. She and Willy had made complaints but nothing had been done. She said she could not bear to sit at her desk for very long and I found this to be true.

I sat down in front of the Hygiaphone. Noreen and Willy went away without telling me anything about what I was supposed to do. Every morning they went down to the mailroom and helped to count the cheques and cash and postal orders and milk bottle tops and foreign stamps and matchbook collections and mantelpiece ornaments and old blankets and worn-out shoes and other valuables sent in by donors to further the cause of medical research. I was alone for an hour. All my senses were heightened. I felt the same kind of paranoia that I felt on starting every job – this was a test, a trick, a dream. Or I was really a specimen in one of the laboratories, a special kind of cancer, and the drugs they were giving me induced the hallucination that I had been abandoned in a cashier's box. Or I had been committed to a psychiatric institute. I loosened my collar and took deep breaths. I went to the door but it was locked. I rattled it. On the frame was a digital lock with a button pad like a telephone. I punched in 1987 and 1066 and 4711 and other likely numbers but it stayed shut. Retaining sufficient grip on myself not to hammer on the walls screaming Let me out, Let me out, I lay down on the floor in the narrow space between my chair and the screen and did the relaxation exercises I had learned at natural childbirth classes.

When I recovered I examined my new working environment. The narrow desk between me and the Hygiaphone was cluttered with files and wire baskets. They made no sense. An adding machine, a large box of rubber bands, a plastic cup with two broken pocket staplers, another cup of pointless pencils. In the desk drawers were blank forms of impenetrable mystery and brown envelopes stuffed with used forms. Then I made a wonderful discovery. Beside the cash window was a green baize noticeboard. Pinned on it, covered up with yellow and curling notices about the foundation's new tax number and what to do with forged twenty-pound notes were three sheets of lined foolscap covered in neat ballpoint writing. It was a detailed description of the cashier's job. It was either written for Margaret when she took over or by Margaret for her replacement when she went on holiday. It was several months old. I read it very carefully several times and then hid it in a drawer. I was not going to tell Willy and Noreen I had found it. I wanted to surprise them with how fast I picked things up.

When Noreen came back she showed me how to open the door. The number was 999. Then she showed me how to open the walk-in vault in Willy's office. The key was kept in a key box in the top drawer of my desk. Inside the vault was a large safe for which only Willy and

Ernest had the combination. On the floor were heaps of cardboard boxes spilling records and forms and print-outs. On shelves were the board minutes of the foundation, bound in leather. I found out what happened to the postage stamps and silver balls of compressed milk bottle tops and worthless jewellery that arrived in the morning mail. Sacks of accumulated rubbish were stacked in the vault. As it had a notional value, unlike the old shoes and blankets, the Cashier's Department did not have the authority to throw it away when it came in. Noreen's face fell when she heard I did not collect stamps. Every so often, when they couldn't get the door of the safe open, they passed a board resolution to dispose of it and paid a totter twenty quid to cart it away.

Inside the safe were the petty cash boxes of which I was the custodian for the coming week. Noreen helped me to carry them to my desk. The smallest was for books of stamps which we sold as a service. The medium-sized one was for the day's float and carried about £200. The largest was the Main Box. It held about £1,500. The two smaller boxes were carefully locked at lunchtime and at night and the keys kept in the key box with the vault key. We did not lock the Main Box since someone had lost the key several months ago. In addition, there was a cardboard box with little brown envelopes of unclaimed expenses and wads of luncheon vouchers secured with elastic bands. The vouchers were for use in the staff canteen. In fifteen years of international banking I had never been as close to real money. Nervously I counted the luncheon vouchers and the contents of the cash boxes several times. The totals were different each time. I kept counting until I got a total that duplicated a previous one. I plumped for that and hoped for the best.

Noreen ran through my duties. I was grateful that I had a crib hidden in the desk. Familiar and routine to her, they were bewilderingly incoherent to me. This was not unusual. I met no-one at any level in my temping career who was capable of explaining their own or any other job succinctly and clearly. The most common transactions were the reimbursement of petty cash expenses, the sale of stamps and the issue of luncheon vouchers. I had to make sure the petty cash vouchers were properly filled in and completed. If they were to my satisfaction I was to stamp a number on them and hand over the cash. The stamps were straightforward. The luncheon vouchers had to be registered in a loose-leaf book. They were worth twenty pence each and employees were entitled to twenty-five per month. I was strictly forbidden to issue vouchers for any but the current month.

Noreen opened the door into the corridor to expose me to the public. I felt a tremor of excitement. This soon subsided as no one required my services for the next hour and a half. I passed the time by making anagrams of Hygiaphone. It read backwards from where I sat, which gave the game a spice of novelty. Then I worked out how many letters of the alphabet looked the same written backwards (eleven). Then I meditated. I sat perfectly still and softly hummed a mantra and fixed on the crutch of the Y in Hygiaphone as the centre of the universe. The idea that I had most frequently to chase from my mind was that I had engaged myself to spend thirty-five hours of my life like this. It was very soothing. I sank gently into a contented stupor. Sometimes people passed by as they went down the corridor. I must have looked like a waxwork in a glass case.

Noreen came back to her desk in the middle of the morning. I found that if I turned round and pressed my eye to the join in the screen behind I could see her. The crack was so small she could not see me. When she wasn't smoking cigarettes she chewed the end of her little finger while she worked. But mostly we talked to each other as if we were on the telephone. I opened the conversation with the conventional temp's gambit of asking where the toilets were. She explained and said I could leave the Hygiaphone in her care while I went.

For the first day I was very nervous about being in a place devoted to cancer. I always looked away if I saw the word. I used to pity people born between 22 June and 23 July. Here I was surrounded by it. I shuddered every time people answered the phone. 'Cancer. Can I help you?' The Jackson Pollocks on the walls of the corridor were blown-up pictures of cancer cells. Facing me through the Hygiaphone was a colourful rendering of a malignant carcinoma of the liver, magnified several hundred times. I felt dizzy again when I read the title. The illustrated life story of a cervical cancer cell was posted up by the coffee machine at the top of the stairs. I walked round with downcast eyes. My hand shook the first time I reimbursed a research assistant for his taxi fare to collect a sample of a prostate tumour from a London hospital. I wished I hadn't touched the money a scientist handed over for a book of second-class stamps. At lunchtime I went to the library and looked on the magazine racks for a *Punch* or a *Private Eye* but all they had were rows of periodicals with titles like *Carcinoma News* and *Cancer Today*. I fled and went for a long walk.

By the middle of the second day it had worn off. The pictures looked quite pretty. The patient, painstaking logic underlying the treatise by the coffee machine was fascinating, even though I could only understand half the words. I started to read the magazines in the library and the leaflets in the lobby and the annual report of the foundation. It said that one person in three in the UK dies of cancer. Smoking was blamed as the greatest single cause. Smoking was banned in the corridors and public places like the canteen and coffee lounge. But Ernest smoked a pipe and Willy smoked Embassy and Noreen smoked John Players. A grey pall of smoke hung over the ceiling of Records next door. At least two of the messengers smoked in their cubbyhole in the basement. I didn't have a cigar for two days but then I started again. If a cancer research organization cannot get its employees to stop smoking, what chance has any company of getting its corporate messages across? The natural immunity of employees to the exhortations of management should never be underestimated.

It was the friendliest place I had worked in. In the morning we exchanged information about our health and the weather. Strangers said hello to me in the corridors. I did not once hear myself referred to as 'The Temp'. I was usually called by my first name. Noreen called me 'the little ray of sunshine' because she heard me whistling. The epithet stuck, at least in informal interchanges. When people came into the office from other departments I was introduced to them. On my first day Willy wanted to change a pound coin in my petty cash box.

'Excuse me,' he said as he helped himself to change, 'I'm not undermining your authority.' Everyone was very considerate about each other's feelings. It was quite unlike the City offices I was used to.

Grateful that I was treated considerately and bored with contemplating the Hygiaphone I asked for work to keep me busy. It was hard to get. Noreen said it was all so complicated that it was hard to single out something for me to do. Willy told me to relax, read a book, enjoy the rest. They themselves worked very hard. Willy was in charge of gathering and recording and banking donations and bequests and the profits of the foundation's charity shops. Noreen was in charge of the payroll. After much insistence I was entrusted with counting the postal orders every morning. I made myself miserable reading the letters that came with them, in loving memory, so that others might be spared, before passing them on to Fund Raising for acknowledgement. I felt I had been accepted. Jokes were made about my staying on full-time. Noreen offered to get me coffee.

Why were people more civilized to each other in the foundation than elsewhere? The majority of people in the building were scientific staff. Most of them were in their thirties or under. The scientists were indistinguishable from each other and the lab technicians. They wore sweaters and jeans and trainers under white lab coats with a radiation recorder clipped to the pocket. They took their coats off as soon as they left the labs. The older scientists wore ties and slacks but were often seen without jackets. I wondered whether this informality gave the tone. But the personnel and finance and administrative staff all wore formal business clothes.

The foundation was a charity and its mission was finding a cure for cancer. Did this give people a greater sense of community? Did they feel a greater self-esteem that they were working for something more worthwhile than employees of banks which fulfil a useful, but hardly uplifting, function? I did not feel this, although I might not have been there long enough. It certainly did not feel like voluntary work. I found no evidence that the administrative staff were informed about the work of the institute and its achievements. At the front door were a few brochures about clinical work, such as screening, the work on children's cancer and so on. But it was very hard to find information about what actually went on in the building and whether it was getting anywhere. I asked for an annual report from the Public Relations Department but it was not helpful. Inside our office it was hard to tell what sort of organization we were in.

I usually went to the canteen for lunch. It was heavily subsidized, providing a solid three-course meal for less than a pound. It was always busy with staff and visitors, many of whom were voluntary workers visiting the Head Office. One day the only free space I could find was at a table for four already occupied by two people. One was a youngish man who looked like an accountant in a dark blue suit and white shirt and maroon tie. He had a flat, classless accent. He was sitting opposite a younger man decorated with spiked hair, designer stubble and a sapphire earring. He was a Brummie. They were talking about the football team they both played for. Then an older man sat down opposite me. He was slim and elegant and greying.

'I don't know your face,' he said to me.

'I'm not surprised. I've only been here a couple of days. I'm temping in Accounts.'

I was not sure if he was disappointed with my reply or the texture of his bubble and squeak.

'What do you do?' I asked.

'I'm the Director,' he said.

The foundation had two directors. One was a scientist who directed the research work. My lunch companion was in charge of the rest. My first reaction was to be impressed that he ate in the canteen with everyone else. The second was that I couldn't believe my luck.

'What do you do all day?' I asked him.

'Meet and greet, empty the in-tray, go to meetings.' He went on to describe a rag-bag of chores familiar to any chief executive.

'What is your greatest challenge?'

'Long-range planning. Matching the resources to the objectives set by the scientists.' He elaborated on this theme but, try as I might, I could not get him to focus on issues of personnel management. The punk from Birmingham excused himself and left.

'Who was that young man?' asked the Director, earnestly, as if he really wanted to know the answer.

'He's got a couple of doctorates in immunology,' said the accountant. 'He's starting a virus project. He comes under me. He was with Wellcome for a couple of years, but he's come back to us.' I found out later that the accountant was a Laboratory Head, a very senior post.

'They like it here,' said the Director.

'Why do they like it here?' I asked. They both thought for a few seconds.

'Because they don't have money problems. They're not fighting for money,' said the Director. 'I don't mean their salaries. I mean they know there will be enough money to finish the project. It's not like a university where they worry about budget cuts every year.'

The Laboratory Head had a different answer. 'Because they have a full support staff here. Their sterilization, glass blowing, computing is done for them by professional staff. They can get on with their work.'

They were both saying similar things. Impediments to doing their job had been removed. They assumed that once the working environment had been made as attractive and supportive as possible, motivation and job satisfaction would take care of themselves. I, having read management books, knew they were talking through their hats. The theory says that pay and conditions and the work environment are de-motivating if they are unsatisfactory but have no effect if they are adequate. Motivation and job satisfaction and self-fulfilment and so on are only achieved by positive factors such as recognition and achievement and good target setting.

'Yes,' I said, 'but once you've provided the money and the support, what motivates them?'

'They motivate themselves, don't they?'

There were certainly no material incentives for working in cancer research. After a degree and a doctorate, and if you were exceptionally talented, you might be taken on at the salary I used to pay my secretary. If you were outstanding and remained with the foundation and became one of their senior scientists you would earn in your mid-thirties what I used to pay a junior lending officer.

After lunch I watched the Director wander round the coffee room next to the restaurant, going from group to group. Here was one reason for the friendly atmosphere. The boss used the staff canteen. He made a point of seeking out the new faces. He asked bluntly and plainly who they were. He gave a clear impression of being interested in them as people. He scavenged gossip and facts and scraps of information as he went. He gave out information honestly and directly. I was impressed.

When I got back to the office I said I had sat next to the boss.

'He seems very nice,' I said.

'I don't trust him,' said Noreen.

'Why not?'

'He's sacked too many people. I don't trust him.'

'Why did he do that?'

'Their faces didn't fit.'

'Is that all?'

'Culling, it's called. Thinning out.'

'He's a new broom,' said Willy.

'How long has he been here?' I asked.

'Eighteen months.'

'He was a top brass in the Army.'

'He's ruthless,' said Noreen.

'Mind you, knowing some of them, it wasn't a bad thing.'

'He's reorganizing things.'

'He's not like the fellow he took over from.'

'He was a gentleman.'

'One of the old school. Know what I mean?'

'Never did a blind thing.'

'You'd never catch him in the canteen.'

Ask someone why they go to work and they will probably say 'for the money'. The money gets us in the door in the morning and keeps us there until knocking-off time. But does it make us work harder or more happily while we are there?

Assuming they have the capability to do either, why do people choose to be prime ministers rather than barristers, writers rather than international bank managers, cancer researchers rather than dentists, teachers rather than accountants, nurses rather than executive secretaries, executive secretaries rather than croupiers, when the money is so much worse?

Why do people who have enough money to live in luxury for the rest of their lives carry on working harder than most of the rest of us?

Money is one of the reasons why people work but it is clearly not the only one. Many theories of motivation have been

developed. They all work on the underlying assumption that there is a pattern of needs or drives or motives to be found and on which human behaviour can be predicted. In all the places I have worked I have found immense difficulty in applying any behavioural theory of motivation to actual circumstances. People's apparent needs and drives and motivations seem to change, not only over time, but from day-to-day or hour-to-hour. Sometimes needs seem to co-exist with equal force, at other times one need will override the others.

In the same person contradictory needs can co-exist for:

conformity	individuality
stability	novelty
tradition	change
habit	learning
peace	excitement
security	danger
being controlled	controlling
status	self-abasement

Anybody who goes to work should think very hard why they are doing it and what they get out of it. The study of motivation in oneself and others is fascinating and rewarding. But it has no part in the manager's job description. Motivation theory is too incomplete, unreliable and inconclusive to rely on as a basis for prediction and executive action. This is not because the theories are half-baked or the theoreticians incapable. Human-beings are a turmoil of contradictions. We have the capability of holding two contradictory views simultaneously, of feeling contradictory feelings, of saying contradictory things. We have contradictory sets of values for different circumstances, contradictory identities. We try and paste over these contradictions with a veneer of consistency in our habits and principles and prejudices and the other things we live by. Upbringing, experience, religious or ethical conviction, the need for consistency keep these forces in check, more or less. Our individual personalities are not the sum of our inner drives and needs but a trade-off, a fragile balance between them. The balance is constantly shifting, as one particular drive or combination of drives surfaces and disappears again.

Morale

I came to the foundation at a busy time. Pay-day was the following week. The deadline was immovable. It was Noreen's responsibility to complete the salary sheets to give to the bank on the third Friday of the month. This was secret and confidential work, which is why she sat behind a screen. It was also very complicated work. A new computerized staff administration system had been installed six months before. It had been designed by Computer Services from a specification designed by the Personnel Department. The heart of the system was a master file of employees. It contained everything that the Personnel Department could possibly wish to know about the staff and at the touch of a button could regurgitate the information in any number of ways. Unfortunately it did not contain items of information essential for the Payroll Department.

'It's a pity they didn't ask our opinion,' said Noreen, wistfully.

'You mean they didn't consult you?' I asked. 'That's incredible.'

'So innocent,' sighed Noreen, shaking her head. I thought it was Noreen having a moan. I checked later with Willy and Ernest. It was true. The first they had heard of the new payroll system was when it had been programmed.

The master listing was supplemented with hand-written lists and computations and record cards. A new hire or a departmental transfer or a return from maternity leave or a pay-rise had to be entered in several different records. Overtime had to be calculated separately. There was constant checking and rechecking and correcting the same pieces of information recorded separately in different ways. As a result it took a week to do something that should have taken a couple of days. The procedure was so complicated that mistakes were bound to be made. These mistakes had two results. The first was a succession of visits to the Hygiaphone by disgruntled staff waving pay-slips. The second was a constant defensiveness by Willy and Noreen to complaint and fear of criticism from the Personnel Department and the Director's Office.

It was not common practice to admit a mistake. On Thursday, my first task was to order the petty cash requirements for the coming week from Securicor. In addition to replacing the cash I had given out from the box, I had to order cash to reimburse the tuition and travel expenses of a score of day-release students. Noreen forgot to tell me about this and I overlooked it on my secret crib sheet. On Friday, when the cash was delivered, there was a queue of students at the Hygiaphone asking for their money.

'I'm sorry,' I said to the first few, 'I should have ordered your money but I'm new here and I forgot. I'm very sorry. It's my fault. I will make sure it's here next week.' I was not at all comfortable saying this, but I knew from experience that most people only make a fuss if you make excuses. It also helped to know that I would not be there next week to take the blame again. The first two or three students looked very disappointed but accepted my statement and went quietly away.

'Isn't there anything we can do?' I asked Noreen. 'It was our fault. The money means a lot to those students. Can't we make them an advance or something?' Noreen shook her head.

'We're not allowed to. Tell them the requisition was late coming up from Personnel.'

'But we did get the requisition on time.' Noreen sighed and shook her head.

I did not take her advice at first. I personally took the blame for the next two or three. Then I ran out of resilience, my capacity for self-criticism was exhausted and I used Noreen's excuse on the rest. I knew that they would probably hear the true story from the first comers but I didn't care. It was much less stressful to make up an excuse, even though I saw it was flimsy.

After dealing with a maintenance man whose overtime had been miscalculated and who had been asking us for three weeks for it to be put right, Willy muttered to me, 'Take, take, take. All they do is take.' I thought the maintenance man's attitude was legitimate. What did Willy expect him to give to a payroll department?

One afternoon I answered Noreen's phone. A man who had recently retired had a question about his final salary payment. As usual, Noreen was not at her desk. I said that the person who could help was not there but I would take a message and his telephone number and if he had not heard by the end of the day he should phone again. He refused to hang up. He insisted I get Willy and if he was not available, Ernest.

'If I don't get this cleared up now I never will,' he said. 'Wages are very, very difficult to deal with. They are very slow to answer queries. I worked there at the foundation for years. They're well known for it.'

This approach worked. By persistence and obstinacy he got his answer. If Noreen or Willy or Ernest were confronted with a question they could not avoid they would make every effort to answer it immediately. They were courteous and understanding. If there was an immediate solution it was carried out immediately. But if the employee could be fobbed off, he would be.

'We'll get to it today.' (We did not).

'Personnel haven't sent up the records yet.' (They already had).

'It was sent to the wrong unit.' (It was not sent anywhere).

'We're working on them.' (We have lost them).

I puzzled over this. Payroll administration needs extremely conscientious, dedicated people. My colleagues were. They took immense pains to get things right and on time, to check and test. They ran a complicated system and, as far as I could tell, as well as humanly possible. They made very few mistakes considering there were five hundred people to be paid. There was a standard joke that I heard each member of the Payroll Office and several members of the Personnel Department make at least once. Noreen made it several times. While we were checking lists we would come across people with unpronouncable names, usually African or East European. We would come across complicated cases, people who had transferred between units, done overtime and left for maternity leave in the same week, and so on. 'Sack them,' was the joke. The extension of the joke was to propose that everyone on the payroll was fired, rehired at the beginning of a month, and forbidden overtime or expenses or allowances.

Was this a clue to the department's conception of their work? They regarded the exceptions and the anomalies and the mistakes as a nuisance or an irrelevance. Individual queries and complaints were seen as a distraction from their main job, which was to run the payroll system. They did not see payroll as a service. They did not see it as an essential contribution to maintaining staff morale. They saw their job as keeping the payroll system going. It was a quirky, ill-designed, demanding, unforgiving system that took concentration and attention to detail and commitment. They managed to satisfy at least 95 per cent of the staff at any one time. But the other 5 per cent, the people who had escaped the system, were aberrations. And in treating them as aberrations and not as clients, people it was their job to serve, the payroll staff succeeded in undoing much of what they had achieved by getting the system to work.

People in personnel and payroll, all those who administer pay and benefits and perks, are in a difficult position. On the one hand, they provide a service that is vital to morale. What they are in charge of is the first concern of any employee. The nightmare of any organization is missing a pay-day. If they make repeated mistakes and omissions they can undermine everything else the management is trying to do. Like any group that provides a service they are expected to be responsive and understanding and considerate and to have the needs and interests of the employees uppermost in their mind. On the other hand, they are the keepers of the keys. They guard the safe. Payroll administration has a responsibility to make sure that employees receive only what they are entitled to, what they have earned for their work. There is a tension between these two roles. The tension spilled over into indifference and frustration and defensiveness when the system let them down. They evaded this conflict by making excuses, blaming other people and taking refuge in the faults of the sytem.

Faced with a hostile world outside we all mucked in to help. There was a lot of task sharing and co-operation and mutual support. I spent my free moments collating the text of two print-outs, checking identification numbers. Noreen took over from me at the Hygiaphone when I was adding up the till. Ernest answered queries put through to Willy. In addition, we had a part-timer, Alice, who came in every afternoon and helped with the payroll sheets. She was a bright-eyed Cockney lady in her sixties, brilliant at mental arithmetic, partial to glittering sweaters.

'Fancy a trip up the Amazon?' she inquired when we were introduced.

I was puzzled by this invitation until she revealed that she had had a breast removed.

'They saved me, this lot, they did. You wouldn't notice, would you?' she asked, pulling her Lurex sweater tight. As she had the kind of bosom you wouldn't notice even if she had a complete set, I could truthfully reassure her.

Everyone in the office arrived fifteen minutes late in the morning. They took over an hour for lunch. There was a rush for the lift at five. On my first day I diagnosed a low commitment and poor attitude. On my third day I found that they took work home. 'It's easier to get things done,' said Noreen. In the busy week she must have done two hours a night. She phoned in on Wednesday morning to say she was ill. 'Oh, not again,' said Willy. 'She's had fourteen sick days off already this year.' It was the busiest day of the month. I immediately diagnosed absenteeism through work stress and poor working conditions. Later on a friend of hers who worked in Personnel called in for her work to take home for her that night. Noreen came in the following day. She looked ill and was hoarse. She had done yesterday's work between eight and midnight. So much for diagnosis.

At four o'clock one afternoon there was a row. It was the first genuine shouting match I had heard in an office for many years. From time to time we were visited by David, the Assistant Chief Accountant. While they both reported to the Chief Financial Officer, the Cashier's Department and the Accounts Department had an uneasy relationship. The cashiers gathered in the money, disbursed expenses and invested the surplus. The accountants kept the records. Accountants blamed the cashiers for sloppiness, cashiers blamed the accountants for obtuseness. David was a young fogey. He wore a grey three-piece suit and a watch chain and black shoes with toecaps. He was pernickety in manner and speech. With a measured step, as if pacing out the size of the room, he would walk up to Willy wherever he was and look him up and down. 'Good Morrow. William. A trifle here for your attention.' He would then detail yet another transgression of procedure while Willy, unshaven, tie loose, his light brown suit baggy at the knees, looked pained.

At the end of a particularly stressful day David came in with a buff-coloured file and found Willy leaning over the salary sheets on Noreen's desk. He began to ask why Willy had assigned certain codes to some entries. Willy invited him back into his office to discuss it. The door was left open. Their conversation started at a normal level and then rose to a rousing crescendo. There was a noise of a desk being thumped, the slapping of a file against a solid object. Noreen, Alice and I craned to see what was happening. I caught a glimpse of the two of them standing on either side of Willy's desk, their noses almost touching, shouting at each other at the tops of their voices. David was the first to crack. He turned on his heel and stormed out of the office, slamming the door behind him. There was a moment's stunned silence. Then Noreen and Alice broke into loud applause, which I joined in. We went into his office and congratulated him.

'About time too,' said Alice.

'It's been a long time coming,' said Noreen. Willy was embarrassed. He looked dazed and thoughtful for the rest of the afternoon. He was normally a gentle, cheerful person and his emotions had caught him by surprise. At five o'clock we all left the office together. We were going down the corridor to the lift when Willy suddenly stopped. He turned back and we saw him go down to David's office.

'The creep,' said Noreen.

'He's going to kiss and make up,' said Alice. 'Yuch.'

On the same afternoon an old friend of Alice's who worked in the library came to pick up her luncheon vouchers.

'Hello love, how are you doin'?'

'Same as ever. Terrible,' whispered Alice over my shoulder.

'What's the trouble?'

'It's such a bleeding mess. I hate it. You spend all day just sorting it out.'

'Ask for a transfer. They'll give you one.'

'I dunno. I suppose I enjoy it although it needs so much sorting out.'

'Well, if you enjoy it, it doesn't matter that you don't get any job satisfaction at the end of the day.'

'I suppose you're right there.'

I thought Alice's 'although' in her sentence, 'I enjoy it although it needs so much sorting out' actually meant 'because', as in the sentence, 'I like him although he's so naughty.' Every afternoon she dived into the print-outs and papers in search of nuggets of information she needed for the salary sheets with exclamations of mock annoyance and delight. 'Where's the little bugger disappeared – oh, look what those cretins in Personnel have gone and done – ah, the cheeky sod . . .' Like many of the people I came across she enjoyed unravelling mysteries and solving problems. A smooth-running procedure is deadly boring.

I could not decide whether the morale in the Cashier's Department was high or low. The evidence was as contradictory as Alice's conversation with her friend.

Although there was a lot of work to be done they all rushed out of the office on the dot of five. But they took work home with them. Noreen was frequently off sick. She was away with a cold on a critical day. But she asked for work to be sent home to her which she completed that evening. And so on.

The factors contributing to high morale were:

- **There was a clear and common objective to meet the payroll deadline.**
- **It was understood that what they were doing was very important.**
- **It was clear on pay-day whether they had succeeded.**
- **Each person was very clear about their own and the others' role in achieving the objective.**
- **At the same time, each person was willing and able to help the others.**
- **It was a small group. They seemed to know each other well. They were friendly and considerate.**

- They were physically close in a small office cut off from the outside by programmable door locks and the Hygiaphone.

The factors contributing to low morale were:

- Low pay. They were among the lowest paid of the staff.
- Their working conditions were cramped, airless, and with no outside light. More important, they had deteriorated considerably in the recent past.
- The system they had to work was ill-designed and error-prone and unnecessarily complicated. They had made no contribution to its recent design.
- Direct contact with their 'customers' was usually negative, dealing with complaints.
- I had no evidence while I was there of contact with senior management. They feared such contact because it was usually in the form of criticism for mistakes.
- They were physically cut off from outside contact.

I found it immensely difficult to evaluate the impact of these factors. Was being cut off from the rest a positive or a negative factor? Or was it both positive and negative? Or was it neutral? Did these factors cause variations in morale? Or did variations in morale exaggerate and diminish the importance of these factors?

Perhaps Alice's friend was right. They enjoyed the work but had no job satisfaction. Or perhaps vice versa.

Hard Work

'Any experience of new issues?' asked Jenny.

'You mean shares?'

'Privatization. That sort of thing.'

'Triffic. Life's work. Man and boy. Nothing I don't know.'

I had learned not to lie about what I could do. It was not worth the shame and embarrassment of being found out. But this was an exception. From a management anthropologist's point of view it would be fascinating to see what impact change and improvisation had on working methods and attitudes. Privatization demanded all the talents and expertise and flair the City could muster, not to speak of large gangs of people thrown together to get through the paperwork. I also wanted to get into the heart of the City, the romance and the glamour and excitement of international share dealing, the turmoil of the Big Bang that was shaking the Square Mile to its foundations.

My career in the hurly-burly of the new capitalist revolution started up the Edgware Road, where London melts like a neglected brie into Middlesex. Every morning I trudged from the station past enormous hangars housing furniture showrooms and DIY stores and car repair shops. The office was above a second-hand car showroom. Five of us started together. The others were young women. Two were students with long scarves and layers of jumble sale clothes and big straw bags. One was an Asian clad from head to toe in red leather. One was black, dressed in a pressed beige suit and sitting erect with her legs together and her hands on her lap as if she had been to a convent school. We sat nervously without speaking to each other in a small room with a coffee machine and a row of hooks on the wall loaded with coats. Old newspapers and overflowing ashtrays and empty crisp packets littered the low tables between us.

After half an hour a soft-spoken young man with neatly permed hair and a bright yellow cardigan came to fetch us. His name was Colin. We were led into a large, bright room. Tinsel Christmas decorations fluttered from the ceiling in the draught from the air-conditioning. The room was divided into two by free-standing acoustic partitions. In one half of the room about fifty people sat at three long rows of white formica-topped tables. Each had a telephone and a pad of pink paper. Some of them talked on the telephone, scribbling on the pads. Others talked quietly among themselves. Most of them were men, of all ages. The older they were the more respectable they looked. In the other half of the room another fifty people sat at two rows of tables in front of computer terminals. Two of them were men. About a dozen wore bright yellow cardigans like Colin. They tapped away at their keyboards looking down at piles of pink papers. A few of the terminals were untenanted. Colin invited us to sit down in front of them. I sat down between a young Asian woman and a man with a leather waistcoat and several earrings and a teeny weeny kiss curl on the nape of his neck. They looked up and nodded and got back to their work. Colin came to me first.

'You put the title in and press return. Then the initial. Then the name and so on. The county is the most important. No full stops. OK? Off you go.' That was training and induction. But I was a pro.

'Where are the toilets?'

'By the stairs. OK?'

The information that I was to input into the terminal was the names and addresses of people who called in for share prospectuses for a big privatization bonanza. We were expected to work a minimum of nine hours a day with half an hour for lunch and a ten minute break every two hours. The lunch break was unpaid. The ten minutes were at the company's expense. There was no overtime payment. I was getting less than £3 an hour. Some people were getting £2 an hour. I was not the only one to cross London for the work. People came from Tooting and Ilford and Dartford, three hours commute a day. It took an hour's work just to pay the fare. Another hour to buy a can of cola and a packet of cigarettes. Temping for new issues is not as profitable as stagging them.

This was temporary work in every sense. Only the few people in yellow cardigans were regular employees of the computer bureau. The majority of us were casual labour. We had no idea of how our jobs fitted in, what other people did in the building, how our input was stored and processed and used and what it resulted in. We did not know each other's names. We did not know the hierarchy. We had not been told what company employed us and what its relationship was with the company being privatized. Because the employment agency handled all our tax and national insurance and so on there was no formal link with the bureau. They had our names on sheets on a clipboard on which they recorded the time we worked and this was sent to the agency. We were thrown together to do a specific, well-defined task of limited duration. The job would finish in six weeks. There was no organization, no culture, no image, no long-term goals, no traditional ways of doing things, no existing social patterns, no future, no long-term objectives to distort the picture of how people behaved when they worked together.

There were two sorts of work. Newspaper and television advertisements enticed people to telephone a toll free number for a prospectus and a share application. The calls were taken on the other side of the large room by the people with the telephones. The names and addresses were written down on the pink pads, four applicants to a sheet. The papers were collected by a supervisor and put in a red plastic washing-up bowl on a small table under a portrait of Winston Churchill. The telephone answerers were trained. They were given scripts. A notice on the wall said that they were legally required to stick to them. They learned how to discriminate between genuine capitalists and troublemakers, how to cope with objectionable and offensive callers. Their work was unpredictable. In the early days of the campaign, if it was very slack, they were sent back home without pay. At other times, during commercial breaks or after the morning papers were delivered, it would be pandemonium. There were one or two retired people, a few were unemployed. Most were students. Who else would work for that money?

We VDU operators collected the pink papers from the washing-up bowl. We were paid more, presumably because we had a skill. There were a few men, a dozen black and Asian women and the rest were white. Some of the women had received letters asking them to wear white tops and black skirts or trousers. The regular staff wore little black string ties as well as yellow cardigans. I asked why they had to wear uniform.

'It's a foreign company, isn't it?'

'You have to be smart to deal with the public.'

'They make rules for the sake of it.'

'I like it. It makes us a bit different, doesn't it.'

None of the temps made any attempt to wear uniform. On my first day, in deference to the new capitalism, I wore a suit and a college tie. People asked me where the toilets were and whether there was time and a half on Sunday. After that I came in jeans and no one bothered me. On Sundays, although as far as the work was concerned there was no difference to any other day of the week, nobody wore uniform. On Sunday afternoon Belinda, one of the supervisors, brought in a radio. I asked on Monday if we could have the radio again and was told it wasn't allowed on a weekday.

The work was unremitting. We never got to the bottom of the red washing-up bowl. It was intensely boring. One way of coping with it was self-hypnosis. I tried to short circuit the link between the eyes and the fingers, like a musician reading music. I drove all thoughts out of my mind, closed down as many brain circuits as I could, hummed a mantra, lapsed into a trance. But there were too many distractions. I found the best way to cope with it was to work as hard as I could, to see how many names and addresses I could do in a set time. I found that at the beginning I could do sixty names and addresses an hour and by the time I finished about ninety.

There was no financial incentive to work hard. There were no targets, no monitoring of the work rate, no performance requirement. I had to ask three times before I was told that the expected input rate was eighty names and addresses an hour. One day Belinda took it into her head to tell us how many we had processed. At lunchtime she announced we had made nearly four thousand entries so far that day. The record was eight thousand. 'So what,' whispered Debbie opposite me. It was the only indication I ever heard of how we were doing. Some worked slower than others and nobody minded. It was up to us. Almost everyone tapped away as if we were on piecework.

The job was not purely mechanical. Initiative was required to decipher the writing on the input sheets. There were a lot of foreign students among the telephone answerers. They did not recognize the names and towns of the callers and were embarrassed to ask them to spell each word. They did the best they could phonetically. Someone who had worked down there told me that during the busy times when everyone was speaking and the phones were ringing it was difficult to hear, even if the line was good. So we had towns like Wuster and Gilfud and Warsaw and others which were indecipherable. The handwriting was appalling so that even correct spellings would be camouflaged with scrawl. Occasionally there were sheets covered with neat, copperplate handwriting like my father's. These were rare and wonderful. Every time I went to the washing-up bowl I rummaged to find them.

The task of deciphering the addresses was not made easier by our own ignorance. Cries for help rose above the pattering of keyboards.

'What county is Derby in?'

'Is Aberystwyth in Scotland?'

'Is Exeter a county?'

We helped each other. I was usually the authority on the English places, although the new counties were a trial and I could never remember the various Yorkshires. I was not so good at Wales and hopeless on Scotland. We were all totally ignorant about Northern Ireland but we had two people from Belfast to put us right. It became a game, your starter for ten, is Dundee a county? When everyone passed someone said 'the postman will know'. I estimated that more than half the entries had at least one error and a significant proportion were sheer nonsense.

We did not always ask for help. There were periods during the day when the room lapsed into a tapping, bleeping, paper shuffling catalepsy when no one seemed to care what they put in. As there did not seem to be any quality control the temptation to liven up the dull moments with a few deliberate mistakes was overwhelming. I sent a prospectus to our dog Guinness and S.Holmes in Baker Street and various relatives I honoured with peerages. Majors and colonels were demoted a rank or two. Vicars became rabbis and rabbis became ayatollahs. *Telegraph* readers who lived in Old Vicarages were rechristened with subcontinental names. But this soon palled. We ran out of ideas. The feeling of power was soon deadened by guilt and boredom.

We sat at a different place each day, usually next to different people. There was very little conversation, in short bursts at the deadest parts of the day, the middle of the morning and the middle of the afternoon. The Asian woman I sat next to on the first morning, Bhati, was doing a postgraduate degree in genetic engineering at London University. Ron, the man with the kiss curl on his neck was an Australian loss adjuster working his way round the world. The black girl who started at the same time as me had indeed been educated by the nuns in Nigeria. Her father was a paramount chief and a property developer in Edgware. He picked her up in his Mercedes each evening. Mary was a refugee from the Falls Road. She sat small and quiet and aspirated her haitches. Steven and Wallace from Dollis Hill wore identical moustaches and leather waistcoats and always sat together. They came to work in the ice cream van they owned. It was their livelihood in the summer. We called them the Whippy Twins. Eileen had seventeen grandchildren and every twenty minutes went to the toilets for a smoke. Three Sharons, two Debbies and a Tracey from Dollis Hill wanted to be air hostesses.

'What about you?'

'I'm a writer.'

'Oh yeah. What do you write?'

'Right now I'm writing a book about what it's like to work in an office.'

'Oh yeah.'

Several people, like the Whippy Twins, had come to the job with a friend. Many of those who came alone paired off after two or three days. Couples sat together, took their breaks together, arranged to come in at the same time the next day. There was no greater level of intimacy that I could detect, nor could I analyse what determined the match other than a general similarity of social class and educational background. Even this did not apply to every case. My mate was Mac. We were dissimilar in every way except that we constituted a minority of heterosexual males. Mac was a Scotsman from Aberdeen. He had been a roustabout on an oil rig in the heady days of North Sea oil until his marginal field collapsed with the oil price and he was out of a job. He had come south and taken a secretarial course. The money wasn't as good but it was indoor work.

'And you got a better crack at the crumpet, mon, than you did on an oil rig. You're surrounded by it, mon, just reach out and take your pick. I've never put it around so much in my life.'

There was only one person I came across out of fifty who consciously slacked. Diana stopped for a minute's rest after every entry. She dawdled and chatted and found excuses to leave the table and talk to the supervisor. She had recently graduated from a Midlands polytechnic and, unable to find a job, learned to type and wanted to be a secretary. She talked with great repetitiveness about the rates of pay at the various jobs she had had. The rest of us resented the distraction. She was not pulling her weight. Two people wondered out loud why she was not thrown out, why she was not reprimanded. Her low productivity did not slow us down, did not materially affect us. We did not have a quota. Yet we found her annoying and disturbing. She was not playing along with the rest of us. I remembered how I had irritated Greta, the hyperactive reconciliations clerk, by my slowness at the bank where I had been sacked.

She was a lonely person. She found no one to team up with. She was restless and ill-at-ease, bored and fretful. I asked her what she looked for in a job and she gave a stock answer.

'It has to involve you and interest you. You have to learn something. You have to work with nice people. And of course the money. The money shows how much they appreciate you.'

'Why are you doing this boring, low-paid job then?'

'It's all there is. Besides it's good keyboard practice. I find I'm getting faster and more accurate. I always fail the typing tests they give me at the agencies.'

'How do you fail a typing test?'

'I don't do as well as I know I can.'

She was not the only one to look for reasons other than the money for what she was doing. Six people said it improved their typing speed. Three others said it gave them familiarity with a word processing keyboard which they had not come across before. Several of the telephone answerers thought they could get into telephone sales as a result of the experience. We all agreed it was boring, low-paid, menial, frustrating work but we refused to accept that it was a completely dead end. Even in this job most people were looking for new things to learn. Money was not sufficient justification. My consolation was that it improved my knowledge of Scottish counties.

The thirst for knowledge and the temptations of sabotage were not enough to distract us. Complaining helped to relieve the boredom. We complained more as we became more familiar with each other and the environment and less in awe of our employers. Variations in the heat, the light, the brightness of the screens became more and more important as the day wore on. But there was a limit to the number of times we could ask for the fans to be turned up or down or the windows to be open or closed. We exchanged details of our terms and conditions of work. We discovered we were getting different rates of pay, some lower by fifty pence an hour. Some of us could choose our hours, others were expected to work only nine until six. These complaints were deflected by our supervisors to our official employers, the agencies.

Diana, the slacker, had other ways of testing authority, of asserting her individuality. After lunch on the first day she looked round and then dived furtively into her bag. She brought out a bag of crisps.

'I bet you're not allowed to eat up here. The last place I was at like this someone tipped up a can of Coke over a personal computer. It went all over the keyboard and down into the processor. They said it cost four thousand pounds of damage.'

She ate the crisps one by one, sitting back from the table, waiting to be picked on by a supervisor. She finished the bag without interruption. It was a triumph but she looked disappointed. After tea-break she looked round, dived into her bag and brought out a can of cola.

'You can't,' I whispered.

'It's all right,' she whispered back, snapping the ring with a last gasp, 'it's Diet.'

I devoted myself to the screen and waited for the worst

and hoped it did not go over my trousers. She was halfway through the can when Belinda, the supervisor, came over. She was very apologetic. 'Didn't they tell you? There's no eating or drinking up here. That's why we give you the ten minutes breaks and a refreshment room. I'm sorry. It might go over the machines.'

Diana put the half finished can carefully upright in her bag. When Belinda had gone she smirked at me.

'There. Didn't I tell you?' At six o'clock, when it was time to go, she picked up her bag. She rummaged inside it for her scarf.

'O shit,' she said.

'What?' I asked innocently.

'Nothing.'

I did not see Diana again for a few days. We sat with our backs to each other and had different breaks. I tried to avoid her. I wanted to see if I could get up to a hundred an hour. Her chattering slowed me down and her slowness irritated me. On my last day I had no choice. The only vacant place was next to her. Halfway through the morning she ferreted in her bag and came up with a paper bag. She took out a brown bread sandwich.

'Honey,' she said. 'I'll have to be careful. It's very runny.'

She snatched a bite, like a dog snapping at a titbit, and put it back in her bag.

'Watch it,' said the girl opposite, a regular in a yellow cardigan. 'You'll really cop it if they catch you eating up here.'

'Oh. I didn't know,' said Diana, and licked her palm.

I liked our supervisors, Colin and Belinda. Belinda was a big, gawky girl in her mid-twenties. They worked twelve-hour shifts and although they were often tired and under pressure, were always courteous to us. They kept a meticulous record of the hours we worked and made sure we did not overstay our breaks but they did so equally meticulously with everyone. They listened seriously to our complaints and tried to do something about them. They made efforts to call us by our names. They were knowledgeable about postcodes and Northern Irish counties. When they were not attending to us they seemed to be very busy on tasks of their own. But I conceived an instant loathing for a middle-aged woman who came on patrol every afternoon after lunch. She was carefully dressed in a grey dress with a little black tie. Her hair looked like a Barbie Doll wig. She had spectacles with clear frames. She looked the kind of person you wait to be seated by in hotel coffee shops. She walked slowly down towards us, walked up and down between the tables, and then stood behind each of us in turn. The first time she did it I waited for something to whack down on my head. She never said anything or did anything. We did not know who she was or where she came from.

'Who is she? Who's she checking up on?' said Diana.

On the second afternoon I swivelled round.

'Are you in authority here?' I asked.

'Why?' she replied.

'Are you in charge. Do you have an executive position?'

'Why do you ask?'

'Yes or no?'

'Is there something the matter?'

It was like talking to matron.

'The writing on these sheets is terrible. They are full of mis-spellings and mistakes. It's very hard to input them correctly. People don't like having their names got wrong. It reflects very badly on the company. Look here.' I picked a sheet at random out of the pile. It was in beautiful senior citizen copperplate. I tossed it away and picked up another. It was not copperplate but it was legible.

'These are the exceptions.'

'Tell your supervisor,' she said grandly and stalked away.

I learned a useful lesson. For complaints to be an effective diversion from boredom and a test of authority they should not be impromptu. They must be well founded and incapable of easy solution. I bided my time and after a few days found a perfect one. I was sitting next to Mac. We had our backs to the other table where most of the girls were regulars with yellow cardigans and transparent blouses. They were in their late teens and early twenties. They chatted while they worked. Their language surprised even the roustabout. 'They dinna swear so much on a rig, mon.' It was casual swearing, not meant to shock, obscenities used as grace words.

'I went to f***ing Sainsbury's for a frozen pizza, didn't I, and they were f***ing closed. I had to go all the way to f***ing Brent Cross.'

'Amanda, you are a dick head. The f***ing Spar's open till nine.'

Mac and I were part amused and part uncomfortable at this idle girlish chat. Then Sharon and Debbie began to discuss each other's farting habits.

'You're just a smelly prick, you are,' said Debbie.

'Jesus, mon,' said Mac, 'I'm going to tell them to wash their mouths out.' I put a restraining hand on his arm. 'Wait. There are channels.'

I stood up and went over to the washing-up bowl where Belinda and the middle-aged woman in the Barbie Doll wig were talking. They ignored me at first and then Matron turned round with a glassy stare.

'I should like to make a formal complaint,' I said.

'Tell your supervisor,' she said and turned to walk away. But I stopped her in her tracks.

'The bad language in here is terrible. I don't like it. It puts me off my work. I find it offensive.'

'Who do you mean?' said Matron. Belinda looked over at Mac.

'The girls behind us. I don't mind how women talk to each other in the ladies' room but in mixed company it lowers the tone. It's very embarrassing. I think the men in here are entitled to some respect. I mean, there are standards.'

Belinda looked as though she wanted to pinch herself. Matron blinked.

'And Mac and I find it personally offensive when they use the name of the male private parts as a term of abuse.'

I turned on my heel and went back to my seat. Until lunchtime I worked conscientiously and tried to avoid looking at Belinda. The girls behind continued to swear. At lunchtime Mac clapped me on the back and bought me a pint. When we came back from lunch the girls in yellow cardigans had been moved to another bank of terminals on the other side of the room. Belinda never mentioned the incident. It kept me going for the rest of the afternoon. I felt I had won a victory. Over what or whom I am not sure, but it felt like a victory.

'There was no organization, no culture, no image, no long-term goals, no traditional ways of doing things, no existing social patterns, no future, no long-term objectives to distort the picture of how people behaved when they worked together . . . There was no financial incentive to work hard. There were no targets, no monitoring of the work rate, no performance requirement.'

And what was the result?

- **Almost everyone worked extremely hard.**
- **The slacker was ostracized by the rest of us.**
- **Even though the work was essentially non-collaborative, we helped each other.**
- **We paired off for companionship and support.**
- **We set our own targets.**
- **We strove to learn and improve our skills.**
- **Organizers of the work, Colin and Belinda, were respected and obeyed. Ritual displays of status and authority by Matron were disturbing and disruptive.**

The quality of the output was poor. The main reason for this was the conception and structure of the job. Information initiated orally was transcribed twice by inexperienced people in difficult conditions. There was no quality standard or control.

Some of the poor quality was due to indifference, some to deliberate sabotage resulting from boredom and frustration and resentment of authority. But outbreaks were spasmodic, occurring mainly in the middle of the afternoon, the low point of the day. For most of the time people made a conscious effort to do the best job they could.

Dedication

At the heart of the system is the dealing room. This is where bankers and businessmen and traders and presidents and finance ministers and economists and politicians and all the other great and good of the Western capitalist system come to judgement. Exchange rates go up and down as a direct result of economic and political events. Verdicts are instantaneous. Within seconds of news, currencies are bought or sold, driving rates up or down. If the trade figures are good, buy Deutschmarks. If the President sees the proctologist, sell dollars. If the EEC freezes car imports, sell yen. If Labour does well in the polls, sell sterling. If the Russians put the squeeze on Poland, buy gold. It is a pure market. With present day communications everyone has access to all the information. There are so many players in so many dealing rooms that it cannot be dominated by a minority. Governments or central banks sometimes get together to swing things their way but it does not last very long. Moralists and socialists and patriots and spendthrift finance ministers and lazy exporters rail against the faceless, uncaring, unprincipled speculators of the market. But there is no room for passion or principle in the dealing room, except the lust for making money and the cardinal virtue of self-interest.

'How do you feel about dealing rooms, John?'

'The cardiograph of capitalism, Jenny. Flickering and fluttering from second to second. The vital signs.'

'I mean for a job.'

'Triffic, Jenny.'

I dressed the part. Beige suit, grey shoes and a gold Rolex. The worst part was getting up early. I had to be in at eight. I waited in the lobby for my new boss, Roberta. She was in charge of foreign exchange operations. She was a tall, thin, nervous woman in her mid-thirties, clad in a dark blue tube of jersey wool. Her fine boned, dark-eyed Mediterranean face was topped with a frizz of brown hair. She went away to comb it down every hour, I observed later, and it rose remorselessly again in ten minutes.

'I hope you stay longer than the others,' she said in the lift. 'We've had three already. They were hopeless. Everyone has to pull their weight around here. There are no passengers.' I looked forward to an interesting but brief career.

She led me into the dealing room. The immediate impression was of noise and clutter and chaos. VDU screens blinked brown and green, dealers shouted at each other and gabbled into their phones above the nattering of loudspeakers and the clatter of telexes. I breathed in the comforting smell of new carpet and stale tobacco and sweat and the ozone of electronic machinery and the thrilling pheromones exuded by vast quantities of money. Roberta took me to a small table, hardly bigger than a school desk, by a window overlooking a bowling green three stories below. Two men were already playing in the fresh morning sunshine, bending gently at the knee to swing the woods in their inevitable curve towards the tiny white jack.

The dealing room was L-shaped. My desk was at the elbow of the L, in front of Roberta. In the long bit were four clusters of dealing desks, each seating seven people, three down each side and one at the end. In front of each dealer were three VDU screens controlled by a complicated coloured keyboard. Another keyboard controlled three telephones. Intercoms enable dealers to communicate with each other without shouting, and to listen to brokers' natter on the loudspeakers. On the wall above them were four clocks showing the time in New York, London, the Middle East and the Far East. Below the clocks were six telexes and two facsimile machines.

The group nearest me did foreign exchange. There was one dealer for each of the main currencies we traded, dollars, sterling, Deutschmarks, and yen. The others had two currencies each, the swissy and the scandy, the franc and the guilder, the Hong Kong dollar and the lira. Their deals were priced in fractions of a penny and involved all the major banks of the world. There was no mystique in what they did. They bought cheap and sold dear.

Sometimes they bought dear and waited to sell, expecting the rate to go up. Sometimes they sold cheap and waited to buy, expecting the rate to go down. Money they had bought but not sold, or sold and not bought, was called the position. Unless you had very good reasons you did not keep a position overnight. You closed off your position, ended the day square. Buying and selling for immediate value is called spot trading. Buying and selling for a value date in the future is called forward trading. They did other more complicated things too, which I won't go into now, mainly because I never understood them even when it was my business to do so at the bank I managed.

The next group of dealers did the money market. Banks take in deposits and lend the money out again. If they do not get money from ordinary customers, like the High Street banks, they have to buy it in from other banks or companies so they can lend it out at a profit. They keep positions, too, by buying and not selling or selling and not buying. There were dealers for sterling and dollars and government securities. The money market dealers worked closely with the foreign exchange desk. It is very hard to make a profit by taking in money and lending it out again immediately. One thing you can do if the rates are right, say, is to take in a sterling deposit, change it into dollars, lend out the dollars, and do a forward contract to change the dollars you get repaid back into sterling so you can pay back the money you first borrowed. They did lots of other things too which we won't go into for the reason mentioned in the previous paragraph.

The next group traded gold and silver. They bought it for resale and kept positions and traded options and futures. Bullion dealing is as sophisticated and fast moving as foreign exchange but it feels more like real money. There is more of a thrill in contracting to buy half a ton of gold than fifty million dollars. Somewhere in the world are vaults full of the stuff and men in overalls trundling it around on trolleys. There are coins in safes and mattresses, Krugerrands and Sovereigns and Napoleons. The customers are more mysterious, more romantic than in other markets. Arabs and Russians and South Africans rub shoulders on equal terms with Swiss and Americans.

The last group were banknote dealers. This was real money, carried around in bags and wallets and suitcases. The amounts they dealt in were small. In the foreign exchange markets a quarter of a million dollars is peanuts but it means a lot of used fivers in the banknote market. The amounts dealt may be small but the margins are high and it is a profitable trade. There are no fancy forward markets. The notes are bought and sold for actual delivery. The market not only makes sure that tourists get their spending money. Banknotes are the monetary instrument of choice for currency smugglers and money launderers and tax evaders and drug dealers, and anyone else who wishes their wealth not to be traced. Switzerland is the biggest market-place for banknotes.

There was another group of six people in the room, sitting behind me in the short bit of the L. They belonged to Operations and worked for Roberta. When the dealers did a deal they scribbled down the details on a deal ticket. The tickets were passed behind me to be input by my new colleagues into the computer system. They had to make sure that our counter-party's address and bank account details were correct. They also swapped instructions, in other words exchanged details, by telephone, their conversations recorded on tape in case there was a dispute later.

And what was my role in this hurly-burly? I was nothing less than the link between dealers and Operations. The awesome technology of worldwide telecommunications systems with their satellites and lasers and microwaves was connected with the equally awesome technology of a state-of-the-art mainframe computer across my little desk. I was a live Interface. I had no screens or telephones or keyboards. Instead I had a numbering machine. It imprinted a number and the date and time on anything that was thin enough to be thrust between its narrow jaws. They chomped down with a satisfying clunk. I still have a pale grey silk tie bearing the number 78453, the work of an idle moment, three forty-nine to be precise. The proper recipient of that time and number should have been a deal ticket. The other tools of my trade were an in-tray stacked on top of an out-tray. The deal tickets were dumped into the in-tray. It was my job to push them into the numbering machine, tick off the numbers on a tally sheet, and put the forms in the out-tray. They were then passed back to the Operations Group who put the details into the system, identifying them with the unique number I had so deftly assigned. Without a unique number assigned by me the transaction could not be recorded in the system. I felt like the focus of all the intense effort going on around me.

I could not understand why the previous incumbents had found the job so difficult. A certain manual dexterity was required but no great intelligence or skill. I got on famously until lunchtime, and what the task itself lacked in intrinsic job satisfaction was compensated by the spectator sports of bowls outside the window and dealing inside. But Roberta was breaking me in gently, testing me out before she introduced me to my second responsibility.

'John,' she said solemnly, as if I were being

consecrated, 'I want you to be in charge of the limits.' She let this sink in for a few moments before explaining my new duties.

This is the background. A gold dealer in Jeddah takes it into his head to buy a few pounds of gold. He picks up the telephone and arranges the deal with one of the people sitting opposite me. They agree on a price and a date on which the gold is to be delivered and the money handed over in exchange. This is the value date. But we take a risk that on the value date the Saudi might go bankrupt or renege on the deal, taking our gold and keeping his money. And he takes the same risk with us, that we go bankrupt or renege on the deal and take his money and keep our gold. This risk is called the exposure. So banks establish the creditworthiness of the people they deal with. They set the maximum amount they will risk with any one client at any one time. This is called the limit. They allow their dealers to do as many deals as they like with a customer as long as the total amount at risk, the exposure, does not exceed the limit.

With due ceremony, Roberta handed me a card file packed with dog-eared postcards. There was a card for each customer with its limit written on the top. For the time being I was entrusted only with the foreign exchange and the money market deals limits. After I had christened the deal with a number I wrote, with a chewed, stubby pencil, its amount and value date on the appropriate card. I added it to previous deals if there were any. If a deal on the card had a value date in the past we assumed that had gone through satisfactorily. I turned the pencil the other way round and rubbed it out. I then made sure that the total exposure did not exceed the limit. If the limit was exceeded I took out a piece of paper called an Exception Slip and recorded the transgression. At the end of the day the slips were sent up to the General Manager. I did not write the first few clearly enough. On one I crossed out a mistake and wrote the correction over it. Roberta breathed in sharply.

'These go to management,' she said, awe and anger mingling in her voice. 'Write them out again neatly. And never cross out, always use Tippex.'

Each day there was a sheaf of about fifty reports. The General Manager initialled them and sent them back down to us. I put them in a box file to prove to the auditors that we were assiduously monitoring the limits and management was approving excesses. When it was part of my life's work to initial exception reports I timed myself to see how fast I could do them. I got it down to an average of two a second. This of course precluded reading them. If I had read them I would not have known what I was supposed to do with the information thus acquired. I had never been told or read in any procedure manual why I was supposed to initial them. I asked my predecessor and he did not know either. I assumed that my name was on the top of the exception report and many other reports like it, not because I was supposed to do anything but in order to keep the lower orders honest. As long as they thought someone was taking action they would carry out the procedures. I thought of explaining this to Roberta but feared she would not understand.

I also told the dealers that they were over the limit with the customer. This happened quite often. The dealers were never happy to be told this. They would scowl when they saw me coming, as if I had been personally responsible for setting the limits. Some of them made cringing excuses and other blustered. As I was only a temporary operations clerk and they were, deep breath, dealers, I found this very satisfactory. It made me feel powerful and important.

Dealers have to have good nerves, a quick brain, a zest for doing deals, and the will to make money for the sake of it. They are highly paid. They earn their money with the profits they make, the stress of their occupation, the money they are trusted with. A dealer cannot usually ruin his employer in seconds, since most banks have adequate checks and controls, but he or she can severely dent its reputation in the market. With a little ingenuity a dealer can line his or her own pockets with no greater punishment, if discovered, than a discreet sacking, quietly, in case the market finds out. Because dealers are judged on their results the dealing community is classless. Those with aptitude, whatever their background or experience or age, are soon accepted and can rise very quickly to responsible and well-paid jobs.

Since continental Europe is an hour ahead, most of them started before eight. Many of the others got in before seven to catch the tail-end of Hong Kong and Singapore. Bursts of intense activity, demanding peak concentration and effort and split second decision-making were interspersed with periods of idleness and boredom. Dealing started in earnest at around eight when the European centres opened. The London market itself was busiest between nine and eleven and then again at three. It also perked up when other international markets opened and closed, especially New York. At these times the atmosphere was electric. They gabbled into their telephones and shouted rates to each other and punched their keyboards with the loudspeakers egging them on like commentators in a betting shop. Lunchtime and late afternoon were usually very dull. The dealers moped and read the paper and boasted of their good deals and brooded quietly on the bad.

They could make a week's profit in a few deals on a Monday morning, close out the position and sit on it until Friday. Or they could lose last month's profit in a single trade and spend the next three weeks trying to claw back the loss. They had immediate feedback on how they had done. The time horizon for most of them was close of business on the same day when they closed out their position.

It was a collaborative effort. No dealer can work effectively on his own. When the market was busy the dealers were constantly calling rates out to each other, backing each other up, calling for help, answering each other's phones, congratulating and commiserating with each other. There was a high level of verbal intimacy. Questions and answers were direct and to the point. There was no time for formality or circumlocution. Communication was frank and open, sometimes to the point of abuse in moments of great tension. A camaraderie develops from interdependence and lack of formality that is vital to their work and which shuts out other groups in the organization. 'The dealers. They're something else. They're a law unto themselves,' is heard in banks all over the world. Intense personal loyalties develop so that if one person leaves to join another bank others will often follow.

Jacques was the Chief Dealer. He had the job of co-ordinating the activity in the room. He set dealing strategies, recommended policies, made sure that the rules and safeguards and limits were kept. He was a Lebanese in his late fifties. He only used his private office to entertain visitors and fire people. Most of the time he sat at the head of the bullion dealing desk. He came into the dealing room at eight, sallow-skinned, slack bellied, bags under his brown, watery eyes, blinking as if he had come from a dark place. He smiled shyly at everyone and greeted those nearest in halting English. He sat down in front of the screen and pressed a few buttons on the keyboard. After the first deal he was transformed. The brown watery eyes narrowed and glittered, the jaw tightened, the slack on his cheeks disappeared. He visibly metamorphosed into a predator.

Tim was the most junior dealer. He looked after overnight sterling, taking in deposits for repayment the next day. He was nineteen and came from South London. He was tall with a shock of spiky blond hair. His passions were soccer and Heavy Metal. He had left school eighteen months before with two indifferent 'A' level passes and had failed a third. The Monday after school finished he started a labouring job for a couple of months. He did not bother to sign on, none of his mates did. He had a couple of weeks holiday. Then he went to an agency in the City. The same day they sent him for an interview as an accounting trainee at a retail store chain. He was told he was too bright for the job. Within a week he had three other job offers. Two were as trainee accountants in banks and the third was a trainee dealer which he accepted. He had been doing it for over a year now and liked it. He seemed good at it. He was numerate and relaxed and sociable and self-confident. In a couple of years he would be earning a very large salary. It was interesting to compare his fortunes with Roy, one of the input clerks. He had graduated from Manchester University with an economics degree at the same time Tim had left school. He spent a year looking for a job up north, any kind of job, and then came to London where he was hired by the bank the day he arrived. He wanted to get into investment analysis but had been turned down several times. He was small and shy and unassertive.

It was a cosmopolitan mix of dealers. We had American and French and Italian and Swiss and Lebanese dealers as well as the Brits, who made up the largest single group. There was an Australian, a Japanese and an Israeli. One of the Americans and two of the French were girls. The Swiss and French were wealthy, middle class, university graduates, owned houses in expensive parts of London and pedigree dogs. They talked French to each other about the quality of last night's snow in Verbier and where you could keep a horse in London. The Lebanese were also wealthy and were the most dedicated to money. They often gathered round a single screen and had vociferous discussions in Arabic. The Americans rented flats in Central London and spent their leisure finding new restaurants. The Brits lived in commuter villages outside London. Their background and education were very different from the Europeans'. Bank dealing rooms have tended to be staffed by school leavers who spent a couple of years as clerks before being promoted. No clique seemed to have much in common with each other. But in working hours they had much more in common with each other than with us.

A young dealer started at the same time that I did. She was half-American, half-French and had worked for the bank in New York. We met at the coffee machine. She was having black no sugar. I concealed my choice of double soup with creamer. She was petite and dark and pretty with neat stylish clothes and scraped-back hair. She had been in New York for five years.

'Why did you come here?' I asked.

'I asked for a transfer. You get too comfortable in New York. I had a job and an apartment and everything material in life. But there is no emotional life in New York. Everyone is very defensive. They live in a hard shell. No feelings, you know? I guess there are better priorities in Europe.'

'How do you like it so far?'

'It's tough. Real tough. I just opened my personal account with the High Street bank. The service was terrible. I waited for ten days but no one notified me that the account was open and a cheque book was waiting. I mean, I am a Yuppie. I have potential. They should take good care of me. In the future I am going to be worth much more. That would never happen in New York.'

I had thought Yuppie was a term of abuse. I would not have expected anyone to stick the label on themselves. It was like puffing your chest out and saying 'I'm a Sloane Ranger,' or 'I'm a Hooray Henry.' When she walked away I was pleased to see the hem of her skirt was coming down at the back.

The Operations Group had a close working relationship with the dealers. We executed the deals which they did, making sure that the money or the commodities they exchanged actually changed hands through the international network of bank accounts. If we bought dollars in exchange for marks from a French bank, we would instruct the bank in Germany, where we had a mark account, to pay the money into the French bank's mark account. We would tell the bank where we had our dollar account to expect the dollars. And we would confirm the deal direct with the French bank. The slightest mistake could send the money to the wrong place, take days to find, and cost far more in interest charges than the profit on the deal. The deals had to be put through the system on the day they were done. The input group was consistently busy throughout the day. They arrived at half-past eight and were often still there at half-past six. The official hours were nine to five.

We were lucky to be upstairs with the dealers. The urgency and immediacy of the dealing room was contagious. It was exciting to be part of it. Most of the Operations staff worked in a green-painted, windowless basement next to the computer room. Pipes ran across the ceiling. Desks were crammed together. The central heating did not work down there so they had portable paraffin heaters. Printers and terminals were not acoustically shielded. It was noisy and stuffy and uncomfortable. There were no lunch or recreation facilities. Physical conditions afforded neither comfort nor status.

There was a mutual dependence between the dealers and Operations. Our work derived directly from theirs. The effectiveness of their work depended on ours. We sat in the same room. We could see and hear their work being done. If we had a question about a deal we could get up and ask or shout if the dealer sat near. They often shouted queries to us or walked over to where we sat. When a dealer had done a few deals he stood up and walked over to my desk with the deal tickets and put them in my in-tray. Relationships were informal, first names for everyone.

Yet there was a yawning chasm between the two groups in terms of pay, status and conditions of work. The lowest paid dealer probably earned twice as much as the highest paid clerk. The lowest paid clerk (me) earned a tenth as much as the highest paid dealer. They were the stars, the prima donnas, we were the stage hands. We came in within an hour of the time they did in the morning, and left two hours later. Our work was a constant treadmill throughout the day, theirs was intermittent. They went out to lunch, often on expenses, we had sandwiches at our desk. We joked and talked among ourselves but never with them, nor did they with us. There was no socializing between the groups after work. During my time in the dealing room I did not come across a single instance, however trivial, of rancour or envy or non-cooperation or ill-feeling or complaint among the clerks. On the contrary, they made what I thought were extraordinary efforts to accommodate the dealers. On two successive Fridays, an hour after cut-off, we accepted without even a ritual murmur deal tickets which dealers had forgotten to write out earlier in the day. They did not even apologise.

I was caught up in this. On reflection I can't think why I didn't tell them to stuff their deal tickets. I am surprised I stuck it for so long. I find money markets fascinating but distasteful, like porno movies or bullfights. I find the mentality of the dealing rooms unpleasant. I feel pity for dealers who spend their lives in a universe dominated by figures and prices and interest rates and gold and silver, completely divorced from the use or meaning of these things. All that technology and human energy with nothing to show. I came out of a day in a dealing room like the Roman soldier who went into the Holy of Holies and found nothing there. This is not a criticism, it is a description of my own feelings. And yet when the last dealer to leave dropped his tickets in the tray on his way out of the door, and it was Friday night and I wanted to go home, I said thank you. And I meant it. I wouldn't have minded had there been more. Indeed I would have taken pleasure in the imposition, showing that I could easily cope with whatever they wanted to give us. It wasn't just pride. There was pleasure in being of service.

One group had much higher status, recognition and reward than the other. I would have predicted the relationship between the two groups to have been marked by jealousy and resentment.

What makes people with little hope of advancement, of inferior status, earning a pittance compared with the people they serve, in 30 per cent more time on the job, with no ties other than a month's notice, willingly and happily dedicate most of their waking hours to making other people's fortunes?

Perhaps it was the excitement of money. Perhaps it was the reflected status of working in the same room. Perhaps it was pride in their own performance, as George Orwell observed in his Paris hotel:

> 'What keeps a hotel going is the fact that employees take a genuine pride in their work, beastly and silly though it is. If a man idles, the others soon find him out and conspire against him to get him sacked. Cooks, waiters and *plongeurs* differ greatly in outlook but they are all alike in being proud of their efficiency.' (George Orwell, *Down and Out in Paris and London.*)

Stress

They were some of the most hard-working and dedicated people I had worked with. Roberta set the tone. She had been with the bank three years. She had been hired as an accounts clerk. The bank was little more than a representative office at that time. She had seven other colleagues. Now there were nearly three hundred and she was in charge of all the dealing room operations. It had been a rapid rise.

'That must have been an interesting time.'

'It was a real learning experience. We invented the whole thing from scratch,' she confided over a doughnut one morning.

'How did you learn? How did you cope?'

'Hard work and common sense. It was a real mess. It still is.'

'What training did you have?'

'Training? When do we have time for training? What sort of training, anyway?'

'Any sort. Systems training or computer training or management training.'

'You must be joking. Here. Your in-tray's full. Come on, John, you're creating a bottleneck. You have to be quicker than this, you know.'

The back-office systems had not kept pace with expansion. The first step to computerization had been an off-the-shelf package bought from a software house that specialized in banks. It had been continually enhanced with add-on programs that were outgrown before they were commissioned. The enhancements had to be run in parallel with the manual system for a few weeks to iron out the bugs, which doubled the work-load. In the first eighteen months Roberta regularly worked from six in the morning until eleven at night.

'It was a goal, wasn't it, to get things sorted out. And it's an achievement when you see it start to work properly. You learn a terrific amount, too. I know it's hard work but I've always enjoyed it. It's going to take another couple of years at least. You get a lot of satisfaction from the achievement. Less so now, though. We seem to be going backwards, or at least standing still.'

She exuded suppressed rage. The indignation she felt at the inefficiency and carelessness and stupidity and ignorance of others was very personal. She had a real talent for spotting mistakes and sloppiness. She was cross with a different person every day. One day it was her boss, the Head of Operations. She had wanted to change the work flow in the investigations section. These are the people who track down missing payments and other errors.

'He just hummed and hahed. I expect to have a boss who I can discuss things with and who'll give me his views and opinions. I put a lot of work into that work flow chart. I was here until eleven three nights. I take my work seriously. He just wasn't interested. Now I've lost all self-confidence, all enthusiasm.' She soon got it back.

On another occasion there was a senior management meeting about limits, the ones written on my dog-eared postcards. Jacques wanted them changed. Roberta was not invited, although she had set up the system and developed the procedure three months before. She had spent three weekends writing out the cards. She found out about it the next day. She was furious.

'I take my work seriously. I like to think I do my work and complete it and achieve something. I worked weekends on this. Saturdays and Sundays, my own time. We don't get overtime. How would you feel? I'm really mad.

We set this up three months ago. Management didn't care. Now they finally had to do something about it. They're squeezed to the wall. We were on at them to do something. The trouble is, management won't stand up to the dealers . . .'

Roberta's deputy was Ronald. He sat downstairs in the basement. He was bustling and bird-like, dressed at the height of youthful fashion. He had a flat-top haircut and baggy jacket and amply cut trousers and black shoes with blue tongues. This may have been because he took the same size as his teenage son. He was in his middle forties. At least twice a day he would report to Roberta's desk for a tongue lashing.

'You seem to get on well with Roberta,' I commented one day when he was waiting for her to come back.

'She's all right. She's a bit of a perfectionist that's all. A stickler for accuracy. She rules with a rod of iron. I catch most of the welly.'

'How long have you worked for her?'

'Since I joined. She took me on nearly three years ago. We've seem some things together. We certainly have seen some things.'

I was surprised that Ronald and the others took so much stick without walking out. I think it was because it was delivered without malice and apparently derived not from personal antagonism but a dispassionate belief in high standards of performance. At first she did not know me well enough to give me the full treatment and also I was older than her, which may have inhibited her usual style. The best time to talk to her was early in the morning before the work-load built up. I bought her doughnuts and sympathized with her problems. I commiserated with her about the long hours and stress of her job. When the pressure was off she was quiet and gauche and shy.

This was not a side of her character that her subordinates usually saw. She was impatient with anyone who did not have her dedication to the job. The most important quality she looked for in her staff was reliability. Roberta carried everyone's sick days and holidays around in her head. She did not need to look them up in the attendance diary. She reminded Ronald about a day off one of the girls had had four months before.

The most recent recruit to Operations was Paul, a young man of about twenty. He had been a Marine until he fell off a helicopter and was invalided out. He loathed office work. He had applied to join the police and was confident he would be accepted. The last hurdle was submitting colour photographs of his tattoos. He had a Marine bulldog on his upper arm and was worried because he had been told a bulldog is a National Front emblem. Nobody minded about the red devil tattooed on his left buttock. One day he asked Roberta a favour. On Friday he was going to a twenty-first on the other side of London. He wanted to leave at six so he could get home and change first. Roberta thought, frowned for a few seconds and then gave her permission. The official leaving time on a Friday was a quarter to five. It must have been a good party because he called in sick on Monday.

'These youngsters,' moaned Roberta. 'He's only been there a month, he's still on probation, and he's had seven days off sick already. Some young people are reliable, they take work seriously, they have it here,' she thumped her chest, 'but others just think it's a job. They'll learn, they have to learn. Now Ronald,' she tapped her forehead with her forefinger, 'doesn't have much up here but he turns up every day without fail. Otherwise I can only rely on two others out of the twenty. If they call in sick it means they're really ill. They still come to work if they have a headache or a runny nose. All right, so you throw up in the toilets, it doesn't stop you doing a day's work.'

Freda from telex had heard that Paul might be leaving. She came to sound Roberta out for a transfer to dealer input. She was about nineteen, coltishly pretty.

'I want to further my career, Roberta.'

'This has to be confidential, Freda. Off the record. Until your boss says you can leave and the General Manager agrees I'm not allowed to talk to you.' She explained bluntly what the job entailed. 'It's not easy. We work long hours. We rotate the jobs. You have to go where you are needed. Every job is important, there are no status differences. The decision whether to apply is up to you.'

Had I been Freda I would have joined Roberta. She seemed very open and direct. You knew where you were with Roberta. And the hours and inconvenience never seem to matter at interview time.

While I was there Roberta arrived at seven and never left before eight in the evening. Sometimes she was there until after nine. I never saw her take more than half an hour for lunch. Ronald worked the same hours. They both commuted for at least three hours a day. They would get home for dinner at about ten, go to bed and be up at six the next morning. Instead of the contractual thirty-five-hour week they worked at least fifty-five hours. By Friday morning they were visibly exhausted.

'I went home last night and Joe was ready to go out,' said Roberta. 'We were only meeting our friends in the pub. We were already an hour late. I went up for a quick bath but I was too tired to come down again. He left on his own. I went straight to bed. I didn't even have any supper. I was asleep when he came in. I had to get up at six this morning to get here.'

'I didn't even see my wife,' replied Ronald. 'It was twelve when I got home last night, she was already asleep. She was still asleep when I left this morning.'

Roberta and Ronald were not paid overtime. They were supervisors. People sometimes refused promotion because the loss of overtime meant a drop in pay. Ronald said he earned less in his first year as Operations Supervisor than he did as a clerk.

'Why do you do it then?' I asked.

'I don't do it for my health, that's for sure,' he said.

Why did they do this to themselves?

Dealing is a stressful occupation. The dealers worked in short, intense bursts. They were constantly on the alert. There was intense pressure to make profits, stay ahead of the game, beat the competition. They knew within seconds or at the end of the day whether they had made or lost money. If they were carrying positions they worried continually about whether to hold or close out. But when they were square or the markets were quiet or there were public holidays in Europe or New York they had little to do. For a couple of weeks over Christmas and the Year End it is very quiet. In many dealing rooms they play cards or go home early when there is nothing to do.

Roberta and Ronald suffered stress of a different kind. They were workaholics. They worked unremittingly for twelve hours a day. They had to finish the day's through-put before they went home. They spent most of their day sorting out a succession of technical and human errors. There was little excitement or glamour or status compared with the dealers. At least on the management floor the material rewards and status compensated in small measure for the detrimental effects on health and family life, but it was curious to see it in the basement. The stress they suffered was unrewarded, unrecorded and much more harmful. Work had alienated them from the rest of their lives.

Who Do You Think You Are?

Jimmy came round with a juicy tit-bit about the General Manager. Jimmy was the internal messenger and the bank driver. ''Ello Girls' was the signal for a thud of print-out to land on the desk or a wodge of brown envelopes to smother the in-tray. He regarded it as part of his job description to cheer people up with jokes and ribaldry and gossip as he made his rounds.

'He tells me yesterday I have to go to the airport this morning to pick up one of the directors from New York. He's coming in about eight but I have to be there at seven just in case. He tells me to go and hire a car. I says what about the bank car? He says I'm using that to come into the office. So I have to go out and hire a car, a BMW, eighty quid plus the VAT and the insurance and everything to pick up this geezer from the airport and take him to his hotel. Eighty quid! You'd think Peterson could have come in on the tube for once. Or spent a fiver on a taxi. Eighty quid! They say we're cutting costs. Look here! Don't use so much toilet paper, they say.'

He pulled a memo out of the pile of papers he was carrying. It reminded staff of the need to cut costs and specifically stated that toilet paper was not to be removed from the toilets and kept in people's desks for use as paper handkerchiefs. Staff with runny noses were expected to provide their own tissues.

'They'll be cutting out the toilet paper altogether next,' said the girl behind me.

'Don't worry. There's plenty of memos. We'll ask

them to type them on soft paper,' said Jimmy.

I am sure the General Manager had very good reasons for not sending the bank car. One of his children had been sick on the back seat or it was covered in dog hairs or his wife was going to the supermarket or the director was known for asking at board meetings why the overseas branches had to have bank cars or he was on the board of General Motors and the car was a Ford. Jimmy had only got half the story. But it was enough to undermine that week's cost-cutting drive.

In the few weeks I was at the company I saw the General Manager once. He was in his mid-forties, tall and imposing. He was walking down a corridor, unsmiling, stern and purposeful. He nodded curtly to me and the others he passed. He rarely came down to our floor. He communicated in laconic, almost cryptic memos and notices. One morning his secretary called our supervisor, saying that the General Manager wanted to see him.

'What's it about? What kind of a mood is he in?' he asked. He spent ten minutes in the lavatory preparing himself. He left looking nervous. He came back after half an hour looking smug and serious. We all waited anxiously to hear what it was about. After a pause for effect, looking at the telephone messages on his desk, he told us.

'He wanted to know what I was doing this year about the presents for the kids' Christmas party. He's going to be Santa Claus.'

'Him? Santa Claus?' hooted our youngest colleague.

I contrasted this with the informal style I cultivated at the bank I managed. I made a point of being seen on every floor at least twice a week. I thought I had a good feel for what was going on. I tried to remember every one's Christian names. I made funny speeches at the Christmas party. I thought I got on well with people, made them relaxed. I brought a sense of fun to the organization, a touch of healthy informality. When I started temping I bought some of my former colleagues a drink and asked them how I had appeared to them.

'You always had something on your mind.'

'I never knew you had a sense of humour.'

'You often looked bored.'

'Formal.'

'Distant.'

'Aloof.'

'Typical English manager.'

If this wasn't surprise enough I then asked them what they looked for in a boss. Out of a score of people half used the same word: royalty. Most of the others used a similar analogy. They ranged from a senior bank officer to a messenger and included both men and women, Americans and Brits, people I knew well and those I did not. They looked for dignity and authority and distance.

'People should be in awe of the manager.'

'You were just a figurehead.'

'There's got to be someone who lays down the law.'

'It was a good sign when they were nervous when they saw you.'

'You've got to show authority.'

'You didn't have any charisma.'

'Your predecessor was all-American and laid back. That's no good.'

'There's got to be respect.'

'You shouldn't have made your own tea.'

'You didn't impact us much at all. It's your immediate boss who matters most.'

The word that people used most often after 'royalty' was 'character', not in the moral sense, but in phrases like 'he was a character, he was'. There was nostalgia for an ex-Bank of England man, who told ribald stories about the Deputy Governor and kept a shrunken penis in a lacquer box to shock spinsters. And a manager with a wooden leg that he would take off in the middle of meetings and use to bang the table. And a manager famous for his regular Wednesday afternoon tantrum.

There was a general regret for the replacement of 'characters' by faceless bureaucrats and conformist Yuppies. I was not a character. Riding a bike to the office in track suit and balaclava was only undignified.

I thought that temping was a good opportunity to try out a few other characters.

'So what do you do, John?' asked Jenny.

I leant back in my chair and put my left thumb in the fob pocket of my purple brocade waistcoat. I took the treacly black Brazilian cigar out of my mouth and puffed a smoke ring to the ceiling, watching it curl and dissolve before it hit the textured ceiling tiles.

'Oh, a little bit of this, a little bit of that.'

Another day, another Jenny. I sat on the edge of my chair hiding my chewed fingers in clenched fists, one knee jigging nervously up and down. I was wearing my best suit trousers with my best suit jacket. They were from different suits. I steeled myself to look her in the eye, but I could not help looking down again at the application form in front of her.

'I'll do anything. Really. Anything at all.'

I strode up to the desk in tight jeans, a shiny borrowed ski jacket and a healthy glow from taking the dog for walks in Brockwell Park.

'So you like paragliding and downhill racing, John.'

'Right on, Jenny.' It's true. I always look out for them on Grandstand.

'You want office work?'

'Between seasons, right? Makes a change.'

So who shall I be today? Will it be the blue cord jacket, a packet of Gitanes and a dab of Pernod behind the ears? The Hush Puppy suedes and a blazer and a dark blue tie with red-lightning zig-zags? The gold-rimmed tinted glasses and the leather jacket? The Chester Barry suit too tight to button across the middle and the string vest peeping through the straining buttons of the frayed Gieves and Hawkes shirt? How about a clerical collar? A white stick?

Only once was I rumbled. I had just been telling the person behind me about the pitfalls of professional barracuda fishing off the Florida Coast. A girl who had been a colleague thirteen years before came up to my desk. She had not changed at all. I wanted to sink through the floor. I prayed that my beard and my lowly status would disguise me.

'Hello! Remember me?'

'No. Should I?'

'I recognize you! I've got a picture of you at home. I was looking at it the other day. I used to work in Cash. You're wearing a maroon velvet suit. Well I never. I'll bring it in.'

She went away.

'I thought you'd never worked in banking before,' said the person behind me.

'Did I say that? I meant I'd never done this sort of banking before.'

'I thought you were in Mexico in the early seventies.'

'I was. I went there on holiday.'

She brought the picture in the next day. She was wearing a long black dress set off with a spray of orchids. My maroon velvet suit looked terrible. It must have been a Christmas party but I couldn't remember anything about the occasion. I was grinning and had my arm round my secretary. Neither of us recognized the other man.

'Why did you keep the photograph?' I asked, flattered that I had been secretly desired all those years.

'I always loved that dress. Don't you think it's nice? It's the only picture I've got of it.'

She promised to come back the next day so we could go out to lunch. But she must have found out that I was a temp. She was now an Assistant Vice-President. I only saw her once again, in the corridor. She smiled briefly and passed on.

I made it a rule never to tell lies. I always answered direct questions with the truth. But they were rarely asked. People drew their own conclusions. I started at one office the day after the launching party of my second novel. The signs of a good time were etched all over my face. I went to lunch early.

'Where did you go, John?' asked Brenda.

'The Samuel Pepys. Hair of the dog, Brenda.'

'I thought so. There's more in you than there is in Watneys.'

For the rest of my stay I was an alcoholic. It explained why a reasonably well-spoken, middle-aged man was doing temporary clerical work and had not held a job down for more than a few weeks.

In another office we were discussing insider dealing. There was some uncertainty about what insider dealing was, which I attempted to clear up with a case history or two. I pointed out that it had only been a criminal offence for less than five years. Not so long ago one of the perks of being Something in the City was knowing what the ordinary punter had no means of knowing. It was considered no worse than stable lads putting a few bob on what they saw at the morning canter. Now, all of a sudden, you got sent to jail. For the next few days I noticed that conversations would veer towards discussions of the prison system, on which my opinions were highly valued. One nervous lady would not stay alone in the same room with me.

After a few different jobs I discovered that I did not have to invent identities for myself. They were invented for me. After a very short time people picked up a handful of clues which they used to support their expectations of what I was, how I got there, how I would behave. They behaved towards me accordingly. And even more fascinating was that I began to respond involuntarily in the light of their expectations. When I was judged a boozer I felt like drinking at lunchtime. When I was judged a felon I felt guilty and introverted. When I was judged a shiftless good-for-nothing I slacked and made mistakes. I was not consciously playing up to them. It usually took some time to realize what I was supposed to be.

In some places I volunteered the information that I was a writer working on a book about office life. Only one person clammed up. A few did not believe me, a few were amused. Most people wanted to tell me their life stories. They wanted to be in the book. Do you want to be a goodie or a baddie? I asked. They did not mind as long as they were characters.

I found none of my temporary characters as hard to play as that of a manager. The expectations of what I was supposed to be, including my own preconceptions of how I should behave, were immensely strong from all sides. They conflicted with each other and also with the idea I carried round of the 'real' me. This was more stressful than work-load or responsibility or any of the other conventional sources of stress. When I left the bank the biggest weight I felt lifted from my shoulders had nothing to do with the work itself, it was the feeling of having to wear several different identities. It is hard at any level of the hierarchy. One evening I sat before the fireplace of a small hotel bar with two men who had been Executive Vice-Presidents of a once great American bank. One had taken the other's job but they had remained friends. They were now with other companies.

'When I told him I was quitting it felt like an immense burden being lifted.'

'I know what you mean. I felt ten years younger.'

'You got torn all ways. You could never do what was really you, you know.'

'You'd go into a staff meeting and have to explain all that stuff and you knew it was crap.'

'You know what the worst is? Why I really quit? I hadn't the nerve to tell the people who worked for me that I didn't believe what I was telling them. And I didn't have the guts to tell the Chairman he was talking bullshit.'

Big Bang Excitement

The call came on Monday morning. A High Street bank had acquired a firm of stockbrokers and a firm of jobbers in the Big Bang. They were in the process of merging them with their own merchant bank and investment department. At the same time they had installed a new computer system to keep track of their share deals. It was like doing brain surgery at the same time as a heart and lung transplant. Their share dealing system was on the point of collapse. Millions of pounds and thousands of share deals had disappeared into the hyperactive gut of the main computer and was being regurgitated as half-masticated rubbish. The directors, the auditors, the bank inspectors were in uproar. Panic and scandal scented the air like sulphur. The bank had already hired three different firms of accountants. Even this was not enough. They wanted more qualified and part-qualified accountants. Could I start right away? To the rescue. It was the summons I had been waiting for. Yes, I was part-qualified. Sort of. I had done a term of elementary book-keeping at a business school in France in 1969. It was French book-keeping but the idea was the same. The bottom number on the right-hand side is always the same as the bottom number on the left-hand side. Yes, I knew all about share dealing systems. I've got two hundred British Telecom shares to prove it. Yes, I worked in a bank. And yes, I knew all about systems fiascos. I have personally contributed to several in my time.

There was a double bonus in my new job. My

employer was not the bank itself but Waterhouse, Lybrand and Mitchell, the prestigious firm of accountants they had hired to sort out the mess. Not only was I getting to the white-hot core of the Big Bang but I was going to be an accountant for a few weeks. In my old bank we called accountants Bean Counters, although not to their faces. It was a favourite expression of the Deputy Chairman who had come up through the marketing side. Beneath the mild contempt was an undercurrent of fear. The bean counters were remorseless realists. Not for them the heady excitement of done deals and whipping the competition and roping in new customers.

They were recording angels, quiet, soft-spoken introverts, their fingers wandering over clicking calculators and writing down strings of neat little numbers. They were unmoved by the cut and thrust of the market, the triumphs and disasters of the moment. They lived in the past, days, months, years behind the rest of us. They constructed marvellous and complicated and confusing lattices of ledgers and journals and accounts which seemed to bear little resemblance to the world in which everyone else lived. My heart sank whenever a bean counter wanted to talk to me. Even if my conscience was clear about my expense returns or the petty cash or overdue interest payments on my mortgage I dreaded the tedium and embarrassment of not understanding what they were talking about and the compounded confusion when it was explained to me. I was curious to know how they thought and worked. With luck I would get the chance to shove a sheet of closely typed figures under the nose of some supercilious and innumerate marketing type.

I had to look the part. I had a haircut, dusted off my best blue suit and crested tie, bought a stripy shirt with a white collar. With a felt tip I wrote a small D, standing for debit, on my little fingernail of my left hand. C, standing for credit, on my right hand would have been a dead give-away so I left the fingernail clean and relied on my powers of deduction. Debits on the left, Credits on the right. Or is it the other way round?

I arrived at the bank at lunchtime and took the lift to Finance. I walked into a large office full of young men in stripy shirts and red braces poring over large analysis sheets. A scruffy man in shirt sleeves with a beard and a beer-belly and jogging shoes followed me out of the lift. With finely tuned writer's perspicacity I deduced instantly that he was either a computer whizz brought in to help sort out the program or a messenger delivering stationery. I asked him if he knew the Senior Project Manager.

'That's me,' he said.

With the little finger of my left hand tucked into my palm I introduced myself as his new part-qualified accountant.

'Great,' he grinned. 'My name's Henry. Welcome to the High Street Merchant Bank. You can put your coat in that cupboard, the toilets are first right down the corridor and the coffee machine is the other way.' I was overcome. I thought of asking whether he mistook me for someone else, an accountant from his firm, for example, and not a temp. He clapped his hands and everyone looked up.

'This is John. He's helping us out for a few weeks. Make sure you introduce yourselves to him.' There was a chorus of hellos. He then took me to an empty desk in the centre of the room, opened the top drawer to make sure it was stocked with pens and pencils. 'Spare stationery in the cabinet over there. I do hope you enjoy it here. It's a challenge, but it's fun. If you have any problems at all, come and see me. Right, I'll take you to Graham, the manager you'll be working for.'

Graham had a shock of blond hair and bright blue eyes. He was in his mid-twenties. He had a crazed, startled look as he gazed intently at a massive print-out on his desk, as though it were about to spring the secret of the Universe upon him. He handed me two folders. One was a procedure manual for the bank's new back-office system for keeping track of its share dealings, which they called Miracle, and the other a description of Talisman, the Stock Exchange's system.

'Here. Spend a couple of hours with these. Get to know the two systems before you start. It's our job to reconcile the two. We have some boring tasks to do. But it helps if you understand why you're doing them.'

This was disconcerting. I was used to being ignored when I started a new job. I was used to being the invisible temp. I was used to being an extension of the telephone or the photocopier or the terminal. I was used to being kept in the dark. Now I had the unusual experience of being treated like a colleague. I was surprised to feel resentment. It was partly because it didn't make as good a story for my book. If people in offices were warm and friendly and efficient and hard-working there would be nothing to write about. But it was also because I did not want to get sucked in to their project. What did I care if their computer system was up the spout? It was none of my business. I was only a temp, a good day's work for a good day's pay and home at half-past five. It was somehow threatening to be made to feel involved.

Two young people sat at the next desk. They both wore plain blue pressed suits and crisp white shirts that made me feel scruffy. They both had print-outs in front of them. One of them read out numbers which the other one checked. They nodded and introduced themselves. Julia had a Scottish accent, Tom was a South Londoner. I discovered later that she had a chemistry degree from Oxford and he had a physics degree from Cambridge. They were trainee accountants at Waterhouse, Lybrand and Mitchell. They continued chanting for the rest of the afternoon, taking it in turns. At first I found it distracting while I struggled with the intricacies of matched and unmatched bargains, deliveries and settlements. Then it became soothing, a numbing, mysterious litany.

'Don't you find it boring?' I interrupted after an hour.

'Not as boring as some of the things we've done,' said Julia.

'You just let yourself sink into it,' said Tom.

'How long have you being doing it?'

'Four days. We should be finished the day after tomorrow.' I could see the next three weeks stretching into the distance like an infinite desert. I was too old to spend fifteen days of my life intoning numbers like a human prayer wheel. And what if I was given one of the more boring jobs?

'How are you getting on?' asked Graham. 'Any questions?'

'Why is the bank system called Miracle?'

'Because it's a miracle if it works.'

The Stock Exchange's system, Talisman, records the deals done by all the stockbrokers and jobbers. There is a large computer in the Stock Exchange building. Stockbrokers and jobbers have access to the computer through terminals in their own offices. When a stockbroker strikes a bargain with a jobber, both of them input separately details of the transaction. If the computer finds that the two sets of details are identical it is called a matched bargain. If the details are different or missing it is an unmatched bargain and the two sides have to straighten out the differences before they settle up. All the companies in the system get a print-out which lists the deals they have reported.

Miracle was supposed to tie in with Talisman as well as producing information for the bank's own use. For example, it was meant to allocate bargains to different accounts. It was meant to match up a customer's payment for shares with the bargain in which the shares were bought for him. It was meant to highlight unmatched bargains. And so on. But this was not happening properly. Deals had gone missing or were in the wrong accounts. To find out what had gone astray the first job was to reconcile Talisman with Miracle for the past six months. This is what Julia and Tom were doing, deal by deal. And this is what I had been hired to do.

I was assigned to work with Seamus. We asked to work in a small room next to the main office with Laura, Henry's secretary. She was glad of the company. Seamus's excuse was that we did not want to distract the others. The real reason was so that we were not under the eyes of Henry or Graham. Seamus had done five years training in a Dublin accountancy firm. He was an expert at enlivening boring jobs. I asked him what the difference was between working in Dublin and working in London.

'The crack. Here there's no crack at all. God, in Ireland there's crack all the time. Here they wouldn't know what crack was if it bit them on the leg.'

'What's crack?' I asked..

'What did I tell you?' he said.

For the first couple of days we had plenty of crack while we ticked off Talisman against Miracle. We told jokes and stories all day, breaking off into strings of numbers if anyone came near or looked our way.

'I had an auntie in Acocks Green, one two seven nine. She either liked people or she hated them, three four one five. She kept two sets of rosary beads, five five six two. One black one white, six two four three. Every night she prayed for those she liked on the white beads, nine five four one, and then on the black beads prayed for terrible things to happen to the others, five six nine nine. She was a very religious person one three three three.'

'I had an aunt in Westport who was bent double with arthritis, four four seven six. When she died they had to tie her down on the bed when they laid her out so she'd lie flat, eight four three one. My cousin Sean hid under the bed before the wake, five one zero zero. When everyone arrived he cut the rope round her chest, zero nine two six. The corpse sat up and everyone ran out of the room in a panic, eight eight six six . . .'

If we thought we were falling behind the others we would put on a spurt of number chanting and then relapse into conversation. We would always try to look as though we were working. It was an immature and probably unnecessary subterfuge. It is perfectly reasonable to do long boring jobs in spurts with breaks for rest. It had the thrill of talking in the back of the class.

'The difference between manual work and office work, one one two three, is that labourers are paid to work and clerks are paid to look as though they're working.'

The work was insufferably boring. By eleven in the morning my eyes and legs and back and stomach ached and I wanted to stand up on the desks and scream. There were another eight hours to endure. It was entirely unskilled work. There was nothing to give it meaning or dignity. I was not learning anything, contributing anything, improving anything. Conversation with Seamus died away, smothered by a blanket of boredom. I could not let my mind wander away to other things, as one can in boring manual work. We had to concentrate hard since a single mistake would make the whole job meaningless. There was no physical effort or skill required. At least doing video input for the share bonanza I could take pride in dexterity. We took it in half-hour turns to call the numbers. We were both hoarse. We abandoned the bingo caller's jocular monotone and conserved our voices by whispering.

The only respite was a walk through the main office and down the corridor to the coffee machine. We rationed our trips to one an hour. On the first day we went every half an hour and by the afternoon felt sick and dehydrated. There was a choice of eight beverages contained in inverted plastic bottles. You put the cup under a bottle and pressed a button to release a dose of powder. You then put the cup under a funnel of hot or cold water and filled it up. You stirred it with a plastic stick with a slit in the bottom. For a hot drink you put one cup inside another otherwise you burnt your fingers. To alleviate the monotony I tried each beverage in turn.

There was a slight difference in taste between them but not enough to make me feel less bored. So I tried mixing them. Coffee and chocolate is nice. Vegetable soup and non-dairy creamer is nice. Fizzy orange and lemon tea with extra sugar in hot water is borderline. Tea and oxtail soup is to be avoided. Cold cocoa and Ribena is disgusting. Seamus stuck to tea. He had never tasted coffee, they never had it in the house in Ireland. Tea and Guinness and whiskey and poteen were his only drinks.

Laura, the secretary, was a temp too. She was tall and well-groomed and well-spoken. She had also been surprised by Henry's welcoming reception on the day she arrived. She was more suspicious than I was.

'They must have had trouble keeping secretaries,' she confided. She commiserated with our boredom. Her first task had been to type a massive report of several hundred pages, illustrated with tables and figures. Henry had dictated it all into a machine. It had taken her ten days sitting at the word processor with headphones on her ears for eight hours a day.

'That must have been terrible.'

'It was the most boring thing I have ever done,' she said. 'After two days I couldn't get his voice out of my head. It seemed to be coming from somewhere inside me. It was still talking to me when I went to bed at night. That wore off, thank goodness. I was worried I was going mad. Then on the second week I started to get flashbacks to my childhood. I would be typing away and suddenly I would experience something I had completely forgotten about, things that happened when I was a little girl. My dad pushing me on the swing. Going to the zoo with the school. At first I just saw them in pictures but then I heard the sounds coming over Henry's voice. In the end I could taste and smell things I had completely forgotten about.'

'That must have been very frightening.'

'It wasn't at all. They made me very happy. I didn't want them to stop. Like nice dreams when you wake up. I miss it now. I wonder what caused it.'

'You were dying,' said Seamus, 'dying of boredom. Your life was flashing before your eyes.'

'You were asleep,' I ventured. 'You were typing in your sleep. You really were dreaming. It was like hypnosis.'

'My friend says it's the rays from the screen and the tiny charges of electricity in the headphones that stimulate the memory banks in the brain. She says audiotyping can give you hallucinations like a drug. It can cause brain damage.'

'The screens are dangerous for women, anyway,' said Seamus. 'In some offices the women wear aprons like radiographers. Against cancer and miscarriages.'

'There's no protection against boredom,' said Laura.

After lunch on Friday Henry went round with a clipboard checking who would be coming in on Saturday and Sunday. Julia and Tom and Seamus promised to come in at nine. The thought of spending a weekend ticking off numbers and mixing cocktails at the coffee machine filled me with dread and loathing. I rehearsed a little speech. I had never worked on a weekend in my life and I didn't intend to start now. I thought there was more to life than making money. I had a life to live. I had other interests, family, commitments. Henry turned to me.

'Sorry, John. We won't be needing you over the weekend.'

I felt resentful for the rest of the afternoon.

In the old days, banks and stockbrokers and jobbers were independent from each other by law and custom. Jobbers bought shares in companies from stockbrokers and traded them among themselves and sold them back to the stockbrokers at a profit. Stockbrokers were the only ones allowed to deal with the jobbers. They did this on behalf of banks and companies and private individuals.

High Street banks were not allowed to deal in shares for their own account in case they undermined their own financial stability by speculating. Companies who borrowed from the

banks and gave them confidential information were also happy that the same bank was not dealing in their shares.

When a company wants its shares traded on the Stock Exchange it usually goes to a merchant bank for advice. As well as new share issues, merchant banks carry out mergers and acquisitions for clients. In the old days, High Street banks could own merchant banks or set them up from scratch but most of the famous names were independent.

Then came the Big Bang. The laws and regulations that kept banks and merchant banks and stockbrokers and jobbers separate were abolished. The reason for sweeping them away had nothing to do with the reason for having them in the first place, which was to make a fair and orderly market that safeguarded the probity and financial stability of the various institutions. The reason was to make London an international centre for dealing in shares.

Over the past few years, the market in stocks and shares and other securities like government bonds and Eurobonds has become increasingly international. To play in the international market a trader has to have the capital to deal large amounts of stock. It has to have the people and offices to sell shares not only in London but in Geneva and Chicago and Hong Kong. The skills needed to compete in the international markets were divided up between different types of company. So the City was deregulated. High Street banks with capital and an international presence were allowed to buy stockbrokers and jobbers and merchant banks. There was a spate of mergers. Foreign banks took part as well. Only a few institutions stood aloof. Banks can now carry out all the operations involved in buying and selling shares under one roof.

Other constraints were swept away, too. Fixed commissions were abolished so that brokers and banks compete among each other. Trading does not have to be done on the floor of the Stock Exchange, it can be done over the phone. There are no set hours for trading because there is a stock market open somewhere in the world almost all the time.

As if deregulation were not enough, the Stock Exchange and the other participants in the market automated their dealing procedures at the same time. They are now plugged into a network of computers and screens and terminals. They can quote prices to each other and strike bargains and issue confirmations at the touch of a few keys in their own offices.

The chaos and uncertainty and change and anxiety and risks of the Big Bang made headlines and are likely to continue in the indefinite future. The scale and the timing of the changes in the City are astonishingly bold for an industry that was supposed to be jellied in tradition and amateurishness. It will take years before the business implications are fully realized.

But the impact on the people involved has been immediate. People of different professions and backgrounds and experience and culture have suddenly been thrown together. People who grew up in cosy, clubby, old-boyish partnerships are suddenly part of large bureaucracies. People who were used to comfortable procedures and forms and handbooks find themselves next to people used to thinking on their feet and making split-second decisions. People used to doing things on the nod from the senior partner now have to use forms and go through channels and committees. People used to cartel and monopoly and tradition have been pitched suddenly into the free market. People who had competed for generations find themselves on the same side. People who joined old-established British firms when they left school are dealing with American or Australian or German bosses . . .

The success of the City in competing in the international market does not depend on how good the computer systems are or how sharp the dealers or how clever the analysts. It depends on how well the managers in the City cope with the effect of change on the people at all levels of their companies. Before they can cope with it they have to understand it.

The Will To Win

Seamus and I finished our ticking back and I was given a new task. When a deal was done it was entered into the computer. The customer, the amount, the number of shares bought or sold were recorded under a deal number. The same information was recorded in a different ledger under the name of the client. When the client paid for shares this information was entered into both ledgers and the deal was closed. For reasons which I could not discover, sometimes information got into the client ledger without getting into the ticket ledger or into the ticket ledger without getting into the client ledger. It was my job to look through a year-end print-out of the client ledger to see who had not paid for their shares. Then I had to check the deal ledger to see if the print-out was correct, that in fact we had not received the money. Then I was to make out an Aged Debtors List. ('Aged' refers to the debts not the debtors.) This would enable the auditors to calculate a bad debt provision.

'I'm to exclude money that the client ledger says has not been received but the ticket ledger says has been received.'

'Correct.'

'But what about money that the client ledger says has been received but the deal ledger says has not been received?'

'We don't worry about that, either.'

'Why?'

'Because it wouldn't show up on the client ledger. The client ledger would show it as paid.'

'Even though we haven't received the money?'

'Right.'

'Isn't that a bad debt?'

'Not if it doesn't show on the client ledger.'

'Ah.'

If you are confused by this dialogue, think what I felt.

Miracle did not describe real life. It was an analogy, a human invention that tried to make sense of imponderable confusion, like the Theory of Relativity or Money Supply or the Apostles' Creed. What I was doing was not finding out how much money clients owed the bank. I was making sure two sets of computer entries matched. Any resemblance to reality was coincidental. In the absence of reconciled bank accounts it was impossible to check whether the deal ledger or the client ledger were correct. The job of Henry and his team was not to find out what had happened when the shares were bought and sold. This was a by-product. The prime concern was not that the information was wrong, but that it was inconsistent. Hours of laborious work and conjecture and discussion were devoted to how Miracle worked, how its various routines and sub-routines meshed in with each other, why some print-outs had this data and others that, what were the checks and balances. It was like deciphering an ancient text, a riddle, a fiendish puzzle of enormous scope and complexity.

Miracle had been created by the High Street Bank's computer staff and the computer consultancy arm of yet another firm of accountants. They helped us all they could, but even they did not understand why their creation behaved the way it did. The best we could do was cobble together some sort of tidy explanation and hope that the errors we had not found, and did not wish to find, cancelled each other out.

I asked Graham why Miracle was such a fiasco.

'It was put together in a hurry. Between acquiring the brokers and the Big Bang last October there were only a few months. The management thought like most managements that you can solve a problem by throwing money at it. But the worst mistake was asking systems designers and programmers and consultants to build it. They are the last people you want to build a computer system.'

'Who should? Accountants?'

'The end users. They didn't ask the people who used the terminals and the print-outs. Management told the consultants what they wanted. The consultants had their own idea of what was needed. Nobody asked the users. Not only do you get a poor system but when it was installed the users didn't understand it and had no motivation to make it work. One of the problems with Miracle is that the data is not being input correctly. It happens all the time. It's happening all over the City. Miracle is not the worst. It's typical.

'What you should do is design systems from the end and work back. First you ask end users, down to clerks and secretaries, to design the print-outs and screens they want. Then you check these with accountants and auditors and anyone else you can think of who might use the output. Then you look for the information you need. Then you design the system.'

'But it's extremely tedious if you're a user to try and imagine what you will need in two years time, down to the last decimal point.'

'I didn't say it was easy. As the project grows so do the specifications. It takes a long time and the end result is never perfect. People forget things. The situation changes, the business moves on, but you narrow the scope of disaster.'

Henry had a different view.

'It's not a fiasco. All the books and the business schools say you should consult the users and work backwards and so on. What happens then is that you overdesign it. You wait for years for an enormous all-embracing system that's out of date before it's installed. But in real life you can't wait three years. You have to have something tomorrow. So you throw something up, see how it works and then mend it. You do your development live. That way you find out what's really essential. It's cheaper to get us in for a month to sort out a half-baked effort than to go through a big rigmarole. Suck it and see.'

The basic difference between Graham's strategy and Henry's was one of temperament.

Apart from trying to find several hundred million pounds the bank couldn't account for Henry was also advising management on wider issues of how to restructure the new organization. The idea was to merge the parts of the stockbroker and jobber they had acquired with the bank's unit trust and make a new company to be called High Street Financial Services. The Chief Executive of the new organization was Reginald, seconded from the parent bank. He was about fifty. He was tall and erect and held his head stiffly. He had either been a Guards Officer or suffered a whiplash injury. He drove to work in a Range Rover which he parked next to my bicycle in the loading bay at the side of the building. He changed out of green wellies into shiny black shoes to match his shiny Brylcreemed hair. In bad weather he did not change but wore the wellies in the office. Twice a day he came into our office and stalked through us to Henry's desk, looking neither right nor left, brandishing pieces of paper and requesting advice. His way of taking advice was to tell Henry what he had concluded and ask for an opinion. Henry would only go to Reginald's office for formal meetings, in honour of which he did up his tie and put on his jacket.

After one such meeting in Reginald's office Henry asked Seamus and me to leave the room as he had a very confidential memo to dictate to Laura.

'Open management, huh?' said Seamus. I went back to the first desk I had been given, next to Julia and Tom. Half an hour later Laura brought the memo out to Henry, holding it to her chest. Henry scribbled on it and took it back to her, holding it to his chest. Then he went out for lunch.

I was browsing on the *Financial Times* and a hot samosa when Laura came out of her room. She saw that most of the desks were empty, including Henry's. She came up to me.

'Can you read this word?' she pointed to Henry's extrovert scrawl on the second page of the memo.

'It looks like insolvency to me. Let's have a look at the rest, see what makes sense.'

'That's a good idea.'

I turned to the first page. It was crisp and to the point. The auditors were adamant that despite the clean-up we were doing they would qualify the accounts because of inadequate financial and accounting controls. A million or so would have to be spent on a new internal system. There were unexplained losses of over ten million pounds in the broking business. The company as it now stood was technically insolvent. It contravened the Stock Exchange liquidity requirements. On reorganization the parent High Street Bank would have to inject at least fifteen million pounds of new capital. It seemed that what they had paid to acquire brokers and jobbers and merchant banks before the Big Bang was just seed money.

'I think the word is inadequate, Laura.'

'Thanks, John. He needs this by two.'

By the time Henry came back from lunch the memo was ready. He gave a copy to Graham and told him to be careful with it, to lock it away in his case, it was highly confidential.

I was familiar with the experience of a large regional American bank when the Big Bang merger fever started. They were approached by a large firm of stockbrokers who asked whether they would like to buy them. The Chairman and the Deputy Chairman flew over to London for secret meetings, the senior partners went to America. They had a code name for the project. Swat teams of analysts and strategic planners and accountants and other bean counters made projections and studies. They danced round each other for months. It was clear why the brokers wanted to be bought. They needed a heavy capital injection to survive in the new-look deregulated market. The partners would be very rich men overnight. But it was hard to see what was in it for the bank. They gazed at financial projections and watched their competitors scramble for partners. They tried to discover the logic behind what they were doing. They looked hard for a convincing, quantifiable rationale for why they should join in. The general drift of what was going on in London was obvious and the intention of the City in speeches and articles was clear, but there were very few hard facts on which to make a decision.

'Where are the numbers, for Chrissake?' was the plaintive cry from the executive suite. But there weren't any. How do you quantify what doesn't exist yet? So the bank did nothing. And saved themselves some money.

In the middle of the afternoon Reginald stalked through our office in his wellies and stood by Henry's desk. He had to go to Head Office in the morning to explain the confidential memo to the Chief Executive of the High Street Bank. He was probably feeling like a Burgher of Calais after the nooses had been handed round. Oblivious of the flapping ears of the menials around him he poured out his worries to Henry.

'If you were him, what would you say? Fifteen million quid new capital. Talk about a pig in a poke. What will the board say?'

'I'd ask what I got for my money,' said Henry.

They went through the details of the memo. Then Reginald stood up straight and seemed to notice the rest of us for the first time. He looked down his patrician nose at Henry. He threw his shoulders back.

'We'll make a go of it. We've bought it, we've got it and now we'll make it work. We'll make it profitable. I'm sure we will. We always have. That's the way we've always done things.'

Several weeks later I was in a pub in the City. Standing

next to me at the bar was a man I recognized from when I was a bank manager. He was in the International Department of the High Street Bank. He had nothing to do with the Merchant Bank or Financial Services. I asked him how things were going.

'Pretty good. You remember that bank we bought in the States? I'm working on that mess at the moment.'

'How is it going?'

'You know how much money we lost. It's no bed of roses, that's for sure.'

'Will it work out?'

'We've got it and we'll make it work. We'll make it profitable. I'm sure we will. We always have. That's the way we've always done things.' His profession of faith was either a coincidence or it permeated the whole organization.

The High Street Bank has just announced record profits. It forecasts that its Merchant Bank will be in the black next year. Other competitor banks are getting out of the business. The regional American bank is doing worse and worse each quarter.

Strategic planning, decision analysis, environmental forecasts, five-year targets, market niches, product profiles and all the other tools of professional management are worth nothing without the determination to succeed.

Love

Henry came into our room to dictate a memo to Laura. Seamus and I eavesdropped but without much satisfaction since it was addressed to all of us in the Project Team.

'First of all I should like to thank all of you for the effort you have put into the project over the past few weeks. New paragraph. The purpose of this note is to update you on what is happening around the bank and to let you know how your work is fitting in with the overall scheme . . .'

'What does he want?' muttered Seamus, frowning.

'Since we started four weeks ago we have between us examined nearly fifteen thousand share deals, the gross value of which is in excess of seven hundred million pounds . . .'

'Why is he telling us all this?' whispered Seamus.

'We can now reconcile all the activity for the two week period following the Big Bang on 27 October. When we started there were nearly a thousand deals of more than ten thousand pounds which no one understood or which had been lost in the system. Your efforts have cleared all but a handful of these . . .'

'Is it us he's talking about?'

'The new Issues Account should have had a nil balance. This account receives money from customers for New Issues, principally British Gas, in return for delivery of the stock. Unfortunately there were several thousand items unaccounted for and twenty million pounds outstanding . . .'

'They'll be letting us go on Friday. That's what all this is leading up to. You'll see.'

'The Bank accounts had not been reconciled for months. Five million pounds were unaccounted for . . .'

'That'll teach them to fill in the stubs.'

'We are now in a position to consider how we amend Miracle to increase the volume through the back office . . .'

'Scrap the bloody thing.'

'As you may well be aware, in addition to ourselves we are inundated with auditors from Marwick, Haskins and Whinney. The bulk of the audit work needs to be completed by the 12 January. That is why there are substantial overtime opportunities!'

'You see the looks you get if you want to get home early.'

'Graham and I are currently working out what work will be required thereafter and we shall be discussing with each of you how you will fit in to this . . .'

'What did I tell you? Cards on Friday.'

'Conclusion, underlined, new paragraph. I think you have all done an excellent job and each and every one of you has contributed to the foundations on which High Street Financial Services will now be able to build a profitable business.'

'What's he talking about?'

'This is excellent management, Seamus,' I whispered. 'He's thanking us for a specific contribution. He's not just patting us on the back but praising specific achievements. He's telling us how important the job is. He's giving us as much information about the company as he can, even though it's not directly relevant to our tasks. He's putting our menial ticking off into its overall strategic context. He is establishing target dates. He is outlining what still needs to be done. He's promising individual consultation about our specific jobs. He's involving us in his own preoccupations. By a memo to everyone he reinforces the group as well as its individual components. Don't you know how unusual this is?'

‘How do you want it signed?’ asked Laura.

‘Love Henry,’ said Henry.

‘I beg your pardon?’

‘Love Henry.’

‘Love?’

‘Yes, Love. What’s wrong with that?’

‘I just thought . . . I’ve never seen that before on a memo.’

‘Does he think we’re poofters?’

‘Seamus?’

‘Yes, John?’

‘I don’t think you’re familiar with Open Management.’

‘If that means being lovey-dovey with everyone I don’t want to. Open or shut they want their pound of flesh.’

The memo, with love from Henry, and much more detail than I have reported, was circulated the next day. It was read avidly. I heard no-one comment about it or discuss it, among themselves or with Henry. But it was carried round in handbags and inside pockets and for the next few days people would take it out and refresh their memories. I caught Seamus reading it over a sandwich the following week. I knew from my own experience Henry was longing to know what effect it had and would be denied that satisfaction. That kind of communication is rarely two-way, which is a pity. Without feedback managers get discouraged and stop writing chatty memos and newsletters.

On Friday lunchtimes we went to the pub for mugs of beer and wine paid for by Waterhouse, Lybrand and Mitchell. Henry had established the tradition when the project started. Graham thought it was wasteful and unnecessary. We monopolized a small dark room contrived to look like the Old Curiosity Shop. I cornered Henry before a display of Dickensian Toby Jugs, a pitcher in one hand and a bottle in the other, and quizzed him on his management style.

‘It’s necessary in a project like this to create a team. A team needs a common goal, information on how to achieve it and information on how it’s doing. The more open I am, the more open others are. I also need understanding and co-operation between team members. It improves morale and flexibility. I deliberately swap the working pairs around. And this improves lateral communication.'

'Do they teach you this at Waterhouse, Lybrand and Mitchell?'

'Never. I'm doing a part-time MBA.'

'Why do you need an MBA? It's common sense.'

'The one thing about common sense is that it's not common. In business people don't behave like they do at home or at the golf club. They have to learn how to live together from scratch. Here. Your glass is empty.'

He wandered away, dispensing drink and openness to his people. I joined the circle of admirers round Maggie, a beautiful and vivacious redhead drinking Perrier. She had a degree in zoology. She had nurtured a lifelong ambition to be a vet but accountancy was easier to get into.

'I've just been talking to Henry about the way he manages the project. It seems very effective. What do you think?'

'I used to make rats run round mazes.' She wrinkled her freckled nose.

'You think you're being manipulated?'

'It's better than being ignored.'

Many ideas and concepts and words like compassion, altruism, humility, beauty, democracy, love, are considered out of place at work.

Other ideas and concepts and words in common currency at work, like ambition, attitude, productivity, aggressiveness, are considered out of place in other social situations.

Work has its own conventions, etiquette, ethics, behaviour patterns, psychology. The way people behave at work is different from the way they behave elsewhere.

Behaviour at work does not come naturally. It has to be learned. Managers send each other on courses to learn assertiveness and motivation and listening and communication and other skills enabling them to deal with one another.

If the way we behave towards each other at work does not come naturally, if it has to be learned, it can be changed. However deeply entrenched, the traditional, conventional attitudes towards our jobs and each other can be changed.

Right For The Job

We took half an hour for lunch and finished at eight in the evening. I would have left early but Seamus needed the overtime. At half-past six there were sandwiches in the boardroom for the late stayers. There were about twenty of us and I was the oldest.

'What's your background?' asked Dale, a tall, tanned, muscly Australian who I thought would be more at home with a singlet and a surfboard than a calculator.

'I'm a writer,' I said.

'Oh yeah. What do you write?'

'Novels. But right now I'm writing about people who work in offices.'

I predicted two responses for this confession. I would either be disbelieved, a double bluff. Or people would tell me their life story.

'Hey,' said Dale, 'who's your publisher? I'm just finishing a novel. Do you think they'd be interested? It's set in Ancient Egypt. Second Intermediate Period, you know? It's a sort of social history and spy thriller. I've done nearly eleven hundred pages. Is that enough, do you think?' He then treated me to a synopsis of the plot and copious evidence from recent archaeological discoveries that his novel would not be rejected for lack of historical accuracy.

'It sounds great.'

'Shall I bring it in? Do you have time to read it?'

'Sure. Can I start with a synopsis? What are you doing here anyway, ticking off numbers?'

'Money. I spend the weekends in the British Museum. I've got a reader's card.'

He was an untypical bean counter. I needed dull, grey little men to feed my prejudices about accountants. I picked on a balding, shallow-chested young man in white shirt and black-rimmed spectacles. I imagined annual reports on his bedside table, the *Financial Times* in the loo, the 'Money Programme' on the telly.

'What's your background?' he asked.

'I'm a writer,' I said.

'Oh yes. What do you write?'

'Novels. But right now I'm writing about people who work in offices.'

'Really? Who's your publisher? Would they be interested in a book on trees?'

'Trees?'

'British trees. Deciduous mainly.'

'Is it a thriller?'

'Non-fiction. But there are some exciting bits. It's about how trees grow and where they grow and so on. And a lot about the folklore and poetry of trees. It's mainly illustrations. About a thousand.'

'Who did those?'

'I did. Pen and ink mainly. Some acrylic and watercolour. Oaks are my favourite.'

'It sounds great.'

'Shall I bring it in? Would you have time to have a look at it?'

'Sure. Is there a synopsis?' He then taught me more in ten minutes about *Quercus robur*, the common oak, than I thought I would ever know.

'What are you doing here anyway, ticking off numbers?'

'There's not much of a career in forestry. There's only the Forestry Commission and who wants to grow newsprint? When I'm qualified I'd like to get a job dealing with trees. I'd really like to buy some land and plant my own wood somewhere. I spend the weekends in Sussex. There's a farmer who lets me live in a hut in a wood he has.'

This was serious. I had already gathered two thousand pages of heavy reading without finding a decent specimen of bean counter. I tried one of the girls. In my experience female yuppies cannot afford to be interesting in case they are accused of frivolity. The ones I had known in banking were very serious and dedicated. I sidled up to Margaret.

'I'm a writer,' I said.

'Really? What do you write?'

'Novels. But right now I'm writing about people who work in offices.'

'Really? Who's your publisher? Would they be interested in a book about ballet?'

'Five hundred pages?'

'No. I've just done a synopsis.'

'What are you doing here, ticking off numbers?'

'Getting a qualification. I was with Sadler's Wells for five years. Then I tore a ligament in my knee and had to leave.'

'And Waterhouse, Lybrand and Mitchell took you on? Was it an interview or an audition?'

'I did Maths and Economics 'A' levels first. I did them in six months. It was quite a sweat. When I qualify I shall try to get into festival or concert management. What I really want is to start my own ballet school.'

'What's the book about?'

'It's a psychological thriller set in a ballet troupe. Will you read it?'

These accountants were under thirty and still with that heady feeling that the world is full of options and choices and there is all the time in the world to do what you really want to do after a 'useful qualification'. They had not yet handed down to themselves a life sentence. Also they were mainly graduates from Oxbridge, still imbued with the attitude that business is for gentlemen amateurs. It was sad to see the seeds of dissatisfaction and unhappiness and frustration in later life so firmly planted. The attitudes they expressed, the values they ostensibly adhered to were quite different from the American business school graduates I had worked with, for whom a career was a vocation, not something you did to pay for what you really wanted to do.

The firm made presentations and held interviews at Oxbridge every year. Although they hired people from other universities they did not go out to find them. There was a marked preference for scientists and mathematicians, numerate people who could organize masses of data. Henry was on the interviewing team. He enjoyed recruiting. He thought he was good at interviewing. 'I looked for motivation, enthusiasm and intelligence.'

'Why only Oxbridge?'

'That's what our Personnel Manager asks every year. He's not a graduate and he didn't go to a public school so he doesn't understand.'

'But why?'

'We need another dimension to people, not just the brains. We need a bit of class as well. I don't mean in a social, snobby way. But a bit of style.'

'Where did you go?'

'Durham.'

Vijay was the most dedicated trainee accountant I got to know. He did not go to Oxbridge. He came from a family of postmen who had emigrated from Kenya when he was a baby. He was not the sort who get taken on by the big firms who trawl only in the better universities. He was a temp, studying accountancy at a local college. He hoped to get a good reference from Henry when he finished.

'That's worth something, that is, a reference on Waterhouse, Lybrand and Mitchell notepaper.' As far as I could see he deserved it. He understood Miracle almost as well as Graham. His ambition was to own his own business. He was plump and genial and amusing and took in good part the jokes about his street-market suits and his hobby of trading second-hand cars. Half his family had obtained green cards to the USA through an uncle who had emigrated there instead of the UK. Vijay expected to get his in a couple of years.

'I want to make money, own my own business, be independent. You can't do that in this country.'

Graham was a grey man. His attractive smile, his bright blue eyes, slightly crazed like a berserk Viking, his shock of unruly blond hair, concealed the true heart of a genuine bean counter. He was dedicated to financial analysis. He arrived at eight in the morning and left at eight at night. He carried round two identical leather cases. One contained files and papers. The other contained a portable personal computer. He was shy and diffident. Small talk was a burden. He was also remorselessly accurate and painstaking. He was the only person I met, including a consultant who helped design it, who I was really confident knew how Miracle worked in all its perverse detail. It was not that he enjoyed puzzling it out. He seemed to derive greatest pleasure from moaning about its deficiencies.

'Do you enjoy this work?' I asked.

'Not really. It's a mess.'

'What would you rather be doing?'

'Setting up accounting packages for clients.'

His hobby was playing the stock market. He was a chartist, an investor who analyses statistically, with the help of graphs, the behaviour of share prices rather than the underlying characteristics of the companies themselves. He had written a program for his personal computer that drew pictures of fluctuations in share prices. Most chartists use conventional jargon to describe recurring patterns in their diagrams. Graham had invented his own jargon, incantations which he muttered to himself and neat symbols with which he carefully annotated his charts. He was not secretive. One evening he and I were the last to leave. He got out his computer to enter the day's prices of the stocks he was interested in. He was delighted when I asked him about his system and I hadn't the heart to tell him I was dying to go home. Despite the poetry of his private language he lost me in the theory after a few minutes.

'That's what I call a Wet Willie. See it drop at the end. I'd be looking for an Igloo within two weeks to sell. But usually you just get the Mole Hill, sorry about that.'

'Isn't that a Head and Shoulders?' I asked, dredging up the only bit of chartist lore I could remember.

'Too crude. Head and Shoulders can mean anything. That one's a Hunchback. This one's a Keyhole. They're completely different signals.'

He played squash twice a week. He was thinking of taking up golf. He was thirty and married with no children. His wife was a night sister in the nearby hospital. His spare time, when he was not drawing pictures of the stock market, was taken up with redecorating his house in Purley, near Croydon. I imagined a childhood in a thirties semi somewhere in suburbia, the local grammar school, good at maths, average at most other things, hardly noticed except at the end-of-term mental arithmetic quiz, regular bedtimes, a place for everything and everything in its place, plastic planes dangling from the ceiling, a fortnight in Devon in August, artificial Christmas tree, an apple a day, your mother and I think . . .

Writer's perspicacity again. Towards the end of the Waterhouse, Lybrand and Mitchell's Christmas party I sat down next to him. His tie was loose and his collar undone and he was drinking strong lager straight from the bottle.

'Music's pretty loud,' was my scintillating gambit, pointing to the disco speakers.

'That's my brother,' he said. I looked at the disc jockey fiddling with his outsize earphones.

'No, playing,' said Graham, pointing up at the ceiling.

His brother was a bass guitarist in a rock band in the top ten. His sister danced in *Les Miserables*. His father had been an anthropologist until he retired to the Barrier Reef to write mystical books on divine will. His mother was a sculptor who worked with supermarket trolleys. Graham had been born in Brazil, brought up on a Thames barge in Wapping, a game park in Kenya, a croft in the Orkneys, an artist's colony in Madison, Wisconsin. Becoming an accountant was his way of kicking over the traces.

'I look for motivation, enthusiasm and intelligence,' said Henry. His firm seems to have selected people who dedicated these qualities to their hobbies and not to their work.

When I interviewed people for jobs I found there was little correlation between performance at the interview and performance at the job. It was impossible to predict who would stay long and who would quit in a year, who would be successful and who would not.

The usual procedure for recruiting people is:

- Define the job specification in as much detail as possible.
- Find some candidates by advertising or headhunting or going through the write-ins.
- Weed out the obviously unsuitable.
- Interview the short-list.
- Make an offer to the best candidate.

The assumption underlying this procedure is that the employer knows the kind of person who can do the job best and is able to select the right person from the available candidates. It is usually a one-sided process in which the candidate is seen as a supplicant. For example, interviewers are often advised to let the person being interviewed do most of the talking and to answer queries and talk about the company after candidates have been questioned so that their replies are not tailored to suit.

This approach to recruitment ignores the fact that there are two parties to any social and legal contract, including employment. Employers have a right to decide which candidates are right for the job. Candidates have an equal right to decide and they are much better-qualified to do so.

People who work in companies are volunteers. Unless they have outdated skills or live in high unemployment areas, the decision whether to take a job or not is as much the candidate's as the employer's. People select themselves when they apply for the job in the first place. They select themselves when they come along to the interview. They select themselves when they accept an offer. It is the recruiter's job to provide as much information for their decision as possible.

Employees give the company their time, their careers, their futures, their lives, their identities. They can much less afford to make a mistake than the company. The enthusiasm and motivation we are all looking for is going to last much longer if they feel they have made the right decision.

Upwardly Mobile

After a dozen jobs I got used to the life. After the first few days in a new office it felt as if I had been there for ever. It didn't seem strange any more to get up each morning at the same time and leave the house at the same time and arrive at the office at a minute to nine. I began not to mind commuting. It was comforting to be part of the vast migration of people tramping silently along the pavement, waiting on platforms, pressed together on trains. Mute acceptance of one's lot, dependence on unknown people, obedience to the conventions, tolerance of breakdown and inconvenience and delay, made a suitable overture and finale to the working day.

Looking back on the notes I had made when I first started, about how people did not say hello or tell you what the job was or where to find the coffee, about group norms and peer pressure and the infinite distance of managers, my impressions seemed unnaturally vivid, as if they were written by a Martian or a Bushman. Now I didn't notice them. It was nothing to get excited about, life was like that.

The centre of the universe was the desk and the screen and the keyboard and the person opposite and the supervisor. People from other departments, newcomers, visitors, strangers, were on the periphery. You would no more greet them than you would someone you saw on the same train every morning. What counted was to get through the work. The main requirement of you was that you turned up in the morning. Punctuality. Reliability. Neatness.

After a few days in a job I lost track of time. It felt as

though I had been doing the same thing for ever. And that I would continue to do the same thing. It was reassuring to have something to do and to know that everyone round you was doing the same sort of thing. It was satisfying to learn how to do a task more efficiently, but not so efficiently that you were left with nothing to do. There were a few tricks to get over the moments of intense boredom or despair. It was a mistake to run away, to go to the lavatory for a read, to find an excuse for a walk, to daydream about walking up to the supervisor and saying 'I quit'. The best thing was to work harder. To process three deal tickets a minute instead of two. To challenge oneself to make less than ten typing mistakes in a page. After a time these moments became more and more infrequent, no more than once or twice a day.

I began to dread the end of an assignment, the uncertainty of getting another job, the anxiety of telephoning on a Thursday afternoon and a Friday morning and a Friday afternoon, the stress of a new office and new people and new tasks, the fear of being fired. I did think about a different life, about writing a book or going to the cinema in the afternoon or pottering around the Greek islands for the summer. But they were pipe dreams, divorced from reality.

'John. The Manager wants to see you in his office at eleven o'clock,' said my supervisor, putting down the phone.

'What for?'

'Just a chat,' she said.

The three other people in the room concentrated on their work. They said nothing. Just a chat. I'm a bit concerned about your work. I'm afraid this is an official warning. If it happens again. You're not really happy here are you? Are you cut out for this? I'm having to let you go. It's nothing personal. Good luck. I'm sure you'll find something quickly. A person with your talents.

'I'm expecting a call like that,' said Dean. 'Tell him to stuff it. You're quitting anyway.'

I was only a temp. Temps don't get chats with the Manager, the agency tells them not to go back in the morning. It avoids embarrassment. I supposed I had been rumbled. What is an ex-General Manager up to in the Accounts Department?

The Manager's lavatory on the top floor had concealed lighting and a mahogany mirror and a pile of real hand towels. I combed my hair and licked a tomato pip off my tie which made the stain bigger. I rubbed some of the mud off my shoes with toilet paper. My jacket covered the torn pocket of my trousers. There was nothing I could do about the orange socks and the frayed collar.

I waited outside his office on a low chair. On the coffee table were the *Harvard Business Review* and *Fortune* and *Management Today* in neat rows. I was too nervous to read and the Manager's secretary might not like it if I disturbed her arrangement. She came out of the Manager's office with a tray of china cups and a silver coffee pot.

'You can go in now.'

My supervisor was there too, sitting straight and prim in front of the desk. The Manager behind the desk had his back to us. He was looking out of the window and talking on the telephone, something about a bond price. I stood waiting until he had finished. The carpet under my feet was soft. There was a weeping fig in one corner growing in what looked like dry roasted peanuts. The leaves were shiny and there were no sign of the insects that swarmed on the leaves when I had an office like this. A large glass-fronted ebony bookcase contained a full set of procedure manuals bound in imitation leather. On the walls were coloured prints of the City in Victorian times. The Manager put the phone down, wrote in a thick red diary and waved me to the seat beside my supervisor. He was a youngish American with dark hair tinted grey at the temples, a blue shirt with button down collar and a yellow tie with little horsehoes over it. The jacket of his blue suit was on the back of his swivel chair. He looked tanned and fit and groomed and clean. I felt seedy.

'Hi, John?'

'Er. Hello.'

His large teak desk was covered in trophies. They made a barrier between us. There were half a dozen miniature tombstones encased in clear plastic. A tombstone is a newspaper advertisement of a loan or a bond tissue, a list of banks in a finely negotiated hierarchy. There was also a toy tractor, a highly polished cog, a hotel key on an ebony plinth, a miniature bottle of pancake syrup, a tube of toothpaste, a printed circuit in a silver frame, a metal aeroplane in Pan Am livery, a phial of black liquid, a lump of coal on a pedestal and several other things in his memory game I have forgotten. These were his achievements. Next to this miniature junk heap were a gold pen and pencil in a bright green onyx stand, a gold pen and pencil in an ebony stand, an aluminium paper knife shaped like an Indian dagger, a clock that told the time in ten different places, a polished wooden cigar box with his name carved on the top, a black lacquer cigarette box inlaid with a silhouette of an office building, a glass ashtray in the shape of an Arab dhow and other tributes I can remember no longer. These were reminders of the rungs of his career. On the credenza behind him were three free-standing nameplates. On one his name was inscribed in white letters on black plastic. On the second his name was stamped out in white metal. The third nameplate was embossed bronze with the raised letters highly polished. They were next to two complicated telephone sets, each with a little screen and loudspeakers, and a large, green-flickering Reuters screen. Power, status, achievement.

'You're liking it down there, John?' he said, or asked. He intoned all his statements as questions, inviting complicity and agreement.

'Er. Yeah.'

'You got to know how we do things round here?'

'Er. Yeah.'

'This is a fast-growing and dynamic organization?'

'Er. Yeah.'

'You were in banking for a few years? Then you had a, em, break?'

'Er. Yeah.'

'That must have been a tough time? Quite an adjustment?'

'Er. Yeah.'

'You're already quite familiar with the way banks work? With general procedures?'

'Er. Yeah.'

'I want you to know that we're all very pleased with your performance here, John. We need good, dedicated, reliable people. We'd like you to join us on a permanent basis.'

'You're offering me a job?'

'We have a very competitive package? You'd qualify for a bank mortgage after six months and membership of the pension plan after twelve months? And luncheon vouchers from day one?'

'A permanent job?'

'At first you'd carry on doing what you're doing now for a few months? Then cross-train into other parts of accounts? There is lots of opportunity in this organization for people like you with ambition? You could be doing the reconciliations in a year?'

I felt a prickling in the back of my nose, a weakening in the knees.

I felt I had achieved something.

When I started this book I was looking for answers to some basic questions. Why do people work? What makes them happy? What makes them productive?

People motivate themselves. For whatever material or psychological reason, people need to work. They want achievement and companionship and status and recognition and to learn new skills. Different people are motivated by different things and at different times in their lives.

Few people start work looking for an easy life, something for nothing, a clock to watch, something to complain about, a spanner to throw in the works.

Most people, at whatever level, start their first day at a new job eager to do well, work hard, learn new skills, make a good impression, get promoted, do something meaningful.

If they become de-motivated and disillusioned and unproductive it is because of what happens to them at work.

Office work can be as boring and unrewarding and frustrating and meaningless and stressful and alienating as work on an assembly line. But it is not technology or computers or the intrinsic nature of the jobs that makes it so. It is the way people treat each other.

People have a great tolerance for discomfort and tedium and hard work and low pay as long as they can see a purpose to their efforts and are not treated like another raw material in the business, a human resource.

Managers spend a lot of time and effort wondering what they can do to make the organization more efficient and the people in it more productive. They might be better off thinking of what they can stop doing that prevents people working as hard as they can.

Work is purposeful activity. The principal impediment to purposeful work that I came across was ignorance of the purpose. People have a right to know what they are supposed to do and whether they have achieved it.

Management theorists discovered this simple truth generations ago. Common sense supports it. Its absence in practice is lamentable. I rarely came across people who had a clear idea of what was expected of them and could explain the purpose of their job.

Making sure that everyone in the organization knows exactly what their job is and what its purpose is and how it fits in and how they know if they are doing it well is an arduous and never-ending process, but the single most important element in managing people.

Most of the supervisors I worked with had no advice or training in the rudiments of people management. There is very little training in the basic social skills necessary to work in groups within large organizations towards shared goals.

Education is not a perk. It is not only senior managers who need training in behavioural skills.

Management training can only point the way. There are no easy answers, no recipes, no formulas for making a success of managing people, just as there is none for making a success of parenthood or marriage or a love affair or any other social activity.

The Christmas Party

The end of my clerical career was marked with a Christmas party. It was held in a basement disco on the edge of the City. As it was the beginning of March there was no Christmas tree but they had taken the trouble to put up decorations and fairy lights and artificial snow. It looked very festive. There was a free bar until nine and a lavish buffet and a disco.

It was given by one of the Big Bang conglomerates where I'd been an internal messenger the previous autumn. The permanent messengers were given a smart three-piece dark suit and a company tie to wear. I had to make do with a shortie blue cotton jacket with a logo on the collar. I complemented this outfit with grey pinstripe trousers and jogging shoes. I calculated I walked about twenty miles a day pushing a supermarket trolley loaded with envelopes. It gave me an opportunity to confirm an observation I had made in other offices. I had wondered why internal messengers had such a limited repertoire of songs to sing while pushing their trolleys through the corridors of power. They were like street cries or a post horn announcing the mail. From a sample of a dozen different offices I had established a Hit Parade. Top was 'Fly Me To The Moon' followed by 'I Did It My Way' and 'I Left My Heart in San Francisco'. It is not only that messengers are romantics – wanderlust is a desirable attribute in a messenger – but that few other types of song go with a leisurely amble.

One of the documents I delivered was a memo to all

staff announcing a Christmas party and asking them to return the tear-off slip at the bottom if they wanted an invitation. It did not specifically exclude temps so I signed up on the off-chance. Somehow it slipped through. Three months later I was agreeably surprised to receive a ticket in a sealed envelope, forwarded through the agency.

It was two years since I had been to an office party. It was reassuringly familiar. The women were extravagantly dressed and made up, showing they could be sexy as well as businesslike. The lady who cleaned the telephone came in a ball gown sparkling with hand sewn sequins. Young clerks in shimmering jackets and baggy trousers stood stiffly, their hair-dos balanced precariously on their heads. Dealers in shirtsleeves did rowdy dances in an unbreakable circle. Managers wandered dutifully around being amiable. Yuppies sat in cliques in corners round bottles of wine. Brassy blondes from the post room whooped and shrieked and dragged elderly men onto the dance floor.

'What the firkin are you doing here?' asked Jerry, one of the external messengers. 'Don't let George see you. You made a right buttocks of the post ledger. We're still looking for stuff.'

'It's all right. I'm in disguise. Who's that over there?'

I nodded to a bald man standing in the middle of the room smiling and nodding graciously to people as they circulated round him.

'He's the Chairman. The Big Wally.'

I worked my way over to him. Close up it was obvious that his gracious smile was a nervous tic. The corners of his mouth naturally turned down. Every so often they would twitch up involuntarily as if they had been jerked by a string. They twitched even when he was not talking to anyone. I behaved as though he ought to have known me. He did not like to ask me who I was. He was grateful to talk shop.

'How are you coping with the personnel side of the merger? Morale, team-building, that sort of stuff?'

'That was the hardest part. Forget the business side, that's easy. It's the people. We're making headway, but it's tough.'

'You're not the only one,' I consoled him. 'The City's full of firms much worse off. They're sitting on time bombs.'

'Some of them with a very short fuse. Particularly those taken over by the foreign institutions. I never realized the strength of feeling.'

'What did you do?'

'We had consultants in to help. They specialize in post-merger situations. They did attitude surveys. We were astonished at the anti-partner feelings in the brokers. No wonder. They treated their staff like dirt. Dirt.'

'And they resent you, I suppose.'

'We had no problem with bank-to-jobber and bank-to-broker relationships. They liked us coming in. They'd rather have us than the partners. It's the broker-jobber relationship that's the problem. They've got their knives out for each other. It's been like that for generations.'

'Well, good luck. I think you're doing a wonderful job. Keep it up.'

'Thanks. Let's have lunch one day.'

'I'll get my secretary on it.'

'Good show.'

I kept out of his way for the rest of the evening. I sometimes caught him looking at me across the dance floor, trying to remember who I was. Before the dancing started he made a lamentable speech, full of lame jokes and long sentences and exhortations to pull together. While he talked the disc jockeys fiddled with their equipment behind him, clattering waiters cleared the buffet, a tipsy teenager fell off her chair, a glass crashed on the floor, people at the back murmured and giggled, a knot of drunks in shirtsleeves at the bar turned their backs. His ticcy smile flickered incessantly over his face. Having to make the speech at the Christmas party is part of the price of success. The ordeal over he danced once with his secretary and slipped thankfully away.

Of all the opinions and attitudes I collected during my months of research I have most faith in the honesty of those bellowed in my ear while we bopped up and down on the dance floor, pounded by the beat, chopped in pieces by the strobes, soused with free drink, sprinkled with colours by the revolving bowl in the ceiling.

'It's invigorating. Sometimes the speed of change is bewildering. But I love it' – an English rose holding up her Hermes scarf as a yashmak and fluttering her eyelids.

'They just mess us around' – a blonde girl in a silver crochet dress, like glistening spider's webs.

'I work for money. The more I get paid the more I do. The less I get paid the less I do' – a pregnant woman doing the twist.

'The one thing that worries everyone is the job rating system the bank is putting in' – a redhead who danced like a cobra rising from a basket.

'You have to work, don't you? I wouldn't work if I didn't have to' – a Scotswoman in a white blazer she kept for bowling and discos.

'I like it. You learn something new every day' – a fragile-looking girl in a green sari who danced with her eyes cast down.

'My work's interesting, but I don't let it interfere with my life' – a very large black woman in a bright red dress with mesmerizing hips.

'I try to do the best I can regardless of the pay' – the telephone cleaning lady in a glittering ball gown.

It was as confusing as it had been on the day I started.

So what did I learn?

The quality of people-management is lamentable in almost all the companies I worked in. The waste of human resources is scandalous. It is scandalous for the people who work there, forced to fritter away their talents, their desire to succeed, their desire to make a contribution. It is scandalous for the companies who employ them. They are pouring money down the drain in wasted productivity. And they are not bucket shops. Most of the companies I worked for are household names.

I found the simplest, most basic practices of people-management were lacking. Induction is scrappy or non-existent. Promotion is haphazard and ill-prepared. Evaluation and appraisal and career review are non-existent. Even a decent staff handbook is a rarity. There is no training for that crucial, difficult step up to the first people-managing job. All these are as important for cashiers and computer operators as for graduate trainees and branch managers.

I am sure that the companies I worked for spend a lot of money on management training. For most of their employees what they spend on people-related skills, on people-management courses, on organization and development consultants is wasted. There is no trickledown. The inadequacy of basic management training reinforces the British tradition of a small well-educated elite bossing an ill-informed, disillusioned proletariat of workers.

The demand for good management has to come from the bottom. All people, whatever their job or status, have a right not only to decent pay and working conditions but to the essential knowledge and skills necessary to do their job. Only if it is recognized that they are rights and not devices to make people work harder will the quality of people-management improve.

THE END

THANKS EDDIE
by John Mole

No-one knows more about the workings of Dividend Investments than Eddie Fly. He reads all the memos, all the telexes. He hears all the most important telephone calls. He knows all the staff, and all their little weaknesses. His grapevine in the City keeps him informed of all the latest developments in the world of business and finance. But no, he isn't the Chief Executive Officer. He is the head messenger, the life and soul of the company.

When the general manager of Dividend Investments dies in the arms of his secretary, Norah, in the course of some after-hours recreation, and when Percy Wheeler, Dividend's boss, decides to put a woman in his place, Eddie's carefully managed world seems to be running out of control. And has someone been up to some mysterious dealings on the side? There will be much hilarious confusion, and many disasters, before Eddie's multifarious talents can restore order to the little world of Divident Investments, a world that anyone who has ever worked in an office will instantly recognize.

0 593 01636X

BANTAM PRESS HARDCOVER
Available June 1989

UP THE GARDEN PATH
by Sue Limb

Izzy has problems . . . fat and spotty (too many cream cakes), she is hopelessly in love with Michael. Michael, unfortunately, is married to Louise – and intends to stay that way. Meanwhile Izzy has to contend with the assorted delights and terrors of 4C (that would have to be her class!), put up with being adored by Dick (the pottery teacher), and somehow cope with the maniacal, larger-than-life attentions of Hywel and Gwyn, two sex-mad Welshman who force their way into her life and affections, in spite of their very obvious faults . . .

UP THE GARDEN PATH is a brilliant comic debut about men, marriage, sex, eating, love and life.

'LAUGH-OUT-LOUD FUNNY'
MARGARET FORSTER, BOOKS & BOOKMEN

'ENORMOUSLY ENTERTAINING'
FINANCIAL TIMES

'A MARVELLOUS START FOR A NEW WRITER WITH SUCH AN UNMALICIOUS, BUBBLING SENSE OF HUMOUR'
ELIZABETH BERRIDGE, DAILY TELEGRAPH

0 552 12561X